# TEACHING MATHEMATICS SUCCESSFULLY

**ENCYCLOPAEDIA OF TEACHING - IV**

# TEACHING MATHEMATICS SUCCESSFULLY

**Prof. MARLOW EDIGER**
*Ph.D.*
Truman State University Route 2,
Box 38, Kirksville,
Missouri MO 63501-9802.
U.S.A.

**Dr. DIGUMARTI BHASKARA RAO**
*M.Sc., M.A., M.A., M.Ed., Ph.D.*
R.V.R. College of Education,
Nagarjuna University,
Guntur-522006, (A.P.)
INDIA

DISCOVERY PUBLISHING HOUSE
NEW DELHI-1100 02

First Published – 2000

Reprinted – 2017

ISBN: 978-93-5056-516-2 (Set)

ISBN: 978-81-7141-552-6



**Teaching Mathematics Successfully**

*Published by:*

**DISCOVERY PUBLISHING HOUSE PVT. LTD.**
4383/4B, Ansari Road Darya Ganj
New Delhi - 110 002 (India)
Phone: +91-11-23279245, 43596064-65
Fax: +91-11-23253475
*E-mail:* discoverypublishinghouse@gmail.com
sales@discoverypublishinggroup.com
*web:* www.discoverypublishinggroup.com

*Printed at:*
Dynamic Printers
Delhi

# PREFACE

Mathematics is one of the languages of human life and certainly no more marvellous language was ever created by the mind of man. Mathematics cut short the lengthy statements through its symbols, is free from verbosity, helps the expression of ideas in an exact form, and enables to understand and appreciate precision, brevity, sharpness, logic and beauty of mathematics.

Mathematics fulfills the educational values such as practical, disciplinary, cultural, intellectual, moral, aesthetic, social, vocational, inter-disciplinary, etc. In order to realise the educational values and instructional objectives of mathematics, the subject must be practiced in class rooms by utilising the services of traditional methods, educational innovations and technological advancements.

Mathematics instruction must be improved from the present state of affairs as many are raising questions against the present classroom practices. This book, Effective Teaching of Mathematics, is written for pre-service and in-service teachers to answer such questions. We believe the contents herein possess a scope and sequence which guide teachers to provide for individual differences so that each student may achieve as optimally as possible in mathematics. Mathematics teachers need to select the best objectives, and appraisal procedures, with the use of quality criteria, so that students may be successful learners. We sincerely hope each student experiences the best curriculum possible in order to become competent in mathematics in school and in society.

*Prof. Marlow Ediger*
*Dr. D. Bhaskara Rao*

# CONTENTS

# CONTENTS

# Chapter 1

# MOTIVATING PUPILS TO LEARN MATHEMATICS

The mathematics teacher has a major responsibility in assisting pupils to learn in ongoing lessons and units of study. Thus, motivating pupils to achieve optimally is a concern of conscientious teachers. When observing pupils in a classroom, there are highly motivated pupils who work hard on the task at hand and they do well in attaining vital goals of instruction. Others are less motivated and their attention may be divided between the lesson at hand and distractions in the classroom. And yet, these pupils need much guidance to complete assignments on time with minimal quality. A few pupils need much guidance to complete assignments and fail to achieve as well as desired by the mathematics teacher. Each pupil is important and no one should fall through the slats in mathematics. Mathematics is one of the three R's (reading, writing, and arithmetic).

Knowledge, skills, and attitudes as objectives to achieve are vital for each pupil. Learners presently need to attain as optimally as possible so that at the work place as adults, there is a better chance to be successful and receive adequate remuneration to live a decent life style. Thus, pupils need to be motivated to do well in the mathematics curriculum.

## BEHAVIOURISM AND THE MATHEMATICS CURRICULUM

E.L. Thorndike (1874-1949) established foundational ideas for behaviourism as a psychology of learning during the early years of the 1900s. His stimulus/response school of thought in terms of how animals learn was translated to the teaching of pupils in the school setting. Thorndike did much experimenting with cats going through a maze. The cat that followed the maze successfully was rewarded with a fish at the end of the maze. The Law of Effect was then developed by Thorndike in that the cat went through the maze more rapidly, with repeated attempts, than formerly due to the reward at the end of the maze. The effect was the available fish to eat. Thorndike also developed the Law of Frequency (the more often the cat went through the maze, the more likely the animal would learn quickly how to complete the task with minimal errors), the Law of Recency (the more recent the event, the more likely the animal would remember the task - Recency instead of something having happened some time ago). The latter two laws have been discarded since there are other factors that enter in, other than something being learned frequently and recently. The Law of Effect has remained important by behaviourists, in numerous situations.

B.F. Skinner (1902–1986) did many research studies and came up with the concept of operant conditioning. With operant conditioning, Skinner placed major emphasis in learning upon the response in S–R theory of learning as compared to the stimulus. Thus, for example, the mathematics teacher may be assisting pupils with learning what 5 +4 is in a meaningful and interesting procedure of instruction. If the pupil responds with "nine" as the answer, he/she is rewarded. The emphasis here is placed upon the response in operant condition, not the stimulus. The teacher may say, "That is good," when a learner responds correctly. The response then is further reinforced in operant conditioning through verbal praise. With reinforcement theory, pupils learn more quickly and retain learnings longer, according to B.F. Skinner. With operant conditioning, the following steps are salient for the teacher to follow:

1. specifying what pupils are to learn prior to instruction.
2. Writing these ends in measurable terms, with great specificity.
3. teaching each lesson in very small incremental steps.
4. learning by pupils occurs as each small item of content is acquired sequentially.
5. providing feedback continuously to pupils on how well each is doing with verbal praise and with the correct answer.

6. reinforcing positive pupil behaviour in terms of subject matter learned as well as study skills acquired (Ediger, 1997).

Schedules of reinforcement may be in the offing as advocated by behaviourists. The schedule of rewards may be based on a ratio basis such as a verbal reward for every three correct responses given by a pupil. Time may also be used as a basis for rewarding pupils with a verbal reward. Thus, for a pupil with poor study habits in mathematics, if he/she completes three basic addition facts correctly in two minutes, praise is given here. The schedules of reinforcement can be altered depending upon how frequently the pupil needs a reward to continue achieving more optimally.

Presently, behaviourism emphasizes the writing of predetermined, precise objectives for pupils to achieve in mathematics. These specific objectives are written so that teachers and pupils know exactly what pupils are to learn. Objectives then are available to teachers prior to instruction. The teacher may announce what pupils are to achieve within a lesson. This provides security to the learners in terms of knowing what the outcomes of teaching are to be. The following are examples of behaviourally stated objectives for the pupil to achieve within a lesson:

1. The pupil will add correctly nine out of ten addition basic number pairs, each continuing single digit addends.
2. The pupil will check his/her addition by using the commutative property of addition.

Adding correctly none out of ten in the above objective # 1 is a minimum level of acceptance. Ten out of ten is the ideal! There are teachers who provide inexpensive rewards if pupils achieve the desired goal in the stated objective. Pupils should know ahead of time in instruction what the physical reward will be so that maximum effort is put forth to achieve and grow in mathematics.

## HUMANISM IN THE MATHEMATICS CURRICULUM

Some what toward the opposite end of the continuum, humanists advocate their approaches in having pupils achieve more optimally. Maslow"s hierarchy of needs is fundamental to understand in order to attach meaning to humanism as a psychology of learning. Abraham Maslow (1908-1970) developed a motivation theory based on needs of individuals. The first need stressed meeting physiological needs of pupils such as adequate nutrition, clothing, and shelter provisions. Free breakfasts and lunches in school help, but there are too many other meals that poor children may not be getting. Second, Maslow advocated safety needs of pupils be met. Child abuse and loaded pistols along with other arms brought to school by pupils will not help the situation. Neither does bullying by pupils of other children help to make for a safe school enviornment. Third, the need for belonging needs to be met. Here, the teacher needs to accept and care for each child. The teacher also needs to guide pupils to accept each other in school and in committee work. Adequate time should be spent by the teacher in helping pupils feel as if they belong in an accepted group. Fourth esteem needs of pupils must be met. Here, the teacher should recognize pupils for accomplishments in class and in outside class/ school endeavours. Individuals desire to be recognized for something that is done well. No one desires to be ignored in class. Fifth, the need for self actualization is important. The pupil then becomes the kind of person he/she wishes to become. Sixth, the pupil has a need to understand and know. This stage of needs then stresses, among other things, pupils achieving vital mathematics objectives. Maslow in his well developed hierarchy of needs pinpoints how other needs, than to know and understand are also important and they definitely are. We recommend that the need to know and understand be integrated with the first five needs. A quality mathematics curriculum then needs to be in the offing continuously with its knowledge, skills, and attitudinal objectives. We agree strongly that pupils need to have physiological needs, safety needs, belonging needs, and esteem need met so that more optimal achievement in mathematics is possible. How can pupils learn if they are hungry, lack safety, feel as if they do not belong in the classroom, and lack esteem?

Humanism advocates an open ended mathematics curriculum. The following tenets of humanism are important to understand:

1. Pupil/teacher planning of the mathematics curriculum. Thus, there needs to be input from the pupil in terms of what is taught

in the mathematics curriculum. With a learning centers approach, the pupil may sequentially select from the diverse tasks what to learn and what to omit, but still be profitably occupied continuously. As much as possible, there should be pupil directed learning. Pupils should have a voice in goal determination in the mathematics curriculum. As a university supervisors of student teachers, we have noticed a contract system at work in mathematics. Here, the pupil with teacher guidance establishes a contract of what specifically the learner is to complete in mathematics with a due date thereon. The pupil and the teacher both sign the contract. The teacher is there to assist and help the pupil in contract establishment. In all of the work completed and the inherent processes, pupils should be involved in evaluation. The learner is not to be left out of developing the mathematics curriculum. The attitudinal or affective dimension is very important to a humanist. With much pupil input into the mathematics curriculum, humanists believe attitudes improve. A contract may look like the following:

I agree to complete the following in mathematics:

1. do five activities at the enrichment centers.
2. do ten tasks at the learning centers.
3. read and report on two library books on mathematics.
4. view two videotapes on mathematics and write summary statements for each.
5. work in a committee to complete collaboratively pages ten and eleven from the basal.

Signed by the pupil                Signed by the teacher

<u>due date</u>

The above contract indicates that the learner is quite subject centered in achievement, especially when looking at the basal text completions being a part of the contract. A pupil who likes an activity centered curriculum may wish to do more construction, visual arts, demonstrations, dramatic activities, and projects as they relate to the ongoing unit of study (Ediger, 1991).

Carl Rogers (1902-1987) was also a leading advocate of humanism, as a psychology of learning, to be emphasized in the classroom.

Rogers believed pupils to be naturally curious and thus a child centered mathematics curriculum was needed. Pupils then liked to explore the environment and satisfy their academic needs. The teacher needs to assist pupils to satisfy their curiosity for learning.

Rogers believed that change in society is rather rapid and what the schools stress may soon become outdated. Therefore, pupils need to accept the concept of *change* and become lifelike learners. Pupils should be able to try out their own ideas without fear of failure or ridicule. The learning environment must therefore be free from threat and criticism.

How to learn and how to become a lifelike learner are very important to humanists, such as Carl Rogers. Self directed learning as an ideal to stress in the classroom and choosing what to learn is highly motivating to pupils. Learner motivation increases with pupils being involved in the making of choices. Self reliance and independence are two concepts strongly advocated by Rogers and they result from self directed learning. The implications here for mathematics teachers, pertaining to humanism in the classroom, are the following:

1. Provide as many opportunities as possible for pupils to select and pursue their very own individual interests. We would like to suggest using, among other approaches, a learning centers philosophy of teaching whereby a learner sequences his own achievement by choosing sequential tasks in mathematics to pursue at the diverse centers.
2. Guide pupils to become responsible individuals in doing work in the mathematics curriculum. The teacher may set up several enrichment stations which contain learning activities that go beyond those of the tasks at the diverse learning centers. After completion of regular lessons and assignments, the pupil may then go the enrichment center to learn in depth what was stressed at the leaning centers.
3. Encourage life long learning by having the pupil choose a library book on mathematics that is interesting and contains meaning for the involved learner. These library books should be on the individual's reading and understanding level (Rogers, 1983).

## BEHAVIOURISM AND COGNITIVE PSYCHOLOGY IN MATHEMATICS

Rober Gagne (1985) is a leading psychologist today who advocates both tenets of behaviourism and cognitive psychology. He has been very strong in emphasizing that pupils experience quality sequence in learning. Thus, mathematics teachers are to arrange the objectives of instruction on a continuum from the easiest to the more complex. Careful planning is necessary to do this. The teacher needs to have an excellent knowledge of subject matter to use Gagne's hierarchy of objectives approach in teaching and learning. The eight levels of learning are signal learning, stimulus-response, chaining, verbal association learning, multiple discrimination, concept learning, rule learning, and problem solving.

Gagne's lowest level of objectives for pupils to achieve emphasize signal learning. Signal learning is much like Ivan Pavlov's experiments in The Soviet Union in 1927, among other years. Here, Pavlov experimented with dogs and their salivation. A dog salivated with the sight of meat and its accompanying odor. Pavlov experimented with pairing the sound of a bell with the sight of the meat. The dog still salivated and continued to do so with the sound of the bell only. Gradually, the salivation lessened and went away completely. This is classical conditioning. The next level is stimulus-response learning whereby, for example, upon seeing 5+4 on a flash card (the stimulus) a pupil responds immediately with nine as the answer. Five plus four is associated with nine (the response). Stimulus-response learning has many uses in teaching, especially with items that need to be committed to memory. Ultimately, after meaning and use have been made of the basic addition, subtraction, multiplication, and division number pairs, they should be committed to memory by pupils so that rapid recall is there when needed. Chaining stresses the pupil doing a series of tasks in proper order whereby psychomotor learnings are involved. In the making of model geometry figures, there is a better and a worse way of making squares, rectangles, circles, semicircles, triangles, and trapezoids. A skillful learner will soon find, when ready, improved ways of making things and in this case model geometrical figures. Chaining is involved in the physical activity. Verbal association learning emphasizes pupils being able to explain sequentially, for example, a new process in arithmetic. Thus, in long division, the pupil with a series of meaningful statements explains how 45, 637 divided by 84 is done. The explanations involve verbal language and need to follow a definite order so that the listener is clear on the involved steps. Multiple discriminations involve separating the needed from the unneeded in mathematics. When adding, subtracting, multiplying, and dividing, the pupil needs to separate what is necessary from what is incorrect. In doing word problems, there is essential needed information that the problem asks for. The rest needs to be discarded. Multiple discrimination involves critical thinking in separating the relevant from the irrelevant. Level six is concept development of pupils, according to Gagne. Pupils need to learn vital concepts. Concepts are represented by single words or phrases. The following, as examples, are concepts: circumference, area, radius, pi, and diameter. inside of each concept are numerous facts. Thus, in the concept of *circumference of a circle,* the pupil needs to know and understand *diameter* and *pi* together with the operation of *multiplication.* The seventh level of Gagne's model is rule learning. Rules stress pupils developing *generalizations.* Generalizations are broad, meaningful sentences that relate concepts. For example, the formula for determining the area of a cylinder is radius squared times *pi* times height. There are several relevant concepts inside this generalization, such as cylinder, radius, squared, *pi,* times and height. The last and eighth step of developing an instructional sequence is problem solving. Here, lifelike and word problems, based on the readiness level of the pupil may be used.

A major advantage in using Gagne's hierarchy of objectives psychology is that the mathematics teacher is attempting to develop quality sequence for pupil learning. Thus, if a pupil cannot solve the problem, he/she can go back to earlier levels in the hierarchy such as a learner not understanding and knowing the involved generalization. If the pupil does not know and understand the generalization, he/she may be deficient in the related concepts therein. If the mathematical concepts are not understood, perhaps the pupil is not able to distingusih in multiple discriminations the relevant from the irrelevant in information dealing with the inherent concepts being studied in mathematics.

## GUIDELINES FOR TEACHING MATHEMATICS

We have asked many student teachers and co-operating teachers whom we have supervised in the schools about what they perceive to be major problems in teaching pupils. The student teachers and co-operating teachers have generally indicated the following:

1. *Securing Attention of Pupils in Learning Mathematics.* When teaching a set of twenty-five pupils in large group instruction, the mathematics teacher needs to use a teaching strategy with diverse kinds of materials to obtain the interests of learners. We observed classroom whereby the teachers were attempting to have pupils develop a concept of a set of ten. Each pupil was given ten sticks to use as counters. Pupils started to click the sticks so that nothing was achieved in terms of learning about a set of ten. These pupils seemingly were not trying to distract others, but they found it interesting to make these clicking sounds individually. We suggested that the student teacher and the co-operating teacher use a set of large sticks that pupils could see from their desks and then to use discovery methods of learning about what a set of ten is. This avoided the clicking sounds and did help pupils to focus upon the set portrayed by the teacher.
2. *Having Pupils Understand what is Taught.* To understand a set of ten, pupils need to see different materials being used. These materials may include crayons, pencils, chalk, seeds, and paper clips, among other materials. It is important for pupils to perceive that the concept of ten is applicable to all of these materials when saying how may are in a set. Patience is a very important trait of teachers. Pupils learn at different rates of speed and at diverse levels of understanding. If pupils do not learn with one teaching strategy, another needs to be tried. The activity may be made less complex so that understanding is possible. Thus, the teacher may go back to working with pupils in understanding or reviewing what a set of five is.
3. *Guiding Pupils to Perceive Reasons for Leaning that which is Stated in the Objective.* Sometimes, a pupil says, "Do we have to learn this?" We would suggest here to explain to pupils why it is important to learn what a set of ten is. The teacher should not feel threatened in these situations, but realize too that here are

opportunities to reflect one's thinking on objects to be emphasized in the teaching of mathematics.

4. *Sequencing Learning Opportunities in the Teaching of Mathematics.* It takes good sequence when teaching mathematics if pupils are to be successful in learning. How can the teacher(s) properly sequence for each pupil in a class of twenty-five? We would say to do the best possible. If collaborative learning is used, there will be those who learn more rapidly that others. In large group instruction, the top achievers will achieve more rapidly than the rest in the classroom. Even in individualized study, such as a pupil reading a library book on the history of mathematics, written for children, there will be times when the contents will be easier therein as compared to other places in the library book. Then too, the mathematics teacher does not have the 'gauges' to measure precisely where a pupil is in achievement now as compared to a plumber fitting standardized parts together to join pipes. Pupils individually are unique and different from each other. They also possess multiple intelligences such as in art, music, physical education, social studies, science, reading and the language arts, as well as in mathematics. Whatever the mathematics intelligence of the pupil is, he/she should have the best curriculum possible to become proficient in the third of the 3 R's. With a variety of materials of instruction, the teacher should be able to reach many pupils to learn as much as films, filmstrips, workbooks, worksheets, software packages, CD ROMS, concrete realia and objects, dramatizations, drawings, and models, among others. Recommended materials of instruction tend to be neutral, neither good nor bad, and require a good mathematics teacher who is creative to assist pupils individually to learn as much as possible (Ediger, 1995).

## CONSTRUCTIVISM IN MATHEMATICS

A relatively new concept of teaching and evaluation involves constructivism. Constructivism, among other things, involves appraising pupils within a contextual situation, not by external procedures (Ediger, 1998). External procedures involves standardized tests written by specialists far removed from the local classroom scence. Then too, the standardized tests are administered once and sometimes twice a year. If administered once a year, these tests are a one shot approach in determining how well pupils are doing in mathematics, and other curriculum areas.

With constructivism, the mathematics teacher may appraise continuously as pupils are learning in mathematics. Whatever problems pupils reveal in achievement or lack thereof can be monitored by the mathematics teacher. Then too, assistance may be given right away to the pupil experiencing a difficulty in mathematics. The every day evaluation results that the lay public hears little or nothing about comes to light and is indicated with constructivism as a concept in teaching and learning. Constructivism is:

1. pupil centered, in that the focus is upon the individual learner in determining how well he/she is doing.
2. sequential, in that the pupil is assisted when difficulties are faced at that specific moment.
3. continuous, in observing pupil achievement, not a one shot approach in appraising learner progress.
4. contextual, and relates to what has happened previously in the ongoing lesson and unit of study.
5. emphasizes that the mathematics teacher is available at the time of need.
6. Personal, in that the appraisal is valid for a given pupil.

With constructivism, if a pupil does not understand place value such as ones, tens, and hundreds, the teacher, at that specific time, may provide needed assistance. This situation is a motivator for each and every pupil in mathematics.

## CONCLUSION

Pupils need to be motivated to achieve as optimally as possible. There are numerous psychologists in education who have excellent suggestions for motivating learners. Teachers and supervisors need to study and analyze diverse schools of thought in educational psychology to ascertain which procedures work best and with which children in mathematics. They need to do much reading and studying to notice which trends in motivation and teaching of pupils are in vogue. Pupils individually are different from each other and possess diverse learning styles. They also possess different intelligences, such as being able to work better individually or within a committee. Teachers and supervisors need to study pupils in the classroom and know under which conditions pupils achieve best in pertaining to the mathematics curriculum.

## REFERENCES

Bhaskara Rao, Digumarti (1996). *Advanced Educational Psychology*. Guntur : Creative Press, (in Telugu language).

Ediger, Marlow (1997), *Teaching Mathematics in the Elementary School*. Kirksville, Missouri : Simpson Publishing Company, 22-44.

Ediger, Marlow (1991), *Relevancy in the Elementary Curriculum*. Kirksville, Missouri: Simpson Publishing Company, 393 -424.

Ediger, Marlow (1995), *Philosophy in curriculum Development*. Kirksville, Missouri : Simpson Publishing Company, 189-204.

Ediger, Marlow (1998), *Teaching Reading Successfully in the Elementary School*. Kirksville, Missouri : Simposon Publishing Company, 204-220.

Ediger, Marlow and Digumarti Bhaskara Rao (1996). *Science Curriculum*. New Delhi: Discovery Publishing House.

Gagne, Robert (1985), *The Conditions of Learning and Theory of Instruction*. New York: Holt, Rinehart and Winston.

Rogers, Carl (1983), *Freedom to Learn in the Eighties*.

## *Chapter 2*

# PHILOSOPHICAL CONSIDERATIONS IN TEACHING MATHEMATICS

Mathematics as a curriculum area might be taught from the point of view of several philosophies of education. One philosophy is that it is a body of subject matter to be learned. Thus, mathematics has a subject matter component only . There are teachers who teach mathematics as if it contains a scope and sequence of subject matter to be learned by pupils. Thus, mathematics is taught as a separate subject area with little or no relationship to other curriculum areas. Mathematics may also be taught as content in and of itself with little or no relationship to the outside world of being practical. The subject matter is then worthwhile for its own sake. Order and structure are inherent. This can be readily observed when writing the counting numbers horizontally as follows:

| | | | | | | | | | |
|---|---|---|---|---|---|---|---|---|---|
| 1 | 2 | 3 | 4 | 5 | 6 | 7 | 8 | 9 | 10 |
| 11 | 12 | 13 | 14 | 15 | 16 | 17 | 18 | 19 | 20 |
| 21 | 22 | 23 | 24 | 25 | 26 | 27 | 28 | 29 | 30 |
| 31 | 32 | 33 | 34 | 35 | 36 | 37 | 38 | 39 | 40 |
| 41 | 42 | 43 | 44 | 45 | 46 | 47 | 48 | 49 | 50 |

The pattern is just as obvious when reading the counting numerals vertically. There are interesting patterns when observing the numerals in terms of the commutative property of addition in that A + B = B + A, or in multiplication in that A×B=B×A. Learning these properties is important for young pupils as well as for graduate students in mathematics. Thus, 4 + 5 = 5 + 4 learned meaningfully is helpful in later learning that 98,654 + 45,689 = 45, 689+98, 654. Any other values listed in addition, no matter how large may be added using the commutative property of addition. The same would hold true of multiplication in that 2×3= 3×2 or 12345 × 54321 = 54321× 12345. The associate property of addition in that A+B+C = C+B+A or in multiplication in that A×B×C =

C×B×A emphasizes additional order in mathematics. The associative property too states that there can be any number of addends arranged in any order in addition, or factors in multiplication arranged in any order and the sum for addition, as well as the product in multiplication would be the same.

Subject matter objectives receive the most emphasis in teaching and learning, in a subject centered curriculum. These objectives might be further classified in terms of being facts, concepts, and generalizations. The basic facts of addition, subtraction, multiplication, and division need to be mastered in a meaningful way. Concepts chosen for teaching subject matter need to be relevant and worthy of inclusion. Concepts such as radius, squared, *pi*, circumference, as examples, should be taught when pupils are ready. Generalizations stress pupils learning vital broad ideas as subject matter. The following is an example of a generalization which becomes an objective at the appropriate time in mathematics instruction: Radius squared times *pi* times height is the formula for finding the volume of a cylinder. Abstract knowledge is preferable to the concrete and the semiconcrete when the philosophy of a subject centered mathematics curriculum is being emphasized. However, to learn subject matter, a pupil may need objects, items, and realia (concrete materials) to learn the abstract. Illustrations(semiconcrete materials) of what is being learned might also assist the pupil to learn more rapidly in terms of achieving the abstract. Thus actual models and illustrations of cylinders may help pupils to learn more rapidly and meaningfully that "radius squared times *pi* times height is the formula for finding the volume of a cylinder." In a subject centered mathematics curriculum, skills objectives for pupils to attain are also vital. Skills objectives and their implementation assist pupils to learn subject matter more readily. Skills objectives include critical thinking in ongoing lessons and units of study. Critical thought emphasizes that pupils separate fact from opinion, fantasy from reality, and accurate from inaccurate information. Mathematics as subject matter stresses accuracy in terms of what is a correct answer as compared to what is incorrect. Pupils need guidance and good teaching so that pupils make the distinction of fact from opinion, fantasy from reality, and accurate from inaccurate ideas in mathematics.

The subject centered mathematics curriculum has its merits. Certainly, everyone should be for pupils learning more vital content in mathematics. Generally a subject centered approach in learning de-emphasizes the use of concrete and semiconcrete materials of instruction. With concrete materials which relate directly to what is being taught will extend meanings and understandings of learners. Thus, if pupils are learning to add unit fractions, they should have the one-half and one-fourth of a circle or square directly in from of them. These models can be shown when combined to equal three-fourths of the circle or square. Pupils may then see the model circle and square with the one-fourth and one-half combined to equal three fourths. The abstract fractions may be written next to the models, such as $\frac{1}{2} + \frac{1}{4} = \frac{3}{4}$. One-half may be shown to equal two fourths by placing two-fourths over the one-half in a model circle/square. Pupils may then realize that the fractional part of the circle/square being considered in fourths which is the denominator whereas the number of parts being considered is one plus two-fourths or three-fourths. Manipulative materials need to be used in teaching so that a hands on approach in learning mathematics might well be in evidence. Learners should hold and manipulate the models. They should also do the writing on the chalkboard or overhead to show the fractional values of $\frac{1}{2} + \frac{1}{4} = \frac{3}{4}$. Too frequently, a subject centered mathematics curriculum de-emphasizes learner involvement. And yet the focal point in teaching is the learner. The pupil needs to do the learning whereas the teacher sets the stage so that pupils may achieve, grow, and develop. The interests and attention need to be obtained of learners in a caring environment. Very often, the basal text-book is the major means of instruction in a subject centered mathematics curriculum. The basal text is neither good nor bad, but neutral depending upon how it is used and if pupils are achieving vital objectives in mathematics. The teacher may use concrete and semiconcrete materials to supplement the learning opportunities emphasized in the basal. When subject matter is learned for its own sake, the level of application or applying what has been learned is minimized. Ample opportunities need to be provided pupils whereby they may use subject matter learned in practical situations. When knowledge is used, it will tend to be remembered better and recalling what has been learned will be facilitated.

## PHILOSOPHY OF EXPERIMENTALISM

The philosophy of experimentalism takes out many of the weakness of a subject centered procedure in teaching mathematics. Here, within a contextual situation in teaching mathematics, pupils select a problem to solve. The problem is realistic and perplexities exist in how it is to be solved. Pupils individually or collaboratively may work on a problem to be solved in mathematics. Notice, there are perplexities or difficulties involved in how to solve the problem and what the hypothesis should be in answer to the problematic situation. Problem solving does not emphasize rote learning or drill and practice from a workbook exercise (Ediger, 1997).

For example, a pupil or pupils may ask in context, "How does one find the number of square yards of carpet needed for our classroom since it will be recarpeted during vacation time?" This is a good time to emphasize finding the area of square yards or feet in a classroom where practicality is involved. The problem needs to be clearly stated so that pupils know what is wanted in the problem. Vagueness needs to be eliminated. Pupils with teacher assistance then need to discuss possible ways of determining the answer. The mathematics teacher could immediately state the formula for finding the area of the classroom in square units and show on the chalkboard how the computation is done. However, telling is not teaching nor is it problem solving. Pupils need to state the problem and clarify its meaning. The teacher assists, guides, and helps pupils in problem slving. This is a complex role for the teacher. It is much easier for the teacher to jump in and show deductively how the problem is to be solved with pupils following the model presented by the teacher. But, it is the *pupil* who needs to learn how to identify and solve problems. Thus, after the problem has been clearly identified by pupils with teacher guidance, plans need to be developed to solve the problem. The plans may involve pupils looking for patterns, using models, dramatizing the important ideas, drawing a related illustration looking for diverse possibilities, developing a graph or table, and analyzing the component parts. The plans should be understood by the learner. Vagueness needs to be taken out as much as possible as the work on the problem continues. At the beginning as the problem is being identified, there will be perplexities and that is what problem solving is all about. The perplexities then need to be cleared up as the learning activity progresses. Within the data finding involving planning, an hypothesis or tentative answer follows. Learners need to understand that an hypothesis is tentative and not an absolute. The hypothesis needs to be tested in a life like situation. Thus, the hypothesis may be revised, if need be. The hypothesis may also have been correct in its original statement in determining the area of the classroom in square yards or feet.

Mathematics for pupils should be purposeful, meaningful, useful, sequential, and interesting (Ediger, 1998). Experimentalism, as a philosophy of education appears to meet many of these criteria. Thus, in finding the area of the classroom, carpeting would soon be placed therein. A purpose was then involved for learning and that purpose was to find the number of square feet/yards in the classroom. Meaning was emphasized when pupils, with teacher guidance, understood what was involved when computing the area of the classroom. Subject matter learned was useful in that a practical situation was involved whereby carpeting would be installed in the classroom. Pupils with teacher assistance largely did their own sequencing by using flexible steps of problem solving. The effort put forth in solving problems chosen by pupils appears to emphasize the interest factor in learning mathematics.

## PHILOSOPHY OF DECISION MAKING

Experimentalism, as discussed above, does involve the many decision that need to be made by pupils in problem solving. In contrast, a decision making philosphy also emphasizes pupils choosing from among alternatives to puusue in objectives learning opportunities, and appraisal procedures. The decisions and choices may be made individually or within committees. The learner is the chooser and needs to learn to accept responsibilities for choices made. Problem solving activities as well as other kinds of experiences may be chosen by the involved pupil. With pupil choice, purpose and reasons for making the sequential sections might well be in the offing. Pupil purpose in making choices should increase energy levels for learning. Thus, a pupil may omit that which is not perceived as being purposeful. There are an adequate number of learning opportunities to choose from to keep a pupil learning sequentially and be on task. Sequence resides with the pupil, not in the teacher nor the basal textbook.

The mathematics teacher needs to be a good way for pupils to engage in decision making in the curriculum. A learning centers approach might well be be used here. The following learning centers may be developed by the teacher or through teacher/pupil planning, for a unit on *Geometry for Grade Pupils*:

1. *An art Center*. Here, pupils may develop an art project from diverse cutouts of geometrical figures. This may be a good way for pupils to identify squares, rectangles, circles, trapezoids, parallelograms, and triangles. The art projects, after completion, should be displayed in the classroom or hallway near to the classroom door.
2. *A model Making Center*. Here, pupils individually or in a small group may make models of geometrical figures with each labeled properly. The models should be displayed above the chalkborad for pupils to refer to, as needed, when they pursue ongoing lessons in geometry.
3. A work sheet center whereby pupils learn to determine the perimeter of selected geometrical figures presented in picture form. Formulas for determining perimeter may be written clearly on a chart for future reference. The pupils at this center may wish to work collaboratively to determine perimeters. The resulting learnings should be applied to the real world of concrete and semi-concrete materials.
4. *A Dramatization Cnter*. Here, pupils may engage in planning for and dramatizing a play pertaining to geometrical figures. Much creativity is necessary in order to role play a specific geometrical figure such as a square. The others in the classroom may observe the play after its completion and rehearsal.
5. *A Textbook Center*. Here, pupils individually or collectively may work selected exercises from the basal. The exercises relate directly to the ongoing unit being studied. Pupils may help each other as necessary or the teacher may provide needed guidance.
6. *A drawing Center*. Here, pupils may develop diagrams that explain partially what is being learned. Thus, to find the area of a triangle, pupils may develop two triangles from a square

to realize and understand the formula: ½ base times height, or ½ bh.

7. *An Audio-visual Center*. Pupils may observe a video-tape and answer questions at the center related to its contents,
8. *A Computer Center*. Here, pupils may work on drill and practice, tutorial, simulation, and games for review purposes as well as to obtain new subject matter pertaining to the unit being pursued.
9. *A Writing of Problems Center*. Pupils may write problems for others to solve related to the lesson or unit being pursued.
10. *A Reading Center*. Pupils may select and read a library book of their own choosing pertaining to mathematics. These books need to be on diverse reading levels and topics in mathematics.

Pupils need to choose the centers they wish to work on sequentially. If decision making is to be involved, then more tasks need to be available than what a pupils can complete. Tasks that lack perceived purpose may be omitted. If pupils are not on task, the teacher needs to assist these pupils to get back on task. Being at learning centers and completing tasks therein is demanding, not a goof of. The teacher monitors pupil work so that high quality products and processes are in evidence. The pupil is the chooser of which center and tasks to work on. If too many pupils select the same center to work at, the teacher needs to be a good organizer so that pupils are spread out at the different centers. A rotation basis may also be used whereby pupils rotate in working at a center, but still choose what to learn and what to omit. The goal is to have pupils achieve mathematics content and skills more optimally since tasks may be chosen that represent pupil purpose. Decision making is also stressed.

## MEASUREMENT DRIVEN PHILOSOPHY

There are many advocates of measurement driven instruction in mathematics. Highly precise objectives need to be chosen by the teacher, district, or on the state level as mandated objectives. The state level then mandates of requires pupils to take tests to determine how well they are doing in achieving the highly precise objectives of instruction. There is no pupil input into the determination and writing of these objectives. The teacher chooses the learning opportunities which assist pupils to achieve these objectives. Criterion referenced tests (CRTs) are given periodically to pupils to ascertain how much achievement there is on the part of pupils in achieving the stated objectives. Schools within a district or school districts may be compared in test results to notice which schools stress stronger achievement than do others. These comparisons might be very unfair since pupils grow up in different kinds of homes with some providing more educational advantages due to having more income. Money does buy many advantages in life. With more educational advantages for some as compared to others, it is no wonder that mathematics achievement is higher or lower for some pupils as compared to others.

Which basic beliefs are in evidence with measurement driven instruction (MDI)?

1. All pupils experience the same mathematics curriculum, but individuals may work at achieving these objectives at different rates of speed.
2. Sequence in learning with the chosen learning opportunities is determined by the mathematics teacher.
3. The objectives are selected externally in relationship to the pupils in the classroom. Thus, pupil input tends to be omitted in the mathematics curriculum.
4. Being able to measure pupil achievement receives major emphasis since results are stated in numerical terms such as percentiles, grade equivalents, standard deviations, quartile deviations, and stanines.
5. Reporting pupil progress in mathematics to parents is much easier if numbers can be used, as indicators, to show learner achievement.

MDI may stress, too frequently, measurement of facts that pupils have learned since these are easiest to measure in achievement. Higher cognitive objectives and their accomplishment are much more difficult to measure.

Ediger (1995) summarizes the MDI philosophy of instruction with the following statements:

1. precise, measurably stated objectives are written prior to instruction.
2. the teacher may announce prior to teaching what students are to learn as a result of instruction.
3. activities for instruction should contain only that which is stated in the objective.
4. appraisal procedures emphasize evaluating student achievement in terms of what was stated in the objective.
5. sequence of activities provided for students is planned by the teacher.
6. tests are valid if they measure what is stated in the objective.
7. activities are valid if they align directly with the stated objectives.
8. techniques of appraisal need to align very precisely with the objectives.

## ADULT DETERMINED MATHEMATICS CURRICULUM

There are numerous adult centered mathematics curriculum plans of instruction. MDI emphasizes adults, highly capable in mathematics, determining which objectives pupils are to achieve. We would like to discuss another adult determined mathematics curriculum plan. Standards setting has become very important in curriculum development. These standards may not be stated in measurable terms, but represent established goals by adults who are very competent in mathematics. 'High expectations' has become a key word here. The feeling is that if teachers have high expectations for pupils in mathematics, the latter will achieve at a higher level. The stated goals in themselves reflect the thinking that pupils can achieve that which is much more challenging than what is presently emphasized in the classroom. Thus, setting goals at a higher level of complexity as well as higher teacher expections for pupil in mathematics will guide the latter to achieve at a more optimal level. The National Council Teachers of Mathematics (NCTM, 1989), USA developed an excellent set of objectives for pupils to achieve; the following is an example of Communication, Reasoning, and Connections Standards(p. 26):

**KINDERGARTEN THROUGH GRADE FOUR**

Standard 2 : Mathematics as Communication. In grades K–4, the study of mathematics should include numerous opportunities for communication so that students can:

* relate physical materials, pictures, and diagrams to mathematical ideas:
* reflect on and clarify their thinking about mathematical language and symbols:
* realize that representing, discussing, reading, writing, and listening to mathematics are a vital part of learning and using mathematics.

Standard 3 : Mathematics as Reasoning. In grades K-4, the study of mathematics should emphasize reasoning so that students can:

* draw logical conclusions about mathematics:
* use models known as facts, properties, and relationships to explain their thinking...

Standard 4 : Mathematical Connections. In grades K - 4, the study of mathematics should include opportunities to make connections so that students can:

* link conceptual and procedural knowledge;
* relate various representations of concepts and procedures to one another;
* relate various representations among different topics in mathematics;
* use mathematics in other curriculum areas;
* use mathematics in their daily lives.

The above named standards indicate the need for pupils to relate, reflect upon, use, as well as integrate the four vocabularies of listening, speaking, reading, and writing in the curriculum area of mathematics. Logic needs to be stressed heavily in that pupils need to be able to draw conclusions, use models and patterns, justify answers and solution processes, as well as experience mathematics as a meaningful curriculum area. In linking mathematics to other curriculum areas as well as to their daily lives, pupils make connections indeed!

The above example indicates what an adult determined mathematics curriculum has to offer teachers in terms of voluntary standards to emphasize in the classroom. We believe strongly that objectives developed by groups and organizations outside the local classroom and this includes objectives developed on the state level should be voluntary to stress in the classroom. We believe strongly that mathematics teachers should be well grounded in the national and state standards through workshops, faculty meetings, and other means of inservice education. In this way, mathematics teachers have vital goals to select from to improve the curriculum. Much time and effort went into developing these standards for teachers to emphasize in the mathematics curriculum. The teacher might then select and adapt those relevant objectives for pupils to achieve whereby readiness, purpose, and interest in learning is in evidence. Learning opportunities need to be chosen by the mathematics teacher to help pupils achieve these goals (Ediger, 1996).

## CONCLUSION

There are diverse philosophies which teachers and administrators need to consider and appraise. The philosophy or philosophies chosen in instruction need to harmonize with pupils' individual learning styles. Learners need quality objectives, learning opportunities, and evaluation procedures to achieve as optimally as possible in mathematics. There may be times whereby a more open-ended as compared to a highly structures mathematics curriculum needs to be emphasized. At other times, pupils may need a more structured environment in mathematics. The pupil is the focal point of instruction in mathematics. Mathematics is a basic and it is vital for pupils to learn as much as possible therein. Teachers and administrators need to stay abreast of current trends in the teaching of mathematics and implement what is relevant and assists pupils to learn as optimally as possible (Ediger, 1998).

## REFERENCES

Ediger, Marlow (1995), *Philosophy in Curriculum Development.* Kirksville, Missouri: Simpson Publishing Company, 21.

Ediger, Marlow (1997), *Teaching Mathematics in the Elementary School.* Kirksville, Missouri: Simpson Publishing Company, 46-48.

Ediger, Marlow (1996), *Essays in School Administration.* Kirksville, Missouri : Simpson Publishing company, 1-4.

Ediger, Marlow (1998), *"Change and the School Administrator, Education,* 118 (4), 541-48.

National Council Teachers of Mathematics (1989), *Curriculum and Evaluation Standards for School Mathematics.* Reston, Virginia : NCTM, 26.

Rathaiali, Lavu and Digumarti Bhaskara Rao, eds. (1996). *International Innovations in Education.* New Delhi : Discovery Publishing House.

*Chapter 3*

# MATHEMATICS IN THE ELEMENTARY SCHOOL

Teachers and administrators need to determine the best mathematics curriculum possible for each pupil. Additional people to assist in developing the mathematics curriculum include university professors in mathematics, parents, other lay persons, and interested personnel in mathematics education. The mathematics curriculum needs to be studied carefully and objectively to arrive at a consensus involving worthwhile objectives for pupil attainment.

Pupil need to become mathematics literate in a rapidly changing society. The National Council Teachers of Mathematics (NCTM) in 1989 came out with a comprehensive statement of objectives for pupils to achieve. Five broadly stated objectives are the following: Pupils need to:

1. learn to value mathematics.
2. become confident in their ability to do mathematics.
3. become mathematical problem solvers.
4. learn to communicate mathematically.
5. learn to reason mathematically (NCTM, 1989, 23).

Each of the above named objectives is relevant for pupils in kindergarten through grade twelve, and beyond, throughout one's life time. To value mathematics means to have pupils feel it is important in school and in society in an ongoing way. The use of mathematics is practical in that in everyday situations individuals face problems involving number. There are items to purchase and pay for. There are checkbook balances to keep and maintain accurately. Monthly print-outs come from the local bank for individual to verify if the accounts were kept accurately and match what the consumer has record of in his/her checkbook such as lists of canceled checks and money on hand balance. It is always good for the consumer to check the accuracy of his/her checkbook balance with that of the computerized bank statement.

Further utilitarian uses of number include credit card purchases with the accompanying receipts and the monthly statement itemizing purchases and payments made as issued by the credit card company. These are just a few ways that are practical in every day use that indicates the necessity for pupils to appreciate number.

The pupil may also value mathematics for its own sake. There is beauty inherent in seeing order in mathematics. No other academic discipline seemingly has this order in which so consistent. No wonder that Rene Descartes (1596–1650) based his philosophy of idealism on mathematics. Descartes advocated using deductive reasoning in arriving at truth. His model stressed a person starting at a given point in knowledge where certainty was involved. Thus deductively, the individual presents clear and distinct ideas related to the starting point. Each new idea is then different from the previous and at the same time is very clear, not vague nor subject to interpretation (Ediger, 1995).

It is enjoyable to notice order in mathematics, such as in base ten. When counting by twos, the order of numbers in making a table are indeed unique:

| | | | | | | | | | | |
|---|---|---|---|---|---|---|---|---|---|---|
| 2 | 12 | 22 | 32 | 42 | 52 | 62 | 72 | 82 | 92 | 102 |
| 4 | 14 | 24 | 34 | 44 | 54 | 64 | 74 | 84 | 94 | 104 |
| 6 | 16 | 26 | 36 | 46 | 56 | 66 | 76 | 86 | 96 | 106 |
| 8 | 18 | 28 | 38 | 48 | 58 | 68 | 78 | 88 | 98 | 108 |
| 10 | 20 | 30 | 40 | 50 | 60 | 70 | 80 | 90 | 100 | 110 |

There certainly is order also when thinking of structural ideas in mathematics:

1. the commutative property of addition states that the order of two addends can be added in any sequence and the sum is the same. Thus, $a + b = b + a$.
2. the associative property of addition states that three or more addends may be added in any order and the sum will be the same, such as $a + b + c = c + b + a$. There are other arrangements

of ordering the addends for addition and the answer or sum will be the same such as—a + c + b = b + c + a. There may be any number of addends, not just three.

3. the commutative and associative properties hold true for multiplication in the same way as was true of addition. Thus, a×b=b×a for the commutative property in multiplication. And, a×b×c=c×b×a for the associative property of multiplication. There may be other arrangements in considering the order of factors when multiplying such as b×a×c= c×a×b. There also might be any number of factors to multiply, beyond that of three: axb×c×d= d×c×b×a. The symbol 'x' stands for 'times', in multiplication.
4. the property of closure indicates that the answer to an addition problem containing whole numbers will also be a whole number. The whole numbers consist of the set: 0, 1, 2, 3, 5, .. The three dots mean the numbers go on sequentially in an infinite manner.

Becoming confident in performing operations and doing problem solving is a must. Learners need to be successful in daily work in mathematics in order to become confident that they can and do achieve success. The mathematics teacher needs to adjust each pupil's daily work to harmonize with his/her capacity and ability to attain success in goal attainment. The teacher may praise a pupil for doing well in mathematics so that increased confidence is in the offing. The praise needs to be honestly given to the learner who is truly doing better in achievement in mathematics. Praise might then be frequently provided to those who do improve in achieving objectives.

Problem solving in mathematics is always a practical and utilitarian goal. Problems need to be as realistic as possible. Lifelike problems identified by pupils for solving propel learners to put forth effort in learning. These problems are considered intrinsically worthwhile to be significant. There are perplexities here in that the involved learner is not certain of the direction to go which is necessary in offering solutions. Thus, deliberation and reflection are needed. Thinking then centers upon clarifying the meaning of the problem as well as of possible alternatives for solution. The solution or hypothesis being considered is tentative and may be modified if evidence warrants. If the solution/hypothesis holds up under testing in a realistic situation, there might then be evidence that the correctness of the answer is no longer tentative. In mathematics, pupils deal with more exactness and accurateness as compared to other curriculum areas, such as social studies. In social studies, there is not the rightness of an answer as compared to mathematics, such as in the basic addition, subtraction, multiplication, and division facts. Thus, for example, in base ten, five plus five is always ten. There are no exceptions.

Being able to communicate well is important in all curriculum areas. Mathematics is no exception. In the following situations, pupils need to be able to communicate clearly and accurately in mathematics:

1. When working in committees and in large group instruction.
2. when discussing ideas with others.
3. when indicating work performed on paper.
4. when using the word processor to show mathematical operations and problem solving experiences.
5. when developing line, bar and circle graphs to show data and information.
6. when using multiple intelligences (Gardner, 1993) to show mathematical ideas. This includes using written work, art work, dramatizations, songs, interpersonal and interpersonal activities, social studies content, and subject matter from science, information to indicate what has been learned in mathematics. Verbal intelligence, such reading, writing, and taking multiple choice tests, as well as other kinds of tests where reading alone is stressed, should not be used to the extent of crowding out those mentioned previously in multiple intelligences. Nor should verbal intelligence by minimized. Pupils then do possess multiple intelligences and these need to be honored and rewarded by the teacher. Possessing multiple intelligences is quite obvious as one observes professional athletes, musicians, dancers, and individuals in the business and academic worlds reveal their talents.

Sternberg (1997) states that when we expand the range of abilities we test for, we also expand the range of students we identify as smart. Among other curriculum areas, he stresses the following as examples in mathematics:

*Memory:* Remember the mathematical formula (Distance = Rate × Time).

*Analysis:* Solve a mathematical problem (using the $D = RT$ formula).

*Creativity:* Create your own mathematical word problem using the $D = RT$ formula.

*Practicality:* Show how to use the $D=RT$ formula to estimate driving time from one city to another near you.

Pupils then need to learn to communicate clearly and accurately in mathematics. It is a necessity to do so; otherwise misinformation will be presented. Also, the reasoning ability of pupils is important in mathematics. Pupils need to use logic when reasoning inductively or deductively. When reasoning inductively, pupils achieve sequentially from the specific to the general. Thus, with the commutative and associative properties of addition and multiplication, learners may generalize from a few cases where this property works to many situations. The cases/situations may be tested again and again in terms of correctness to notice the worth of the commutative as well as associative properties. With deductive reasoning, the mathematics teacher may present one or two examples in a meaningful way to pupils whereby the latter then makes application to specific situations of these properties. Pupils may be appraised at regular intervals if the commutative and associative properties of mathematics are understood and being applied.

Good attitudes of pupils toward mathematics indicate that this academic discipline is valued or prized. Learner need to trust the self that with continued success in ongoing lessons and units in mathematics, they are becoming increasingly confident. Being a proficient problem solver is at the top of mathematics skills and abilities that need to be achieved. With all facts of learning, pupils need to be able to communicate with others in clear and distinct language using symbols in mathematics. Reasoning abilities also need to be cultivated continuously in ongoing lessons and units of study.

## PRINCIPLES OF LEARNING IN MATHEMATICS

The mathematics teacher has selected guidelines which need to be followed in order that pupils may achieve more optimally. These guidelines come from the psychology of learning as advocated by educational psychologists. First of all, pupils need to perceive learning activities that are meaningful. They need to understand that which is taught. Too frequently, rote learning is stressed in which pupils memorize content in ongoing lessons and units of study. Rote learning is done without pupils realizing what is meant by the content committed to memory. Then too, what is memorized usually is placed in short term memory and forgotten. Whereas, what is understood has a good chance of becoming a part of long term memory. We recommend that teachers select important concepts and generalizations to teach that are taught in a manner whereby pupils attach meaning and understanding. For example, if pupils are to understand the concept of what a *line* is, they should see short and longer lines on the chalkboard as well as on monitors with software presentations. Next, pupils should look at illustrations and identify lines in individual pictures. Lines should be differentiated from line segments and rays. Pupils should also have chances to look at objects in the classroom and identify lines thereon. The teacher needs to observe that pupils do not become tired or become confused over what a line is, but rather keep attention placed upon the concept to be developed.

Second, the mathematics teacher needs to pay attention to the rate of presentation at which pupils may understand and attach meaning to what is taught. We have observed student teachers and co-operating teachers, whom we have supervised in the schools, who are in a hurry to have pupils cover much content. The chances are in a hurried lesson that few pupils will grasp the meaning of what is taught. Rather, the teacher needs to observe pupils to pace learning experiences which assist pupils individually to understood that which is taught. Lessons may be paced too rapidly so that understanding of content by pupils is not possible, or the content may be paced too slowly whereby pupils loose attention and focus.

Third, pupils need to experience a variety of learning opportunities in the mathematics curriculum. There are more activities available for pupils than ever before. The teacher needs to select those which will guide pupils than ever before. The teacher needs to select those which will guide pupils to achieve as optimally as possible. Which kinds of learning opportunities might then be available for pupils?

1. The basal textbook, carefully chosen, may provide rich experiences for pupils. This can be done if the teacher is creative and brings in novel, unique experiences along with using the basal mathematics textbook. Readiness for each learning activity needs to be provided pupils that precede teaching and learning from the basal. The readiness experiences provide sequential learnings for pupils. Concrete and semi concrete materials should be used as readiness experiences as well as during the time that pupils are engaged in using the basal.
2. Videotapes and other audio-visual aids on the understanding level of pupils may provide excellent learning opportunities for pupils. For example, if pupils are studying the area of a square, there are good videotapes that provide interesting ways for pupils to determine the area of a square. Pupils may then observe how the person on in the video measures the length and width of the floor in the house to come up with the area in square feet. There are also films that convey this information clearly and accurately to pupils. In one film, a pupil wishes to find out how many square inches there are on his desktop at home. The pace of the presentation is good in that pupils listening and observing may obtain the necessary information in an unhurried way in order to be able to measure to ascertain square inches of a square or rectangle. I like to use filmstrips in teaching. Here, the teacher may take as long as he/she wishes on a frame to teach a concept or generalization in mathematics. The teacher or the pupil determines when to turn to the next frame in sequence. We have observed student teachers and supervising teachers make their own slides to use in teaching.

These slides then in content pertain to the stated objectives of the ongoing lesson or unit of study.

3. Drawings may be made to illustrate concepts and generalizations to pupils. A paper marked in square inches may be an excellent way for pupils to learn how to determine the number of square inches in a given region. Fraction kits showing a pizza divided in halves, fourths, sixths, eighths, among other divisions, may assist pupils to understand fractional values better. Pupils may make their own fractional kits to use in ongoing lessons. Fractional kits truly represent manipulative materials whereby learners may use a hands on approach in learning. Thus, the parts may be manipulated to show that two-fourths equal one-half; the two-fourths may be placed over the half for meaningful learning.
4. Software and technology may be used wisely in teaching mathematics. Drill and practice experiences provide opportunities for pupils to reflect upon what has not been mastered previously. Each program guides pupils through a set of experiences which assists in remedying what had not been learned previously. Tutorial software guides pupils to understand a new process such as adding fractions with unlike denominators. Sequence in the activities helps pupils to understand why the denominators need to be the same before adding can occur. Simulation emphasizes realistic problem solving activities for pupils. The problem is stated for the pupil but generally needs clarification. The learner, individually or in a committee, may then attempt to locate information to solve the problem. The solution is tentative and subject to testing. If necessary, the solution is modified or changed. Gaming stresses pupils playing a competitive game with two or three sides involved. The game may also be for an individual pupil. Games can be very enjoyable for pupils as well as provide for needed learning experiences. Wholesome competition may be emphasized in that a team may win whereas there are also losers, but if pupils can enjoy and learn effectively, the competition can be quite healthy.

The point to be made from the above discussion is that pupils need to experience a variety of learning activities so that interest and meaning is involved while boredom is kept to a very minimum.

Fourth, pupils need to experience individual and collaborative endeavours. Why? there are times when pupils need to be able to work effectively on individual tasks and activities. Then too, there are times whereby pupils need to work well with others in collaborative settings. Both working individually and with others in a positive way are important. In working with others, it is good to have pupils assist each other as needed as well as work politely with others. Learners should become caring individuals who are there to provided needed assistance. High academic achievement should be possible in either individual or group situations.

Esteem needs of individuals should be met whereby pupils are recognized for their talents and abilities. Being confident of the self helps pupils to reach toward higher goals in mathematics achievement. Multicultural education needs to be stressed in collaborative situations. Learners need to respect and accept those who differ according to race, religious beliefs, abilities, and past accomplishments in mathematics. Pupils who are mainstreamed need to be accepted and assisted as needed. There should be no discrimination among individuals due to differences possessed. Differences need to be prized, not cause stumbling blocks.

Fifth, teachers need to minimize lecture as a method of instruction. Explanations are a form of lecture but need to be used to clarify, enrich, and assist to make for meaning in learning. Explanations are short in length and are given in a precise manner to communicate in a rather brief period of time. How short in duration are explanations? It depends upon the amount of subject matter a pupil needs in order to continue working with the task at hand in mathematics. The teacher needs to avoid lengthy explanations whereby pupils lose interest in learning. Sometimes, the mathematics teacher will need to ask questions of the learner to clarify meanings so that the latter may proceed with the ongoing experience. Pupils should be actively engaged in learning and not be passive recipients of knowledge.

Sixth, pupils need to work in an environment that is conducive to achieving in mathematics. A tense learning environment will not assist pupils to achieve as much as they can. Mathematics anxiety is term given to pupils who fear mathematics and feel inferior in this curriculum area. A hostile learning environment whereby pupils are scolded for making mistakes is hardly conducive to appreciating and liking mathematics. A relaxed environment in which learners desire to achieve and attain is wanted. In this environment, pupils like to work with others in collaborative endeavours. Learners also like to work by themselves on individual tasks. Good, attractive bulletin board displays may also assist pupils to enjoy mathematics. These displays may be used to teach pupils or they may also be used as devices for pupils to learn on their very own. Wholesome attitudes toward mathematics as curriculum area need to be in the offing on the student's part. Being sensitive to pupil's feeling is important. Ridiculing and humiliating pupils is a *no no* in teaching mathematics. Mathematics as a curriculum area should not be used to punish pupils for misdeeds.

Seventh, mathematics for all is important to stress. Mathematics is not just for the gifted and talented, But each and every pupil need to achieve vital objectives in mathematics. To be numeracy literate is very important and each pupil needs to achieve as much as possible. Mathematics is a very useful curriculum area presently for pupils, as well as for the future at a work place.

Equity is important to stress whereby each gender receives good instruction to achieve vital objectives. Evaluation techniques and results indicate where pupils individually need more assistance. Remediation then may follow the diagnosis. Computer use, in particular, needs to stress fairness in time for technology use. Thus, boys and girls need to experience a fair share of time in computer use and develop proficiency in its use for each gender.

Eighth, pupils need to achieve three categories of objectives in mathematics. Knowledge objectives need to be carefully chosen and represent vital facts, concepts, and generalizations for pupils to achieve. The objectives need to reflect arithmetic, algebra, geometry, statistics, and graphing. Each objective is relevant and utilitarian in use. Skills objectives, as a second kind for pupils attainment, need to emphasize critical and creative thinking, as well as problem solving. The third kind to stress are attitudinal objectives. The attitudinal objectives should emphasize positive feelings pupils need, to achieve well in the mathematics curriculum. Quality attitudes are long term and difficult for pupils to develop, but achieving them assists pupils to do well in the knowledge and skills areas. Too frequently, bad attitudes hinder pupils from learning as much as they could. In daily lesson plans and entire units of study, the teacher needs to pay careful attention to what will be taught. Thus, three kinds of objectives- knowledge, skills, and attitudes - need adequate attention in curriculum development.

Ninth, a hands on approach in learning needs to be emphasized. Starting with kindergarten pupils for example, the teacher needs to have an adequate number of materials for pupils for example, the teacher meeds to have an adequate number of materials for pupils to use that identify a set of five objects. Each pupil needs to have five sticks to use in associating the concept of "five" with the actual number of sticks that are there. Pupils may use sticks, and other objects, to add, subtract, multiply,and divide. Objects may also be used for counting, forming geometrical designs, and finding the unknown in algebra.

Tenth, pupils need to apply that which has been learned. To make application in practical situations might well indicate that the pupil understands mathematical content studied. To apply what has been learned, pupils need to attach meaning to subject matter being used. Attaching meaning to content understood indicates that pupils have had and experienced prerequisite tasks such as adding, subtracting, multiplying, and dividing. Thus, a hands on approach in learning has been used .

## CONCLUSION

The mathematics teacher has numerous responsibilities in guiding pupils to achieve sequentially. Principles of learning need to be used to assist pupils to achieve as optimally as possible. Objectives need to be chosen which are vital and relevant. Knowledge, skills, and attitudinal objectives need to be in the offing for pupils to achieve. Rational balance among these kinds of objectives need to be stressed in ongoing lessons and units of study. Learning opportunities need to be varied so that each pupil's learning style is being accommodated. These learning opportunities are varied to provide for individual differences among learners so that each may achieve as much as possible. The mathematics teacher needs to possess a good repertoire of knowledge in mathematics, but there also needs to skill on the teacher's part to have learners achieve stated objectives. Sequential experiences for pupils assist in attaining vital goals of mathematics instruction. In a relaxed environment, pupils should achieve as much as individual abilities permit.

## REFERENCES

Bhaskara Rao, Digumarti (1993). *Teaching of Science*, Guntur, Nagarjuna Publishers (in Telugu language).

Bhaskara Rao, Digumarti, ed. (1997). *District Primary Education Project*, New Delhi; Discovery Publishing House.

Ediger, Marlow (1995), *Philosophy of Curriculum Development*. Kirksville, Missouri; Simpson Publishing Company, Chapters One and Two.

Ediger, Marlow (1997), *The Modern Elementary School*, Kirksville, Missouri; Simpson Publishing Company, Chapter Six.

Ediger, Marlow (1997), *Teaching Mathematics in the Elementary School*, Kirksville, Missouri : Simpson Publishing Company, Chapter Two.

Gardner, Howard (1993), *Multiple Intelligences : Theory in Practice*, New York; Basic Books.

NCTM (1989), *Curriculum and Evaluation Standards for School Mathematics* . Reston, Virginia, 23.

Sternberg, Robert (1997), "What Does it Mean to be Smart?" Educational Leadership, 24 (6), 20-24.

## *Chapter 4*

# ACHIEVING WORLD CLASS STANDARDS IN MATHEMATICS

Much has been written and talks presented on World Class Standards that pupils need to achieve in mathematics. The goal here is to raise standards for pupils to achieve. When international comparisons are being made among different nations on the planet earth, many people, especially from the business world are not satisfied with the results of pupil achievement in mathematics. The Third International Mathematics and Science Study (TIMSS) brought attention to the American public as to how US pupils compare with those of other nations. Pertaining to TIMSS, Bracey (1997) wrote:

The Third International Mathematics and Science Study was the big hit of the year. Most educators who hold press conferences consider themselves lucky if they drew 25 people. Some 300 showed up for the first release of TIMSS data...

For the record, we repeat the major finding of eighth grade test results: American eighth-graders placed 25th of the 41 nations in mathematics...

The press almost uniformly pronounced the eighth graders' performance 'mediocre,' forgetting the 'average' is a statistic and 'mediocre' is a judgement that might or might not be accurate... there are about 30 'mediocre' nations, because the scores of most countries were closely bunched–and close to the scores of the US correct...

The eighth grade data might have been ho-hum. But the fourth grade results were so upbeat that President Clinton made a last minute decision to announce them himself. If one considers only the countries that met all the TIMSS sampling criteria, then US fourth graders were seventh of seventeen in math..

The mood of the USA is to be number one in the world in mathematics and science, among all nations. In 1989 at the National Governor's Conference, then President Bush stated that one of six national goals was for the US to be first in the world in mathematics and science. This means that pupils need to achieve higher standards in test results in mathematics that ever before. Then too, there is fear that the US will not be number one, among nations, in goods and services produced in the economy. There is considerable criticism, be it warranted or unwarranted, from the business world on pupil achievement in US schools.

## WHO SHOULD SET STANDARDS FOR PUPIL ACHIEVEMENT?

When attending elementary school years, grades one through eight, from 1934-1942, there were no state or national standards for pupils to achieve. However, there were county standards in which a pupil had to achieve 70% correct of the test items for all curriculum areas upon graduation. The test was written on the country level and each county wrote their own tests in the state of Kansas.

The major material and perhaps the only material of instruction in mathematics at that time was the basal textbook and an accompanying workbook. Teachers followed these mathematics texts religiously in scope and sequence. The textbooks were state adopted in that the state bought publication rights for the mathematics text chosen for use in classrooms in spite of hearing much criticism.

As parents become more involved in their children's mathematics education, their understanding of the changes occurring in school mathematics increases. As a result, they begin to support and enhance their school's efforts to reform their mathematics programs. A principal expressed this idea while reflecting on the parental support that his school had garnered : You make sure that you involve as many parents from the community as you can. We have parent's night, parent's advisory groups, and small groups... We have parent's night, parent's advisory groups, and small groups... We do an awful lot of public relations. To think the main thing that we did a pretty good job of his keeping parents informed as to what's going on... People are always a little concerned about change, and so you try to have community meetings and try to inform. And there will be people who will challenge it, of course, but ... we worked with out community, and I think for the most part they are in support of it (Peressini, 1997).

## MULTIPLE INTELLIGENCES

The concept of multiple intelligences comes up very frequently in journal articles and speeches given at teacher education conventions. Howard Gardner (1993) has identified eight intelligences; logical/mathematical is the intelligence which will be most pertinent for this writing, of the eight identified intelligences. However, the intelligences may well overlap. Campbell wrote:

"In Eva Reeder's math classes at Mountain lake Terrace High School in Edmonds, Washington, students learn algebra kinesthetically (bodily/kinesthetic is another intelligence identified by Gardner). When studying how to graph equations, they head for the school courtyard. There they identify X and Y co-ordinates in the lines of the large, square, cement blocks that form the pavement. Then they plot themselves as points on the large cement axes. Reader maintains that when her students physically pretend to be graphs, they learn more about equations in a single class session than they do in a month of textbook study..."

Many researchers use the multiple intelligences as entry points into lesson content. As our first example showed, Reeder teaches algebra and geometry kinesthetically. Students who have trouble understanding math through paper/pencil exercises (verbal/linguistic intelligence) often grasp concepts easily when they build models or role play math formulas. Other teachers attempt to engage all eight intelligences in their lessons. Sharon Thetford, a multiage intermediate teacher at Tulip Elementary School, sets up eight learning stations that her students rotate through each day. While such lesson planning admittedly daunting, at first, many teachers report that thinking in multiple modes quickly becomes second nature.

To begin lesson planning, teachers should reflect on a concept that they want to teach and identify the intelligences that seems most appropriate for communicating the content...

Much stress is placed upon learning styles in the curriculum. Silver, Strong, and Perini (1997) present the following model for teachers to use in teaching mathematics when integrating multiple intelligences (logical/mathematical) with four learning style--mastery, interpersonal, understanding, and self-expressive:

**Logical/ mathematical:**

*Mastery*: The ability to use numbers to compute, describe, and document...

*Interpersonal* : The ability to apply mathematics in personal and daily life...

*Understanding* : The ability to use mathematical concepts to make conjectures, establish proofs, and apply mathematics and data to construct arguments...

*Self Expressive* : The ability to be sensitive to the patterns, symmetry, logic, and esthetics of mathematics and to solve problems in design and modeling...

Multiple intelligences and learning styles are pupil centered. They attempt to personalize and engage pupils actively in the learning process. Mathematics teachers have guidelines to go by in the teaching arena when planning and implementing units of study and lessons in the classroom. Both pupils and teachers may reflect upon their work and processes used.

**CONCLUSION**

There are numerous, good sources from which to obtain challenging objectives for pupils to achieve in mathematics. The National Council Teachers of Mathematics (NCTM). We recommend the careful consideration of their publications for teachers to read and voluntarily apply valuable ideas in classroom teaching:

* *Curriculum and Evaluation Standards for School Mathematics* (1989).

Here, the authors point out that educational goals for students reflect the importance of mathematical literacy. Toward this end, the K–12 standards articulate five general goals for all students: (1) that they learn to value mathematics, (2) that they become confident in their ability to do mathematics, (3) that they become mathematical problem solvers, (4) that they learn to communicate mathematically, and (5) that they learn to reason mathematically.

* *Professional Standards for Teaching Mathematics* (1991).
* *Assessment Standards for School Mathematics* (1995).

To achieve quality objectives, pupils need to experience worthwhile learning opportunities. The mathematics teacher needs to choose those activities which will assist pupils to achieve relevant objectives. Thus, the chosen learning opportunities should provide for individual differences in achievement. Pupils differ from each other in terms of the complexity of mathematics problems they can benefit from. They also differ from each other in terms of interests possessed, motivation, and purpose in studying ongoing lessons and units of study in mathematics. It behooves the mathematics teacher to plan well and thoroughly to guide each pupil to learn as much as possible in mathematics (Ediger, 1997).

To guide pupils to achieve as optimally as possible, the mathematics teacher needs to use quality criteria in teaching from the psychology of learning:

1. Meaningful lessons lessons are inherent in ongoing units of study in mathematics.

2. Interesting content and skills need emphasis in mathematics.
3. Purposeful mathematics subject matter should be in the offing.
4. Achievable, challenging objectives must be implemented in teaching and learning.
5. Valid and reliable techniques of evaluation need to be used to ascertain pupil progress (Ediger, 1994).

## REFERENCES


Bracey, Gerald W. (1997), The Seventh Bracey Report on the Condition of Public Education, *Phi Delta Kappan,* 79 (2), 124-25.

Campbell, Linda (1997), *How teachers Interpret MI Theory,* Educational Leadership, 55 (1), 14-15.

Ediger, Marlow (1994), "Early field Experiences in Teacher Education," *College Student Journal.* 28 (3), 302.

Ediger, Marlow (1997), *Teaching Mathematics in the Elementary School.* Kirksville, Missouri : Simpson Publishing Company, 93.

Gardner, Howard (1993), *Multiple Intelligences : The Theory in Practice.* New York: The Basic Books.

National Council Teachers of Mathematics (NCTM) 1989, 1991. and 1995. Reston, Virginia.

Peressini, Dominic (1997), "Parental Reform of Mathematics Education," *The Mathematics Teacher.* 90 (6), 426.

Silver, Harvey, Richard Strong, and Mathew Perini (1997), "Integrating Learning Styles and Multiple Intelligences," *Educational Leadership,* 55 (1), 25.

# Chapter 5

# ORGANIZING FOR INSTRUCTION IN MATHEMATICS

A good mathematics instructor is a proficient organizer of pupils for instruction in mathematics (Ediger, 1997, pp 18–38). Here, the teacher has numerous incidental ways for pupils to learn mathematics. Bulletion board displays which illustrate selected facts, concepts, and generalizations in mathematics can assist pupils to obtain needed background information on their very own. The bulletin board displays may also be used in direct teaching of pupils as they relate to an ongoing lesson or unit of study. The best stimulating bulletin board displays we observed when supervising student teachers and co-operating teachers in the schools emphasized a history of measurement. Many pupils were fascinated with the display by noticing how the centimeter, meter, and kilometer had their beginning or origin. We think the bulletin board displays here helped pupils to learn more about measurement. Many pupils spent much time viewing and discussing the bulletin board displays. The mathematics teacher needs to take down a display when it has served its purpose and prepare a new one which encourages pupil learning.

## USING LEARNING STATIONS

The mathematics teacher may organize pupils for instruction by developing a set of learning stations. Each station needs to be labeled so that pupils know what to expect at the center. We suggest that each learning station have concrete (objects, items, and realia) for pupils to learn from. These concrete materials stimulate and motivate pupil learning. Semiconcrete materials (illustrations, slides, video-tapes, filmstrips, CD Rs, computer software and personal computers, as well as films should also be located at each station, along with abstract learning materials such as text book and work book materials, photo copied problems, reading activities, writing experiences, listening/participating through discussions and cassette recordings, among other tasks. The concrete, semiconcrete, and abstract materials may become a part of the tasks on task cards. One task card per center should be in evidence. A fine set of tasks one co-operating teacher wrote was the following as an example:

**A GEOMETRY CENTER (Grade Three)**

1. take four geometrical figures from this station and find the perimeter of each.
2. select two geometrical figures and find the area of each.
3. make your own geometrical figures and develop an art project which shows a new scene.
4. view the filmstrip entitled *Geometrical Figures* and answer the related questions located next to the projector.
5. view and discuss with five other pupils content in the video-tape entitled *Geometry is fun*. Write five main ideas gathered from your discussion.

The mathematics teacher should have an adequate number of tasks at the different stations so that a pupil may omit what does not possess perceived purpose and yet there are ample activities for time on task for each learner. The mathematics teacher assists and guides pupils to achieve and learn at the diverse stations. He/she does not lecture to pupils. Each pupil should be actively engaged in learning. Peer assistance and help should be welcomed as needed. Learners may choose individual as well as collaborative tasks to pursue (Reys, Suydam, and Lindquist, 1995).

The Philosophy in back of learning station use is that pupils will achieve more if they may choose what to pursue and what to omit. A teacher may arrange stations so that pupils may experience the basics as well as activity centered approaches. Much is written about stressing a hands on approach in guiding pupil learning in mathematics. With ample concrete and semiconcrete experiences available in terms of materials and listed tasks at each station, pupils may certainly experience a hands on approach in learning. At the same time, there are ample opportunities for pupil learning that provide for individual differences and learning styles (Ediger, 1995). If too many pupils wish to work a station, the teacher may assign pupils to the different centers so that a reasonable number may work together. Before pupils start working at a station, the teacher should introduce each station to pupils. The introduction should also encourage and motivate pupils to learn. Individual needs are met of pupils through choice of sequential activities as well as by choosing individual *versus* collaborative endeavours. With an adequate number of tasks available, pupils may omit what does not meet personal needs and learning styles. The teacher evaluates each pupil within the framework of continuous achievement at the diverse stations. Organization of pupils for learning is an important task of the mathematics teacher.

The teacher needs to communicate clearly to pupils proper rules for learning and enforce these regulations. He/she needs to observe learner behaviour and attempt to prevent disruptions form occurring. Many school districts and schools have policies on school discipline that must be enforced. An orderly environment helps pupils to achieve more optimally. The teacher needs to evaluate the learning environment continuously and work in the direction of making changes to continually motivate pupil learning. Materials of instruction should be readily available to pupils. They need to be current and attractive to encourage learning. A safe classroom environment guides pupils to learn. Ridiculing, belittling, and sarcasm are not models for good behaviour. There needs to be respect for pupils as well as for the mathematics teacher. All involved in a class need to experience a wholesome environment for teaching and learning (Ediger, 1996).

The ideal in learning is self discipline. Intrinsic motivation might well then be in evidence. Different positive approaches must be used to reward proper behaviour such as verbal praise for work well done by the learner. All like to be recognized for achievement, and esteem needs of pupils and the teacher must be met in the classroom. Improper behaviour needs to be identified and corrected. The correction (s) made in pupil behaviour must emphasize positive approaches. These approaches serve as models for others to emulate. Discipline problems cannot be overlooked and may need administrative help. School board policies on remedying discipline problems need to be enforced. Teachers need to teach and not be bothered by disrupters in the classroom. The following are pointers for the mathematics teacher to stress:

1. guide pupils to develop a good self concept by being successful in every day experiences in mathematics.
2. work in the direction of pupils individually being responsible for their very own behaviour.
3. know the name of each pupil personally and be familiar with the learner's interests.
4. help pupils to develop respect for each other and for the teacher. Correct unacceptable behaviour of pupils with a positive alternative.
5. be available to assist pupils when this is needed.
6. accept all pupils and show a caring attitude for learner achievement.
7. assist each pupil to achieve high standards in the mathematics curriculum.
8. have high, reasonable expectations for each pupil.
9. reward with praise those pupils who do well in mathematics.
10. emphasize rational balance among knowledge, skills, and attitudinal objectives.

The mathematics teacher should stress meeting esteem needs of pupils. Thus, there is recognition for pupils individually as well as in groups who are achieving vital objectives in mathematics. The emotional well being of a child is of utmost importance when developing the mathematics curriculum. Equally salient is the physiological needs of pupils. These need to be met if pupil are to do well in mathematics. A hungry, malnourished pupil cannot do well in ongoing lessons and units of study. In addition to free and reduced prices of school lunches, free breakfasts should be served to all needy pupils. Why? More optimal achievement in mathematics is then possible. Each pupil needs to have physiological needs met in school as well as in the home setting. We know it is a problem to emphasize adequate food, clothing, and shelter for all pupils. However, teachers do need to inform parents in needy situations of available food pantries and places where clothing is available at no cost. There are numerous churches that provide free clothing to needy people. The Salvation Army also has free clothing available as well as food, in many cases. Again, meeting the physiological needs of pupils is important in guiding pupils to achieve more optimally in mathematics. To meet shelter needs of poor people, in particular, we recommend teachers becoming advocates of meeting the needs of all people.

## ORGANIZING FOR INSTRUCTION IN UNIT TEACHING

To initiate a new unit of study in mathematics, the teacher needs to use initiating activities. We would suggest the following ways to initiate or begin a new unit in mathematics :

1. Complete a bulletin board display. This display should be located where all pupils may see the contents clearly. The contents of the bulletin board may be used for incidental learning as well as for direct teaching. In observational visits made to observe student teachers and co-operating teachers whom supervised in the schools, one bulletin board display truly sticks out in our mind. Here, the teachers had arranged a neat attractive caption entitled "Finding the Circumference of a Circle." A large circle of red colored yarn was shown with a piece of yellow colored yarn going through the midpoint (the radius) of the circle. A colored piece of green yarn emphasized the formula for *pi* (approximately 3.14). Clear descriptions were provided as to what is meant by *pi* and its relationship to squaring the radius and multiplying that value by *pi*. A very meaningful description was given on why the radius was squared and then multiplied by *pi*. Meaning theory is very important in mathematics teaching.

The bulletin board display needs to be appealing, neat, clear, and meaningful to pupils. In addition to the bulletin board display, there should be objects for pupils to manipulate in a hands on approach to learning. To teach the finding of the area of a circle, we suggest that enough small circles be available so that each pupil has one in the classroom. Each circle needs to have the center clearly marked with a point. Straight edges should be readily at the finger tops of pupils so that measurement of the radius is possible. Hand held calculators also should be easily accessible to pupils so that measurement of the radius is possible. Hand held calculators also should be easily accessible to pupils so that they may do the necessary multiplying. Using paper and pencil is also important in learning to do the necessary computation. Personal computers should be there for pupils in order that skill is developed in its use when computing is necessary. Real objects that contain circles need to be present for pupils to observe such as bicycle wheels. Illustrations of the many uses for circles may be shown with car, truck, and tractor wheels.

A rich learning environment of concrete, semiconcrete, and abstract materials need to be in the offing for pupil use in active engagement and problem solving.

Next, the teacher should mention to pupils the objective or objectives to be achieved in the first lesson. This may stress inductive or deductive learning. The teacher may now use the materials mentioned above to begin teaching the new unit of study. Securing the attention of all pupils is important initially and as the lessons progress. Pupils need to be actively engaged in the lesson by observing, measuring, solving problems, as well as thinking creatively and critically. Active involvement by each pupil is necessary. The teacher may model as well as pupils may model to other learners what needs to be done to determine the area of a circle. Pupils in many cases may challenge each other to learn and to achieve. The teacher needs to check to see that each pupil understands and attaches meaning to what is being taught. The teacher should ask pupils what the meaning is of *pi*, as well as of squaring the radius.

Pupils should have ample opportunities to determine the area of circles that are in the classroom, be it in an illustration or realia. Ample use needs to be made by pupils of what has been learned. The level of application in teaching is of utmost importance. Facts acquired by pupils can use and apply the information. emphasizing relevant facts then may be vital in teaching and learning.

In the above implemented lesson, pupils practiced the following skills:

1. problem solving–finding the area of a circle.

2. critical thinking– using relevant information as compared to discarding that which is not useful.
3. Creative thinking–determining novel ways of finding the area of a circle.
4. Interpersonal work whereby pupils work collaboratively.
5. Intrapersonal endeavours in which pupils individually do the task at hand.

In that same lesson, the mathematics teacher stressed the following:

1. an appropriate sequence in learning for pupils was emphasized whereby pupils experienced the concrete, semiconcrete, and abstract facts of achievement in that order.
2. readiness for the new learnings was evaluated.
3. motivation for learning was encouraged with a stimulating environment.
4. diagnosis and remediation was stressed in pupils',work pertaining to determining the area of a circle.
5. a varietv of learning opportunities were in evidence.

In any lesson taught, the teacher needs to be certain that pupils understand what is involved when determining the area of a circle. He/she needs to appraise if pupils understand and are ready to compute the area of the circle with teacher assistance and also independently (Ediger, 1996),

## EVALUATING PROCESSES USED BY PUPILS

Too frequently, educators feel that all is well if co-operative learning is stressed in mathematics. We would suggest teachers evaluate the following in committee endeavours:

1. If all pupils are treated with respect.
2. if each pupil is doing his/her fair share of the work within the committee.
3. if learners are on task and achieving optimally.
4. if peers provide assistance as needed.
5. if learners individually are given a chance at the interesting tasks, not the routine largely or only.

Pupils need to work independently on tasks in mathematics. Life itself emphasizes that individuals be able to profitably use spare and independent time wisely. The following criteria need to be followed by pupils working in an intrapersonal manner:

1. the pupil is working constructively in completing the lesson on time.
2. the pupil is trying to solve problems independently.
3. the pupil asks for help when necessary.
4. the pupil is neat and accurate in school work involving mathematics.
5. the pupil shows positive attitudes toward the work and world of mathematics.

The mathematics teacher needs to be able to manage pupils well and in a caring manner when stressing large group instruction. Here the teacher may

1. introduce the lesson to the entire class using objects, pictures of the realia, and abstract symbols and numerals. Motivating pupils with quality materials of instruction as well as the teacher's effective use of voice can do much to obtain learner attention and interest. The voice of the teacher should emphasize appropriate stress, pitch, and juncture. Stress in language use indicates certain worlds are pronounced louder than others within a sentence. Why? To communicate ideas more effectively to others. Pitch is a term that emphasizes certain words be said at a higher and lower to convey the intended sequence. In oral communication too, words need to be pitched higher and lower so that effective presentation of content is in evidence. In addition to stress and pitch, the mathematics teacher needs to pay attention to juncture. Juncture has to do with pauses at appropriate places such as when there are commas, periods, colons, and semicolons in written discourse. Using stress, pitch, and juncture has to do with oral use of language. We suggest that mathematics teachers use cassettes and videotapes to record their own teaching. The results can be listened to and evaluated such as in the video tape to notice where improvements may be made in oral communication. It is important for a teacher to be a good communicator of ideas, be it in explanations of processes in mathematics or as a leader in a discussion group. The pace or

rapidity/slowness of the communication process also needs adequate emphasis. The point is that pupils need to be able to acquire necessary ideas in oral communication from the teacher in teaching and learning situations.

2. In small group instruction, the mathematics teacher needs to be able to have pupils move toward their designated groups quietly and quickly so that the instructional processes are disrupted minimally. In smaller groups, pupils with teacher guidance may explore and clarify ideas presented in the large group session. Additional activities here include.
   1. completing assignments made in the large group session.
   2. extending learnings presented in the large group session.
   3. experiencing enrichment activities.
   4. developing a committee project.
   5. videotaping a small group discussion.

Learning opportunities need to harmonize with the objectives of instruction. As an example, The National Council Teachers of Mathematics (1989) listed the following for grades K–4:

1 construct number meanings though real world experiences and the use of physical materials.
2. understand our numeration system by relating counting, grouping, and place value concepts.
3. develop number sense.
4. interpret the multiple uses of numbers encountered in the real world.

Small group activities need to present challenge and richness of experiences to pupils in mathematics. In addition to large group and smaller group instruction, the mathematics teacher also needs to organize instruction for individual endeavours of learners. A variety of learning opportunities need to be in the offing to develop and maintain learner interest in learning. We suggest the following for individual activities for pupils:

1. working on a self selected task planned with the mathematics teacher.
2. selecting tasks to complete at an enrichment center.
3. receiving extra credit for additional learning activities completed, other than what is assigned.

4. choosing another pupil to do an agreed upon task extending what had been learned in an ongoing lesson.
5. making mathematical models of what is being stressed in terms of relevant lesson/unit objectives.

Th e mathematics teacher must be a good organizer of pupils in order to stress flexible grouping with large group, small group, and individual method of teaching.

3. The teacher needs to think of a quality way to end a unit of instruction in mathematics. The learning opportunities here to culminate a unit in mathematics may include the following:
   a. review what has been learned.
   b. relate ideas acquired in mathematics.
   c. clarify subject matter not understood.
   d. diagnose and remediate what pupils did not attach meaning to.
   e. evaluate pupils progress through testing, portfolios, checklists, rating scales, and journal entries.

The advantages of using several kinds of assessments, some of which are embedded in instruction, is that student's evolving understanding can continuously be monitored. The disadvantage is that such a procedure is perceived cumbersome. Records of student achievement should be more that a set of numerical grades or checklists; they can include brief notes or samples of students' work. Such records are evidence of students' continuous growth in understanding. Students should also maintain their own records. At all grades, students can keep portfolios of their work; in the higher grades, as they become more verbally fluent, they should be encouraged to keep a mathematics journal. These journals contain goals, discoveries, thoughts, and observations, as well as descriptions of activities. Journals allow students, not only to chart their progress in understanding, but also act as a focus for discussion between student and teacher, thereby fostering communication about mathematics itself (National Council Teachers of Mathematics, 1989).

## CONCLUSION

The mathematics teacher needs to be a good organizer of pupils for instruction. There are many specifics involved in organizing for instruction. Pupils need to grouped properly for instruction into large, small, and individual study groups. Pupils need to be placed into groups so that more optimal achievement is an end result. Unit teaching emphasizes that pupils experience good initiating activities to begin a mathematics unit of study. The initiating activities need to motivate pupils in wanting to achieve. Once the unit of study has been initiated, the teacher emphasizes developmental activities to stress depth teaching and learning. Culminating activities end a unit successfully. With initiating, developmental, and culminating activities, pupils need to experience meaning, interest, and purpose. A variety of learning experiences need to be in the offing including concrete, semiconcrete, and abstract materials of instruction. Diagnosis and remediation pinpoint and remedy errors made by pupils.

## REFERENCES

Bhaskara Rao, Digumarti (1989). *Teaching of Biology,* Guntur : Nagarjuna Publishers (in Telugu language).

Ediger, Marlow (1997), *Teaching Mathematics in the Elementary School.* Kirksville, Missouri : Simpson Publishing Company, 18-38.

Ediger, Marlow (1995) *Philosophy in Curriculum Development,* Kirksville, Missouri : Simpson Publishing Company, 13-15.

Ediger, Marlow (1996) , *Elementary Education,* Kirksville, Missouri : Simpson Publishing Company, 172-92.

Ediger, Marlow (1996), *Essays in School Administration,* Kirksville, Missouri : Simpson Publishing Company, 95-101.

National Council Teachers of Mathematics (1989), *Curriculum and Evaluation Standards for School Mathematics,* Reston, Virginia : NCTM, 23.

National Council Teachers of Mathematics (1989), *Curriculum and Evaluation Standards for School Mathematics,* Reston, Virginia : NCTM, 36.

Reys, Reober E., Marilyn N. 50, and Mary M. 50 (1995), *Activity Cards for Helping Children Learn Mathematics.* Boston : Allyn and Bacon.

# Chapter 6

# DESIGNING THE MATHEMATICS CURRICULUM

There are essential ingredients in designing the mathematics curriculum. Design is necessary so that each pupil may achieve as much as possible in learning. Individual differences need adequate provision since pupils differ from each other in many ways including talents, abilities, interests, and needs. Mathematics is one of the three R's (reading, writing, and arithmetic). We live in a world of mathematics since in every day life goods and services are purchased somewhat continually. To determine the costs of these goods and services, money, in one form or another, is needed, which may be totaled to ascertain what needs to be paid. Much mathematics is then needed to live in a world of purchasing goods and services in an economic world. It almost appears that mathematics knowledge and skills should receive primary stress in the curriculum.

## OBJECTIVES IN THE MATHEMATICS CURRICULUM

In determining the mathematics curriculum, teachers, supervisors, and administrators need to ascertain what pupils need to learn. This is a soul searching process which must not be minimized. Time is of utmost important in school and should be used wisely by pupils. Thus, careful selection of objectives must receive much emphasis in developing the mathematics curriculum.

Objectives for pupil achievement should stress the importance of three categories, clearly defined. The first category is knowledge objectives. Here, determiners of objectives in mathematics should focus on which facts, concepts, and generalizations pupils are to achieve as a result of instruction. The facts, concepts and generalizations need to be:

1. important now as well as in the future.
2. assist pupils to use knowledge in school and in society.
3. relevant in the minds of pupils.
4. emphasize structural ideas in mathematics.
5. selected by teachers, supervisors, administrators with pupil and teacher involvement.
6. Implemented as objectives sequentially so that each pupil may achieve as much as possible.
7. taught as background information which might then be used by pupils.
8. balanced in terms of objectives for pupils to achieve along with skills and attitudes that need to be taught.
9. integrated with subject matter from other academic disciplines as needed to provided a meaningful mathematics curriculum.
10. presented in an interesting manner to capture pupil attention for learning that which is important (Ediger, 1995).

We need to reiterate that the selection of vital objectives for pupils to achieve must be chosen with utmost care. These objectives will determine what pupils will be learning in mathematics.

## LEARNING OPPORTUNITIES TO ACHIEVE OBJECTIVES

In designing the mathematics curriculum, the second item to consider is how pupils are to attain the chosen objectives. Learning opportunities are then needed. These learning opportunities should harmonize with the present achievement level of pupils so that each may benefit as much as possible from instruction and achieve challenging new objectives. A variety of learning opportunities need to be in the offing. A hands on approach is necessary with manipulative materials to guide pupil understanding and concept development. A multimedia approach should also stress the use of videotapes, CD ROMS, films, filmstrips, slides, software and computers, hand held calculators, textbooks, library books, writing activities, discussions, committee work, art and construction experiences in mathematics, as well as dramatizations, among others.

Learning opportunities for pupils should follow desired criteria to a optimalize instruction. These criteria include the following:

1. They should capture and hold pupil attention.
2. They should provide for all pupils so that each may learn as much as possible in mathematics.
3. They should guide pupils to perceive purpose or reasons for learning in mathematics.
4. They should provide for the interests of learners.
5. They should assist pupils to attach meaning and understanding to that which is being learned.
6. They should provide for proper sequence in learning for each pupil.
7. They should help pupils to work effectively with others in collaborative situations.
8. They should also emphasize pupils working well individually to achieve vital objectives.
9. They should aid pupils to develop proper attitudes toward mathematics and toward each other.
10. They should stimulate pupils to achieve vital concepts, generalizations, and facts (Ediger, 1998).

Pupils need to develop skills in higher levels of cognition. Thus, they need to come proficient in critical thinking when separating relevant from irrelevant information, separating necessary from that which is not needed in content for problem solving, and in separating the important from the lesser important. Processes used in rational thinking are important to emphasize in the curriculum. Pupils also need to become proficient in logical thinking in ongoing lessons and units of study. Mathematics with its many patterns and logical thought requires learners to engage in higher levels of cognition.

Creative thinking is very important for pupils in the mathematics curriculum. Here, pupils engage in finding novel and unique solutions to problems. Creativity includes pupils developing original ideas in determining solutions and answers to questions and perplexing situations.

Problem solving is at the apex of higher levels of cognition endeavours for pupils. Learners then with teacher guidance identify a problem in context, that is within a lesson or unit of study. Next data is gathered from a variety of sources to find a solution or answer to the problem. This results in an hypothesis or tentative answer. The hypothesis needs to be tried in a lifelike situation. If the hypothesis is satisfactory, it is left as is. If not, the hypothesis needs to be changed or modified.

Quality learning opportunities assist pupils to develop appropriate attitudes toward mathematics, the self, and others. With success in learning, pupils should achieve quality attitudes in mathematics resulting in continual optimal progress.

## EVALUATION OF PUPIL ACHIEVEMENT

A variety of quality evaluation techniques need to be used to ascertain pupil achievement. The evaluation techniques need to be valid in that they appraise what pupils have had opportunities to learn in the stated objectives. The evaluation techniques need to be reliable, be it split-half, test-retest, or alternative forms reliability. What pupils have had opportunities to learn needs to be inherent in the stated objectives. The following are evaluation techniques that may be used in appraising pupil achievement in mathematics:

1. *Checklists*. Here, the teacher writes specific objectives for pupils to attain. If they have been achieved in mathematics, the teacher may make a check mark next to the objective. The following is an example:

The pupil is able to divide a three place dividend by a one place divisor with a remainder.

2. *Rating Scales*. The teacher needs to write relevant behaviours for pupils to achieve in mathematics. These behaviours will tend to be more opended as compared to checklist objectives. When pupils work collaboratively, the ends sought for may be quite openended and continuously moving closer to the ideal is desired in terms of pupil behaviour. The following is an example:

The pupil works well with others on committees to solve problems in mathematics.

3. *Norm Referenced Tests*. These tests are published by commercial companies and have been standardized on a norm group from which comparisons may be made with pupils' results from the local classroom.
4. *Criterion Referenced Tests* (CRTs) are generally written on the state level by appointed educators throughout the state. Objectives for pupils to achieve have also been written on the state level for teachers to use in planning for instruction. The CRTs measure what pupil have learned as stated in the specific objectives developed on the state level.
5. *Teacher Observation*. On a daily basis, the mathematics teacher should appraise pupil progress through observing learners at work. What should the teacher look for in daily work of pupils in mathematics?
   * Time on task of the pupil.
   * Specific errors made by pupils which need diagnosis and remediation.
   * Ability to work effectively individually as well as in a committee collaboratively.
   * Competence in recalling basic addition, subtraction, multiplication, and division facts.
   * Skill in higher levels of cognition such as critical and creative thinking, as well as problem solving.
   * Legibility in written work in mathematics.
   * Quality of oral communication skills in mathematics.
   * Proficiency in reading mathematics information.
   * Metacognition skills such as monitoring one's own progress in mathematics.
   * Improved attitudes toward learning in mathematics.
   * Quality of listening in ongoing lessons an units in mathematics (Ediger, 1997).
6. *Diary Entries Written by Pupils*. Here, pupils keep record of a selected duration of time as to what was learned in mathematics. Each entry is dated and contains vital content learned. Pupil review and reflect upon what was learned when writing diary entries. Pupils review and reflect upon what was learned when writing diary entries. The quality of entries

provide the teacher with much information as to the learner's progress in mathematics.

7. *Log Entries*. The above named diary entries may be summarized in terms of developing a log. Careful consideration needs to be given to each diary entry when summarizing so that an accurate summary may evolve.
8. *Journal Writing*. Here, each pupil may write of things of personal preference. Thus, the following may be written:
   * Learnings mastered in mathematics and those needing more emphasis.
   * Impressions gained in how to use mathematics in school and in society.
   * Creative endeavours in mathematics such as writing related poems and/ or engaging in art projects.
   * Enjoyment expression pertaining to mathematics such as working together with others to solve problems.
9. *Teacher Written Tests*. There are numerous teacher written test which may be used to evaluate pupil achievement in mathematics. These include the following kinds or types:
   * *Essay Test Items*. These will usually be in word problem form whereby pupils need to write explanations given for each step they used in solving the word problem. The content needs to be clearly written with the use of complete sentences. The processor may be used. If long hand is used in writing, it must be clear and legible. Each paragraph must contain unity of ideas and the paragraphs need to be written sequentially.
   * *Multiple Choice Test Items*. The teacher needs to write multiple choice test items which have four plausible responses. Each response needs to make a complete sentence with the stem of the multiple choice item. Clearly one of the four responses only, is correct.
   * *True/ False Test Items*. Many good appraisal items may be written using true/false test items. The item should be either true or false, with no vagueness in the written test item. The pupil may correct the item if it is incorrect. The following is an example : The minuend minus the subtrahend equals the difference.
   * *Matching Test Items*. Two columns may be written by the teacher such as columns A and B. Pupils may then match

the item in column A which is correct with an item in column B. More items should be in one column as compared to the other so that the process of elimination cannot be used excessively.

* *Completion Test Items.* The pupil may fill in with a short answer to a declarative sentence. The following is an example: The answer in division to a dividend divided by a divisor is the...

10. *Portfolios.* The pupil may develop a portfolio with teacher guidance to show evidence of achievement. Inside of the protfolio may be the following representative items, among others, pertaining to a pupil's achievement.
    * Written work of the pupil's daily achievement in mathematics.
    * Snapshots of construction and art projects completed in mathematics.
    * Drawing of graphs, tables, figures, and concepts in and form ongoing lessons and units in mathematics.
    * Videotapes of the quality of group work engaged in when ongoing lessons and units of study are emphasized (Ediger, 1994-1995).

## UNIT PLANS AND LESSON PLANS

Unit and lesson plans are two valuable devices for teachers to develop in order to plan effectively for teaching mathematics. Each unit and lesson needs to be well planned so that pupils achieve as optimally as possible. The objectives section indeed needs to be carefully developed. Pupils then should achieve that which is important and relevant. Objectives should emphasize understandings or knowledge, skills, and attitudinal ends. Achieving each objective assists pupils to do well presently in the mathematics curriculum as well as do well sequentially in society in the future. The objectives need to be arranged in a sequential manner so that pupils experience appropriate order in ongoing experiences.

Learning opportunities to achieve objectives should capture pupil interest and purpose. These opportunities need to provide for fast, average, an slow learners. Varied activities need to be in the offing.

Why? Pupil interest needs to be developed and maintained in mathematics. Evaluation procedures, valid and reliable, need to be used to appraise pupil achievement. Based on evaluation, the mathematics teacher may be able to make better decisions for teaching pupils.

These are the three sections–objectives or ends for pupils to achieve, learning opportunities to attain objectives, and evaluation procedures to appraise learner achievement- of unit plans. Unit plans are developed to cover a longer period of time, as compared to a daily lesson plan, such as three to four weeks on the average. Shorter and longer units are taught depending upon how well pupils have done in ongoing experiences. If there is a need to do so, a longer period of time may be given to teach a unit.

The daily lesson plan is developed from the unit plan. The lesson plan generally is for one day of teaching pupils in mathematics. It is good procedure to have a fe.. extra leaning opportunities on a daily lesson plan, than the normal teaching time would take; this indicates that the teacher has prepared carefully should pupils need additional activities in the allotted time.

The purpose of a unit plan of instruction in mathematics is to:

1. develop procedures for instruction for an entire period of allotted time, such as for three to four weeks.
2. achieve appropriate sequence for pupils among the different daily lessons when planning for long range instruction, such as in the unit of instruction.
3. take time to plan the mathematics curriculum meticulously.
4. provide opportunities to make revisions, as indicated by ongoing learner progress or lack of it, from the original unit plan.
5. look at the future to ascertain what pupils need to learn in mathematics.

Thus, the unit plan deals with planning ahead in terms of objectives, learning opportunities, and evaluation procedures in the mathematics curriculum. The daily lesson plan, in contrast, emphasizes that which pupils are to learn for a single day and indicates a much shorter range of planning as compared to the unit plan. Both types of planning are equally important. The purpose of the daily lesson plan then are to:

1. Provide mathematics teachers guidance and direction for teaching each specific day of instruction.
2. Design instruction with care by using the unit of instruction as a guide.
3. Give teachers a specific plan to use and implement in teaching and learning in mathematics.
4. Assist the teacher in evaluating the self when assessing what pupils have learned in a single day of instruction.
5. Compare daily pupil achievement with the longer range unit plan of instruction to notice what needs to be diagnosed and remedied in teaching and learning.

## FORMATIVE AND SUMMATIVE EVALUATION

Mathematics teachers need to have good knowledge of the two concepts–formative and summative evaluation. Formative evaluation indicates the teacher is not through teaching the entire unit of study. Changes may still be made then within that unit. Why might changes be in the offing? Perhaps, more time needs to be spent on pupils achieving an objective, or two, than was originally planned. Thus, pupils may not have understood what was taught to the degree the teacher wanted it to be. Or, pupils may have needed more challenging objectives to achieve in mathematics as compared to what had been planned for in the original unit of study. Additional reasons might include the following when formative evaluation has occurred and modifications may still be made in the present unit being taught:

1. More practice is needed for pupils in basic addition, subtraction, multiplication, and division facts.
2. Changes in sequence of learning opportunities might guide pupils to achieve at a higher level of progress.
3. New materials of instruction have arrived and using these might assist pupils to achieve the objectives more thoroughly.
4. Diagnosis indicates that more remedial work should be in the offing.

5. **Through pupil/ teacher planning, it is decided that more emphasis should be placed upon selected concepts than was originally planned, such as place value (Ediger, 1996).**

Formative evaluation is highly important in improving the mathematics curriculum in that changes may be made due to evidence provided by pupil's work in daily lessons in mathematics. It is difficult to foresee all the specifics in teaching and learning in mathematics when planning a unit of study ahead of time. The original planning, however, is of utmost importance. It should not be that a teacher comes to a classroom unprepared, but rather is fully ready to implement quality objectives, learning opportunities, and evaluation procedures. Quality units need to be developed which are flexible in nature. Thus, the mathematics teacher may make changes as needed to provide a quality curriculum for learners.

Summative evaluation, as a concept, should not be minimized. With summative evaluation, the unit has been completed. Now the teacher or teachers on the same grade level who have planned and taught the unit need to decide what changes need to be made if it is taught again. It might also be discussed that a completely different unit should be taught and the old unit scrapped. Why should many changes be made if the old unit of study, complete in teaching, is to be taught again? Why might the unit be completely scrapped?

1. a new philosophy of instruction has come into being and is advocated widely.
2. a new program of mathematics instruction sounds very favorable in terms of stated objectives, learning opportunities, and evaluation procedures. The new program was adopted, after careful study, by teachers and the administration.
3. workshops have been attended by teachers which have influenced the latter in making necessary changes in the mathematics curriculum.
4. research findings have indicated changes be made in the present mathematics curriculum.

5. A lack of pupil motivation may signal the need to make many changes in the mathematics curriculum (Ediger, 1991).

## LEADERSHIP IN IMPROVING THE MATHEMATICS CURRICULUM

Mathematics teachers as well as the principal need to take the lead in studying and making positive needed changes. Band wagon approaches have no role to play in improving instruction. Rather, inservice education, reflection, thought, and deliberation are needed. Attending workshops, faculty meetings, professional meetings for teachers and administrators, conducting research in improving mathematics instruction, grade level meetings, and departmental meetings are just a few ways of improving the mathematics curriculum. The focal point of all inservice education should be to improve teaching and learning situations for pupils. Teaching is a very complex series of actions. The following is written/ stated by Rita Dunn, in advocating implementing instruction based on learning styles of pupils.

Given the statistically higher reading and mathematics standardized test scores of previously failing and poorly achieving students in the United States after their learning styles were addressed, learning styles are likely to become a mandated prerequisite for schooling within the next decade. It will take only one class action suit, led by one small group of angry parents advocates, whose nontraditional children have been demoralized by the imposition of traditional schooling, to cause that change. And it will happen, because learning style is not something that affects other people's children. In every family, mother's and father's learning styles are dramatically different from each other. Siblings do not necessary reflect their parent's styles, and Sibling's styles differ significantly from each other. In most families, one child does extremely well in traditional schooling and another considers academics dull and uninteresting. A third child may be extremely different from the first two; thus, one in three is likely to pursue a totally different path from the parent's and the siblings'. Style affects everyone. Whether or not we acknowledge that each learn differently; certain resources, approaches and teachers are right for some—and very wrong for others (Interview by Michael F. Shaughnessy with Rita Dunn, 1998).

Here, teachers will need to have pupils identify how they wish to learn, based on the preferred style of leaning. The curriculum will need to be redesigned to harmonize with these individual styles of learning. Thus, a pupil may prefer to work by the self or with others, as well as be provided choices in terms of what to learn. Methods of instruction and sequential approaches of individual pupil's learning style will need to be considered in designing the curriculum. Even the time of day needs to be identified as to when pupils individually achieve best.

## CONCLUSION

The mathematics teacher needs to design the curriculum with utmost care and deliberation. The best of objectives, learning opportunities, and evaluation procedures need to be chosen for pupils to achieve as much as possible in ongoing lessons and units of study in mathematics. Individual differences need to be adequately provided for. With new research and thought, the designing of the mathematics curriculum has become quite complex. There are may ingredients that go into planning in providing for each pupil.

Even in the area of indicating what pupils have learned, there are many facets that need to be considered. Thus, Gardner (1993) identified multiple intelligences by which individual pupils may reveal what has been learned. These intelligences indicate that a pupil should use his/her talents in showing what has been learned through:

1. verbal/linguistics intelligence. Here, pupils possessing this intelligence might reveal what has been learned through traditioinal methods such as taking tests involving reading and writing.
2. logical/ mathematical. This approach would fit the mathematics curriculum rather well since what has been in mathematics might be shown in symbolic or written forms, including the taking of tests.
3. visual /spatial. Geometry deals with space figures, be it plain or solid geometry.

4. **musical intelligence. There are counting songs for young children to learn and master the counting numbers.**
5. **bodily/ kinesthetic. Pupils may dramatize a word problem such as dividing cookies into fractional parts.**
6. **interpersonal intelligence. Here, pupils may wish to work on mathematics lessons co-operatively in a committee setting.**
7. **intrapersonal intelligence. Pupils possessing this intelligence like to work by the self. They are then highly responsible and like to work individually in ongoing lessons and units of study in mathematics.**

## REFERENCES

Ediger, Marlow, (1998), "Change and the School Administrator," *Education*, 118 (4), 544-45.

Ediger, Marlow, (1995), *Philosophy in Curriculum Development*, Kirksville, Missouri: Simpson Publishing Company, 1-18.

Ediger, Marlow, (1997), *Teaching Mathematics in the Elementary School*, Kirksville, Missouri : Simpson Publishing Company, 118-38.

Ediger, Marlow, (1994-1995), "Problem Solving in Mathematics," *SMTS Journal*, 30, 66-67.

Ediger, Marlow, (1988), *The Elementary Curriculum*, Second Edition. Kirksville, Missouri : Simpson Publishing Company, 99-104.

Ediger, Marlow, (1996), *Elementary Education*. Kirksville, Missouri: Simpson Publishing Company, 193-207.

Ediger, Marlow, (1991), *Relevancy in the Elementary Curriculum*, Second Edition. Kirksville, Missouri : Simpson Publishing Company, 59-66.

Ediger, Marlow and Digumarti Bhaskara Rao, (1996), *Science Curriculum*, New Delhi: Discovery Publishing House.

Gardner, Howard (1993), *Multiple ntelligences: Theory into Practice*, New York : Basic books.

Shaughnessy, Michael, F. (1998), *The Clearning House*. " An Interview with Rita Dunn about Learning Styles, 71 (3), 145.

*Chapter 7*

# PARENTS, THE TEACHER AND MATHEMATICS

To leave parents out of planning the mathematics curriculum is a mistake. Teachers need to work with parents in determining objectives, learning opportunities, and evaluation procedures in mathematics. Parents need to show a willingness to co-operate in working with the teacher in providing the best curriculum possible for learners. There are definite criteria that both teachers and parents need to follow to make for good human relations. Respect for others is an important criteria that works in most cases. There needs to be consideration and acceptance of diverse personalities. Wanting to work with others in a co-operative manner helps in developing a better working relationship. Good attitudes toward others are a must! Careful listening to what the other person is saying assists in communicating ideas. Content in communication needs to be clear and meaningful. The objective in teachers communicating with parents is to offer the best mathematics curriculum possible to pupils.

## THE PARENT AND TEACHER CONFERENCE

Parent/teacher conferences are generally held once or twice a year. There is no reason why these conferences cannot be more frequent. Teachers may call parents by phone at any time before, during, and after the school day. Many parents are at work during the school day hours; however, a voice recorder may provide the needed message for the pupil. The phone call may deal with the need for the parent to stop in to discuss problems the pupil is experiencing in mathematics. Praise for the pupil in doing better in mathematics is also very appropriate to communicate via telephone. A chance to work together is then possible to assist the pupil to achieve at a more optimal rate. When parents come to school for the regular scheduled conference once or twice a year, there are important guidelines to follow:

1. The teacher needs to be well prepared for the conference and know the sequence of content that will be discussed. Doing one's homework here is very important. An unprepared teacher indicates a lack of sincerity and interest in having the conference.
2. The teacher should show as much completed pupil work in mathematics as possible. Parents should see first- hand how well the child is doing in mathematics. Thus, daily work using paper and pencil, computer printouts, projects completed or ongoing, and construction endeavours should be there for parents to see. Questions may be raised about how well the pupil is doing at any point in the ongoing unit of study.
3. Questions to be answered and problems to be discussed must emphasize politeness and consideration for others. There should be a 'We -ness' in the conversation, not an 'I- ness'. We want to work together for the good of the child in mathematics instruction.
4. There needs to be an agreement as to what should done to assist the pupil to achieve at as an optimal rate as possible. Details should be spelled out as to how the parents can specifically help pupils in mathematics. If a second parent/teacher conference is held later in spring, comparisons may be made of the pupil's achievement at the first as compared to the second conference. Definite achievement toward goals should be in evidence.
5. The more evidence that can be shown as to what a child has learned the more objective the results will be. The teacher needs to thank the parent for coming to the conference and invite future visitations and conferences. There should be an open door in having parents come to school.
6. The teacher should learn as much as possible about the child and his/her parents so that the aspirations of the latter are held in high esteem, providing these are positive (Ediger, 1998).

The above six steps should be kept flexible and not as absolutes. Modifications should be made as the need arises. Teacher education classes should stress working with parents as a three semester hour class. The education literature abounds with articles involving parents in the school setting. There can be profitable as well as unprofitable situations involving parents in the school arena. Ways of positive involvement of parents in the schools should be emphasized so that teachers truly receive the cooperation and help that is deemed desirable.

There should be additional times that parents are definitely invited to school, in addition to parent teacher conferences as well as informally to visit the school setting and the child's classroom. Open house during late September is an ideal time for parents to meet the teacher. It might well be that the time here is too short for a thorough parent/teacher conference. At open house, the teacher may meet the parents of the child being taught. As much time as possible should be spent in talking about the child's progress to parents. Comments made should always be positive and friendly. The teacher is there to help and assist the child to do well in mathematics. Concerns of parents for children should be voiced openly. The principal of the school should introduce each teacher to parents at the introductory session of the open house. Refreshments need to be available to make for informality and cordiality at the open house. Every attempt should be made to have parents visit with the teacher of their child. Feelings of welcome and assistance for teaching children should be felt at open house. More optimal achievement of each pupil should be an end result (Ediger, 1997).

## PARENT/TEACHER ORGANIZATION MEETINGS

Parent/teacher organization meetings (PTO) are generally held monthly throughout the school year. These meetings provide opportunities for the parents to talk with to the teacher about the offspring's progress in school. Here, the teacher, in the limited time available, may discuss the child's progress in mathematics as well as things that parents may do to advance achievement in mathematics of the involved child.

It is important for each pupil to have a role in performing in a PTO meeting during the regular school year. The role need not be a major one, but it should provide the opportunity for the pupil tc be recognized. Esteem or recognition needs should be met for each pupil. We have observed pupils being in roles such as he following in PTO meetings:

1. Telling about what was studied recently in mathematics and how the knowledge and skills may be used.
2. Showing mathematical models constructed in an ongoing unit of study by a committee.
3. Doing a team dramatization on a functional experience in mathematics.
4. Indicating how a mathematical problem was identified and solved in a collaborative setting.
5. Singing a chant, involving kindergarten children, when counting numbers are used in jumping rope.
6. Indicating and showing a completed art project pertaining to multiplication and division of fractions.
7. Revealing skills in computer use pertaining to simulation experiences in mathematics.
8. Writing experiences shown in emphasizing journal entries that relate to a present day unit being studied in mathematics.
9. Presenting oral book reports on mathematics library books.
10. Using a video-tape to show a classroom in action in mathematics instruction.

There are very valuable topics that speakers may cover on the teaching of mathematics at parent/teacher conferences. The following topics have been covered with parental questions as these have arisen during the presentation at PTO meetings:

1. Objectives of mathematics instruction.
2. Variety in learning opportunities used to provide for individual differences.
3. Evaluation procedures used to determine achievement in mathematics.
4. Peer learning in mathematics.
5. Learning by discovery and problem solving.
6. Reasoning and logical thinking in mathematics.
7. A hands on approach in teaching mathematics.
8. Innovations in teaching mathematics.
9. Integrating mathematics with other academic areas.

10. Team and collaborative learning in mathematics (Ediger, 1996).

Each presentation given at a PTO meeting should be brief and to the point. Salient ideas, only should be presented. A clear speaking voice should be used with proper stress, pitch, and juncture. Objects and illustrations should be used where applicable. Presentations are aimed at the audience in which they may ask questions as needed.

## AN INTRODUCTION TO THE NEW SCHOOL YEAR

In observing student teachers and co-operating teachers in the public schools, as a university supervisor, Ediger was invited to a parent/ teacher/ and child conference at the very beginning of the second week of the new school year. Here, the student teacher and co-operating teacher planned an agenda of *Introduction to the New School Year* to inform invited parents of possible expectations for their first grade children. Parents were invited to ask questions during the meeting. The first item on the agenda was to invite parents to the meeting and assure them of always being welcome to communicate with their teacher about the child's progress in mathematics. For the second item on the agenda, the teachers encouraged parents to see to it that the child received adequate sleep and rest so that better achievement in mathematics is possible. A tired child cannot achieve well in school. Proper nutrition was also stressed together with developing feelings of belonging with the child. Thus, good nutrition develops higher energy levels for learning. It may also have a psychological component in that feelings of belonging assist pupils to do better in collaborative endeavours in mathematics. Inclusion efforts might well involve parents and the child working together harmoniously on mathematics problems as part of a school assignment or for enrichment and enjoyment. The physical, emotional, and social well being of the child are important factors directly related to school achievement.

A third agenda item to be discussed with parents in *Introduction to the New school Year* agenda emphasized subject matter that will be taught to these first grades. Parents were shown some of the manipulative materials to be used in teaching pupils. Thus, in learning to count, pupils will be using real objects in each lesson. The goal being to have pupils associate the concrete materials with abstract numerals. Learning to add and subtract will also involve use of these concrete materials. Pupils will learn about patterns in using number. The commutative property of addition will be emphasized. Spatial understandings involving proximity, order, enclosure, and separation will be stressed in ongoing lesson and units of study. Identification of geometrical figures such as squares, rectangles, circles, triangles, and parallelograms will be stressed using concrete figures as well as pictorial images. Set notation involving concrete, pictorial, and abstract numerals will be emphasized with pupils learning to write these related numerals. Pupils will also be engaged in computer use such as appropriate software involving tutorial, drill and practice, problem solving, a and gaming. The word processor will be used for typing exercises and experiences of the pupils, as needed in mathematics. Word problems provided by pupils can see talk written down, which is typed in this case. Questions, discussions, and refreshments ended the *Introduction to the New School Year* (Ediger, School Science, 1997).

## THE LEARNING ENVIRONMENT IN MATHEMATICS

Teachers and administrators need to think of ways to help children begin a new school year in a successful manner. For early primary grade pupils, in particular, it is important for learners to experience success and interest on the first days of school. The school environment should emphasize accepting of learners and caring for others. How might pupils learn to care for others? The objective of caring for others should be started early in the home setting. We will discuss how pupils may care for each other in the mathematics curriculum.

1. Learners need to assist each other to complete assignments in mathematics. Early in the primary grades, pupils should learn to communicate clearly and concisely to assist others in understanding and attaching meaning to ongoing assignments. Pupils should also help each other at enrichment centers so that quality sequence in learning is in evidence. If pupils do not understand a new process in mathematics, the new

learnings may lack order or sequence. This hinders pupils in attaching meaning and understanding to attain relevant objectives in mathematics. By assisting others, a pupil has opportunities to review what was acquired previously as well as to notice if there are personal gaps in understanding facts, concepts, and generalizations in mathematics.

2. A pupil may read, orally, word problems in mathematics as others follow along in their textbooks. Those who have problems with word recognition and identification when reading word problems are helped here in reading as well as in problem solving in mathematics.
3. A learner may befriend a child who is an isolate and not doing well in mathematics. Sometimes, an individual does better in mathematics achievement when *belonging* needs are met and the former isolate feels he/she is a member of a group.
4. When unwholesome disagreements occur in collaborative endeavours, a pupil may assist in getting the group to work successfully on the problem area encountered in mathematics.
5. A pupil volunteers to orally record on cassette tapes so that those who do not comprehend well due to reading problems may follow along in their own textbooks as the recorded voice proceeds.

Each pupil has much worth and may need assistance at intervals in doing well in mathematics. It is important for a pupil to have his/her own mathematics curriculum to achieve as optimally as possible. There are times, too, when caring for others becomes important. Society depends upon individuals who care for each other in many ways. Otherwise human beings could not survive as a civilization. Achievement in learning, too, depends upon caring people who accept each other and assist others to do as well as possible in mathematics as well as in other subject matter areas.

Parents need to know the latest trends in teaching mathematics. Thus, parents in the home setting have a better chance to understand how to assist their children in learning to achieve vital objectives in mathematics.

A difficult task for numerous teachers, principals, and supervisors is to work effectively with parents. Certainly, the home and school need to work together to develop a quality mathematics curriculum for each pupil. If the home and school are at loggerheads pertaining to what and how pupil should learn, achievement for learners cannot be optimal. There needs to be flexible agreement upon objectives, learning opportunities, and evaluation procedures between the home and the school so that learners individually may achieve as much as possible. Open and amiable communication must be in the offing ( Ediger, School Science, 1988).

## THE PSYCHOLOGY OF LEARNING

An interesting learning environment needs to be in the offing so that pupils may learn vicariously from it. The bulletin board display may be used vicariously as well as for direct teaching. A mathematics environment should permeate the school setting to encourage pupil learning. When supervising student teachers and co-operating teachers in the public schools, one of us noticed a fascinating bulletin board display. Display related to the ongoing lesson/unit of study and was entitled, "Measuring in Square Units." There were one inch squares neatly tacked on to the side, and pupils were to determine how many one inch squares there were in a rectangle which was four inches long and three inches wide. The separate one inch squares could be used to determine the asked for area. Additional dimensions were given for the sizes of rectangles and learners were to determine the number of square units within each. Pupils could work individually or collaboratively in coming up with solutions. The bulletin board display emphasized pupils learning vicariously; however, almost all pupils in the classroom desired to work on finding the asked for answers.

In addition to the bulletin board display, there also was an enrichment center for pupils to learn from on their very own. Pupils might then find out in using sand, at the center, how many cups go into a pint or how may pints make a quart. The information was recorded on a chart nearby. There was much enthusiasm at the bulletin board display and at the enrichment center.

Bulletin board displays should capture pupil interest and attention. Thus, there is something to learn from when viewing the bulletin board contents. Enrichment centers should have fascinating materials for teaching mathematics. These materials need to be manipulated freely by pupils in an inviting atmosphere.

Pupils have a better chance of understanding what has been taught if concrete materials (realia, physical objects, and items) are used to clarify abstract learnings (numbers, numerals and symbols). Thus, if meaning is attached to what has been learned, pupils might then attach understanding to ongoing activities and experiences.

Learners should have ample opportunities to practice what has been learned. The practice might involve problem solving. Through problem solving, pupils use what has been learned. With application, pupils truly can apply that which has been learned. Drill may be needed, at times, to fix addition, subtraction, multiplication, and division facts in the minds of pupils. But, this should be done only if pupils understand and attach meaning to ongoing learning opportunities involving these facts.

Pupil should feel that purpose is involved in learning. Thus, there are reasons for achieving each and every objective deemed salient in the mathematics curriculum. The teacher may explain the purpose to involved learners. The explanation should be brief and understandable to pupils. An inductive procedure might be used to vary methods used to have pupils perceive reasons for learning in mathematics. Here, the teacher needs to raise questions of pupils in terms of the worth perceived in the new content or skills to be attained. There are teachers who use extrinsic rewards to motivate pupils in the new lesson or unit. Thus, the teacher explains to pupils what needs to be achieved in order that a reward may be received. The award needs to be seen clearly by pupils in order to motivate achievement in mathematics. What pupils need to learn in order to obtain a reward needs to be explained with clarity so that pupils know with certainty what is to be learned. Extrinsic rewards are advocated by behaviourists as a means of stimulating pupils know with certainty what is to be learned. Extrinsic rewards are advocated by behaviourists as a means of stimulating pupils to achieve and attain more optimally in mathematics and other curriculum areas. Thus, prior to instruction, as an example, the mathematics teacher announces to pupils that if nine out of ten basic number pairs in addition are answered correctly, each will receive three M and M's. To receive the M and M's, pupils need to answer correctly nine out of ten basic number pairs in addition, as a minimum level of achievement.

We advocate that pupils feel motivated from within or intrinsically, rather that extrinsically. With mathematics teachers being well prepared for each day for teaching, pupils see this as a model to follow in that mathematics is important to learn. With careful planning, the teacher has in mind a certain order or sequence of learning opportunities for children to be successful in learning. Using a variety of fascinating learning opportunities on their understanding level assists pupils to become actively involved to learn in ongoing lessons and units of study. Evaluation of pupil achievement should result in using the data to improve instruction in mathematics. The teacher needs to obtain feedback from pupils to ascertain what should come next sequentially in instruction. Diagnosis of pupil achievement should result in remediation efforts in order that each pupil makes continuous progress in mathematics.

When teachers use the psychology of learning in teaching mathematics, it provides a model for parents to use in providing help at home to their offspring in the area of mathematics instruction. Parents also need to assist their children by having them perceive interest, purpose, meaning, and application in hands on approach in learning mathematics. An open door policy needs to be in evidence whereby parents are truly invited to come to school and observe teaching during National Education Week as well as at other times during the ensuing school year (Ediger, *Education*, 1981).

## TEACHER EDUCATION

We have longfelt that students in teacher education should experience gain in working with parents (Buday and Kelley, 1996). The course should involve students actually working with parents in assisting the latter's offspring to achieve more optimally. The evaluation of working with parents should involve assessing if the child does better in mathematics as a result of teacher/ parent interaction. Parents and teachers working with together should not be merely for the sake of doing so, but rather to help children achieve at a higher level due to these conferences. Thus, in teacher education, the student should engage in real experiences with parents. To be sure, students need to possess readiness in working with parents. Students should learn how to conduct parent/ teacher conferences, as well as meet parents at open house, at parent's right, and at PTO meetings. Definite guidelines need to be in evidence for interacting with parents. Problems need to be identified in readiness experiences when teachers work with parents. The results should be positive, but as is true of many things, negative occurrences happen. Remediation of problem areas in these conferences need to be discussed in the teacher education class involving working with parents. The above readiness activities need to be studied involving students with professor assistance in a course which may entitled " Working with Parents and the Child." The readiness facets of the course in teacher education must be followed by direct experiences in working with parents in diverse settings and situations. A major objective here is for the teacher to learn to be polite and accepting of parents in all situations. Teaching involves caring and nurturing children to achieve in mathematics and in all curriculum areas. What needs to be present as elements in a student teacher/ parent interaction?

- Have evidence available of pupil products in mathematics to discuss with the parents.
- Display pupil work in mathematics such as book reports on mathematics content, completed assignments, printouts from the word processor on word problems solved by learners, art and construction projects ongoing or completed by pupils, and show videotapes of pupils at work individually or in a committee in using hands on approaches in learning in mathematics.
- Discuss problems faced by the pupil in mathematics with the parent.
- Detail what the parent(s) can do assist the learner to achieve more optimally in mathematics. It is important to agree upon a plan of action. Results recorded from later parent/ teacher

conferences may be compared with earlier ones to notice progress made by the pupil.

- Conduct the conference in an atmosphere of respect and trust. Hostile statements and remarks have no role to play in a quality parent/teacher conference. Show a caring attitude toward the pupil's progress and toward his/her parents.
- Be well prepared for the conference and adhere to time limits, if others also have come for a scheduled parent/teacher conference.
- Get to know the goals parents have for their offspring. It is salient to notice how parents feel toward their child. The teacher should also notice what benefits the parents are able to provide for the child such as instrumental and vocal lessons as well as tutoring after school.
- Observe if parents expect too much of the child as well as too little in terms of achievement in mathematics. Some parents have said they did not do well in mathematics and do not expect their offspring to achieve.

There should be ample opportunities for university students to be involved in mock parent/teacher conferences as well as in actual situations. A framework needs to exist in conducting these conferences and I suggest using the above eight standards, as needed. Teachers and principals may serve as model parents in mock conferences. I have also observed where parents are wiling to donate time for these simulations. Each conference should be evaluated in terms of desired criteria.

We have used both co-operating teacher/student teacher and ourselves, as supervisors, in co-operatively evaluating student/teacher performance in the internship. We have also observed parent/teacher conferences with pupil involvement. These seem to work satisfactorily in most cases. Individual differences are involved here and selected pupils may not contribute positively in the parent/teacher conference.

In addition to assisting pupils with homework, there are numerous other approaches which parents may use to guide learner progress in mathematics:

- Reading library books orally to pupils that contain content dealing with mathematics. For those who read well, these kinds of library books should be available for pupil reading in school and also in the home setting.
- Taking pupils to the public library to check out books that have fascinating and interesting content on mathematics.
- Assisting pupils who have difficulty in reading word problems as well as with abstract symbols and notation.
- Taking pupils to the supermarket, or other kinds of stores, to notice prices of objects purchased, the total price, and the computer printout of the sale.
- Letting pupils be actively involved in measuring ingredients that go into the making of a soup dish or other kind of food.
- Parents realizing that the pupil needs to do the learning. Ready made answers to homework may not assist pupils in learning. Assistance given as needed is different than giving answers to pupils immediately in word recognition and drill/practice situations in mathematics. pupils need to become as independent as possible and lean upon the self in mathematics achievement.
- Involving pupils in planning the cost and selection of an item, such as replacing a carpet in the hone setting.
- Implementing quality sequence in mathematics lessons and units of study tailored to the individual pupil is a key item in instruction. Teachers and parents need to study the concept of 'sequence' to assist a pupil in developing sequential leanings in order to achieve as optimally as possible.

There are pupils who need to work very hard in mathematics to do well. Even then, diagnosis and remediation may be end result. Pupils grow up in unfortunate home situations with abounding poverty. There may be crime ridden areas with mice and rats in the home and in the neighborhood of these pupils. If pupils do poorly in mathematics after twelve years of schooling, the following questions need to be raised:

1. Did the involved pupil not try or was poor quality teaching involved? I cannot imagine poor teaching for twelve consecutive years of a learner who cannot add, subtract, multiply, and divide.

2. Did parents assist the pupil in any way with homework? Was there encouragement for the learner from either parent?
3. What kind of home life did the pupil have?
4. Did the pupil miss many school days? Missing school days are being tardy frequently hinders the pupil from making sequential progress.
5. Why did the learner not learn mathematics on his/ her own when it is so functional in society?

Teachers need to discuss ways of impressing pupils upon doing their utmost continuously to achieve well in mathematics. Time wasted by the learner cannot make for continuous progress. The pupils needs to take each day of instruction in mathematics seriously. There is much to learn in mathematics and in other curriculum areas. Pupils need to discipline themselves to achieve as well as possible. Parents need to set an example whereby the learner is motivated to achieve, grow, and learn. Among other things, parents need to indicate the many practical uses that can be made of mathematics. They should encourage the pupil to learn as much as possible. Never should the curriculum area of mathematics be minimized in the home setting, but rather it is a basic and is the third R in " reading, writing, and arithmetic." Proficiency in mathematics is essential for successful living presently as well as at the work place. We live in a world of numbers whereby so many items are expressed numerically such as the goods and services purchased, checkbook balances, bank statements, allowances received and spent by children, page numbers in printed materials, and materials ordered from companies, among others.

## HUMAN RELATIONS IN THE MATHEMATICS CURRICULUM

The mathematics teacher needs to stress good human relations in the school setting. Why? Pupils very often work collaboratively on mathematics problems to be solved. Unless pupils respect and accept each other, there is little chance of committee work having positive effects upon learners. Teachers, too, need to work harmoniously with each other so that ideas for teaching mathematics are discussed and appraised. Teacher need to learn from each other in ways of improving instruction in mathematics.

Parents need to be accepted as partners in mathematics education so that their offspring achieves as well as possible. We wish there were a two way street of acceptance in educating children between teachers and pupils, parents and teachers, teachers and teachers, and school administrators and teachers. If parents, for example are rude and crude, the teacher still needs to be polite and accepting of the child as well as of each parent. It would be better if all parents were kind and polite in dealing with the mathematics teacher. Let us look at some guidelines for the mathematics teacher to use in working with others in the school and societal setting:

- Be a caring person who desires the best for each pupil in the mathematics curriculum.
- Be a promoter in stressing quality mathematics instruction for all learners.
- Be highly knowledgeable about mathematics content, skills, and attitudes that pupil need to attain.
- Be proficient in communicating ideas to others be it orally or in writing.
- Be patient in dealing with human beings.

We believe good human relations and mathematics achievement for pupils being one, not separate categories.

## CONCLUSION

There are many avenues available for teachers and parents working together for the good of the child in mathematics achievement. These include the following:

- having quality parent/the conferences.
- meeting parents at PTO meetings.
- initiating an *Introduction* to the New School Year time with parents.
- Implementing an invigorating *Introduction to the New School Year meeting.*
- using the psychology of learning from educational psychology for parents to model in assisting offspring with homework.
- trying to initiate parental education classes in Teacher Education programs at colleges and universities.

– integrating human relations and curricular improvement into teaching and learning situations.

The concept of parent involvement is interrelated with parent and teacher efficacy/involvement. Parental efficacy of self image, locus of control, developmental status, and interpersonal support are linked in more effective parent involvement. Specific strategies in the areas of communication, shared learning, and guidance are specified as ways to nurture parental efficacy and strengthen parent-teacher relations (Swick and Broadway, 1997).

## REFERENCES

Bhaskara Rao, Digumarti (1998) *Teacher Education in India,* New Delhi; Discovery Publishing House.

Buday, Mary Caterine, and James A. Kelley, "National Board Certification and the Teaching Profession's Commitment to Quality Assurance, " *Phi Delta Kappan,* 78 (3), 215-19.

Ediger, Marlow (1998) "The Teacher, Reading, and Parents, " *Teaching Reading Successfully in the Elementary School,* Kirksville Missouri; Simpson Publishing Company, 231- 32.

Ediger, Marlow (1997), *Teaching Mathematics in the Elementary School,* Kirksville, Missouri ; Simpson Publishing Company, 18-19.

Ediger, Marlow (1996), "Goals in the Mathematics Curriculum," *Elementary Education,* Kirksville, Missouri ; Simpson Publishing Company, 156-64.

Ediger, Marlow (1997), "Psychology in Teaching Mathematics," *School Science,* 35 (1), 1-14.

Ediger, Marlow (1998), "Philosophy of Teaching Mathematics, *School Science,* 36 (1), 39-53.

Ediger, Marlow (1998), "Change and the School Administrator, " *Education,* 118 (4), 541-48.

Swick, Karen J., and Francis Broadway (1997), "Parental Efficacy and Successful Parental Involvement, *Journal of Instructional Psychology,* 24 (1), 69.

# Chapter 8

## LEADERSHIP IN TECHNOLOGY USE IN SCHOOL MATHEMATICS

Leadership is needed to provide quality computer service in the curriculum. Teachers alone are not in a position to provide leadership in technology use; although, teacher enthusiasm and participation are musts! Teachers and principals need to work together to provide the necessary ingredients for a good school technology program. Ritchie (1996) wrote the following pertaining to reasons why the use of technology is minimal in schools:

* A lack of administrative support,
* Inadequate staff development and technological support,
* Low quality, quantity, and success of technologies in the classroom,
* Nonexistent or cursory plans for adopting and implementing technology into a school,
* The failure to allocate a technology coordinator to help train teachers and coordinate the technologies,
* A lack of funds and personnel to maintain equipment,
* Continual assessment of content acquisition through traditional methods,
* Establishment of a broader clientele to establish a technology culture ( Haffman, 1996).

The first starred item indicates the need for principal/supervisor leadership and participation to implement a quality program of technology use in the curriculum. Mehlinger (1996) wrote:

> "Without going into any detail regarding specific pieces of hardware, I can say with confidence that schools can expect more integration, interaction, and intelligence from future technology. In their early days in school, computers and

> video were regarded as separate entities, and it was assumed they would stay that way. In fact, we can expect a continuing integration of these technologies. Voice, data, and images will be brought together into one package. One current example of this process is desk top video. In a single, relatively inexpensive unit, one has telephone (voice), computer data (storage and manipulation), and video (sending and receiving moving images) capabilities. Those who use the machine can talk to people at a distance, exchange documents, work collaboratively, and even see collaborators on the screen.

A very important fact of leadership in mathematics will continually be to provide quality, sequential programs of instruction using technology.

## STAFF DEVELOPMENT AND TECHNOLOGY

There are several excellent ways to emphasize inservice education for teachers. In supervising student reaches in the public schools, I(Ediger) took careful notice of one school that had a good professional library for teachers. There were publications available for teachers to read and use. These included the *Teaching Children Mathematics, Mathematics Teaching in the Middle School, Social Education, Science and Children, The Language Arts,* and *The Instructor,* among others. I noticed teachers during free time browsing and reading selected of these professional journals. The principal of the school sent memos at monthly intervals to teachers as to valuable articles to read on technology use in the school. The principal of the school needs to secure a professional library for teachers and get teachers involved in reading articles on improving instruction through technology. Hopefully, teachers will try out new ideas in their very own classrooms, from their reading. Feedback may be given to others in terms of how the innovation worked out in the classroom setting.

There are more and more articles written on technology use in the classroom. A teacher may become very versatile in using technology in the classroom from reading and experimenting with new ideas in teaching/learning situations.

The workshop concept can be used wisely to help teachers use technology more effectively in the classroom. The workshop should be very flexible and openeded so that there is wide participation from participants. We suggest, first of all, to have a general session with all teachers and the administrator participating. This provides opportunities for participants to explore and select vital problems to solve in technology use. Each person here should be stimulated and encouraged to identify problem areas in technology use. The problems may arise from teachers who have definite needs pertaining to technology use in the classroom. Teachers may have read articles in the professional library about technology use that they would like to implement in teaching and learning, but need assistance to do so. Adequate time needs to be given to problem identification during the general session.

Problem areas identified might be the following:

1. Using data bases, E-mail, and computer networks (Each of these may be separated as problem areas to be solved).
2. Using internet and Web sites.
3. Using the word processor to motivate pupils in learning.
4. Evaluating and using quality soft ware to improve the curriculum.
5. Using the concept of integration of technology into the curriculum.
6. Using interactive videos.
7. Using the word processor to communicate with parents.

From the general session, participants may choose the problem area they wish to work on. Committees may be formed for each problem area identified in the general session. The number of each committee should be held flexible, but small enough so that the number is not unwieldy or too large. We believe each committee should report to the other committees as to what has been found as answers to each problem area in technology use. Questions might then be raised by other committees on data gathered for problem solving. Wide use should be made of ideas secured for computer use in mathematics.

Throughout the workshop, consultant help must be available. The consultant(s) need to be highly knowledgeable and have a caring attitude in desiring to be of assistance.

In addition to the general session and committee endeavours to work collaboratively, there needs to be time for individual participants to select problem areas of their very own to work on. Consultant help must be given on a one on one basis. The goal is to assist teachers to do a better job of making full use of technology in the classroom as well as increase learner achievement.

Many participants have been highly satisfied with the workshop idea on developing technology skills on the part of individual teachers. A rating scale may be used to evaluate the quality of the workshop. Items on the scale need to be clearly written so that a rating may be given each item. The following are examples of items to be rated on a five point scale:

1. I learned to use the word processor in ways to motivate pupil writing in mathematics in the classroom.
2. I learned to assist pupils in sending messages through E-mail.
3. I learned to use the internet as a proficient way of teaching and learning.

Participants giving a five rating to any of the above the items received much help from the workshop to assist pupils in the classroom. A 'One' rating would indicate the assistance given was well below average. A three rating would indicate 'average' help received during the workshop participants indicate what assistance needs to be given in the school setting. During actual class time as well as before and after school, teachers should ask for assistance from the designated school leader to become more proficient in computer use in the mathematics curriculum.

## FACULTY MEETINGS TO IMPROVE TECHNOLOGY USE IN MATHEMATICS

There should be time on an agenda for a faculty meeting to guide more optimal use of technology in the classroom setting. Agenda items need to be in the hands of participants at least one day prior to the faculty meeting. In this way, participants have time to think through possible solutions to identified problem areas. An improved mathematics curriculum should be an end result. Each faculty member should have ample opportunities to place items on the agendas. At the faculty meeting, consultant help needs to be available in the area of technological services. Committees may work after the faculty meeting in gathering information in answer to each problem area in the use of technology.

Out of committee member concerns, teachers have been able to take time off from teaching to observe a classroom setting where the teacher is known to do well in integrating technology into the mathematics curriculum. Meetings have been attended at district expense on technology and computer services in the classroom. Those attending should report back to other faculty members on what was learned and put to use in the classroom. Opportunities need to be available for teachers and administrators to learn about and implement technology in the classroom.

Teachers need to know procedures involved in obtaining assistance when technological problems arise. Problems pertaining to making maximal use of the computer as well as when computers go on the blink should be in the offing.

## ASSISTING TEACHERS AS NEEDED

Leadership must be provided when teachers need help in the classroom setting. These are some of the more opportune times to assist teachers contextually in ongoing lessons and units of study in mathematics. The teacher who experiences a problem at a given moment should be given assistance if at all possible. Some of the items of assistance might be the following:

1. how to retrieve a needed document that appears to be "lost" in the data base.
2. how to use CD ROMS to maximize pupil learning.
3. how to develop an electronic portfolio.
4. how to develop a classroom mathematics dictionary, using the word processor.
5. how to use selected items on the control panel.
6. how to start file sharing.
7. how to use the power secretary.

The individual teacher or the team of teachers need to make their needs known in terms of specific help needed in using the word processor. If the assistance is not available as needed for computer assistance, the teacher(s) need to write down help that is needed to develop sequentially in successful use of technology in the mathematics curriculum. Skilled teachers may also help those who need assistance in context when computer use is in evidence.

We are truly in an information age in which there are so many outstanding sources of content for pupil acquisition. Pupils need to have ample opportunities to secure a variety of subject matter on a topic. It does cost money to have the latest of technology in our schools. But can we afford to be without it? pupils today, in a few years, will be in the work place where the information age will be even more clearly defined as compared today. Pupils of every race, creed, and religion must have the chances in an equitable manner to be able to use the latest data securing sources. The upper income level of pupils will have these opportunities of securing information through Word Wide Web and internet in the home setting. Other pupils should have equality of opportunity to use state of the art sources to obtain information (Ediger, 1997).

## TECHNOLOGY AND SCHOOL/CLASSROOM NEWSLETTERS

School newsletters are essential in communicating with parents and others in the community. The goal of the Newsletter publication should be to inform parents at to what is being taught and emphasized in teaching and learning situations. Comments from receivers of the Newsletter should be valued. A school should be open ended in terms of parents visiting and corresponding with teachers and administrators in school. Certainly, the public schools are not closed societies. Feedback from the lay public may provide ideas on improving the curriculum. Adequate information in the Newsletter should pertain to what is being emphasized in the mathematics curriculum. The word processor and printed along with photocopying are excellent devises to use as technology to communicate with parents using the Newsletter approach.

As university supervisors of student teachers and co-operating teachers, one of us saw an example of how the classroom can communicate with parents of children and in this case fifth grade pupils. For the mathematics section of the newsletter, pupils stated what had been learned during the concluding week. The teacher then typed on a word processor what had been said by these fifth grade pupils. What then went to the classroom Newsletter which was taken home by the child to his/her parents? The following had been experienced during the week of March 15-19:

We studied division of fractions and realized its close relationship to multiplication of fractions. We also learned how important it is to be able to divide fractions and use this information in and outside of school. We were given five cookies for each set of four pupils. Now we had to find how much each person received of the total number of cookies. The division had to be made sot hat each one could receive his/her share of the cookies. At the beginning, we did much guessing as to how the five cookies should be divided. The teacher helped us in our thinking until we figured out how to be exact when coming up with the final answer. Each pupil individually or in a committee wrote five lifelike problems emphasizing division of fractions. The written work was typed into the word processor. Printouts were exchanged with other learners to complete the problems in division of fractions.

With word processor use, the documents look very neat and attractive for pupils to take home to their parents.

## CONCLUSION

Schools need to make full use of technology to guide pupils to learn as much as possible. Leadership needs to be available to teachers so that technology use is operating as well as possible. Leadership is also needed to provide inservice education in technology use (Ediger, 1996).

Promoters of computer use in the classroom claim that exposing pupils to Web sites, e-mail and news groups promises more than the means to securing a job in the next century. Technology boosters also predict that the use and mastery of the internet and the World Wide Web will produce affective changes that can be measured to produce increased student self esteem and confidence. Whether working at home or at school, as an individual or in co-operative learning or team setting, students will become 'Infotectives,' *i.e.*, independent thinkers, researchers, inventors, inquirers, capable of solving problems that often require the active direction of a teacher or superior..

In expanding the learning environment to include data bases, computer networks, and other library resources throughout the world, the internet makes it possible for students to shape their own education. Once the easy accessing protocols are learned, the student can dive into the resources in his or her home and/or library without the constant supervision and intervention of the teacher. Lao Tzui's dictum, "He who teaches least teaches better," describes student centered teaching, learning, and assessment environment in which the student can access information from multiple perspectives and learn to use this information to solve complex problems (Maskin, 1996).

## REFERENCES

Ediger, Marlow (1997), *Teaching mathematics in the Elementary School*, Kirksville, Missouri; Simpson Publishing Company, 204.

Ediger, Marlow (1996), *Elementary Education*. Kirksville, Missouri; Simpson Publishing Company, 209-14.

Hoffman, Bob (1996), "School Technology Integration : An Automated Needs Assessment and Planning Tool," *Technology and Teacher Education Annual*, edited by Robin, Price, Willis, and Willis. Charlottesville, Virginia : Association for the Advancement of Computing in Education, 81

Maskin, Melvin (1996), "Infotechtives on the Infobahn; Designing Internet Aided projects for the Social Studies Curriculum," *National Association Secondary School Principal's Bulletin*, 77 (6), 59-69.

Mehlinger, Howard (1996). "School Reform in the Information Age," *Phi Delta Kappan*, 77 (6), 405-06.

Ritchie, Don (1996), "The Administrative Role in Integration of Technology, " *Bulletin of the National Associatio.. of Secondary School Principals*, 80 (582), 43.

## Chapter 9

# APPRAISING PUPIL PROGRESS IN MATHEMATICS

A good mathematics teacher is a proficient evaluator of pupil achievement in mathematics. A variety of procedures need to be used in the evaluation process. Why? One technique or approach to evaluation may measure diverse facets of growth as compared to another, such as an achievement test of pupil *knowledge* of mathematics versus teacher observation of learner *attitudes*. There are evaluation devices that emphasize a score or numerical result that a pupil has achieved, such as per cent correct, percentile rank, standard deviation results, stanine rankings, and quartile deviations. Other evaluation result do not stress numerical figures such as using teacher observation recorded in journal writing. The latter may stress valid results about how well a pupil is doing in mathematics. However, two teachers observing the same pupil may not come up with the same results due to diverse perceptions. Even if a teacher attempts to measure pupil achievement in mathematics whereby a numerical result would be in the offing, it is good procedure to check one approach against another. A specific numerical result may not be a good indicator of pupil achievement since it is a one shot case to ascertain pupil progress in mathematics. The teacher needs to be careful that too much time is not given to testing and measuring. Adequate time for instruction is a must! Quality objectives need to be in the offing in any lesson or unit of study so that each pupil may achieve as optimally as possible. Evaluation is stressed further in terms of appraising the quality of objectives, of instructional activities, and the evaluation techniques themselves.

## BEHAVIOURALLY STATED OBJECTIVES AND THE MATHEMATICS CURRICULUM

Many states presently have behaviourally stated objectives for pupils to achieve. These objectives are available to teachers prior to instruction. The objectives generally are developed on the state level with the involvement of leading teachers, supervisors, and administrators in the state. Each objective is stated very precisely, generally, with much specificity. At selected intervals during the school year, pupils are tested to determine if the stated objectives have been achieved and to what extent. Numerical data is then available pertaining to each child's progress in mathematics. These tests are called criterion referenced tests (CRTs). The following are objectives that are stated precisely and in measurable terms:

1. The pupil will add correctly nine out of ten addition problem containing two single digit numerals. After instruction the teacher may measure to ascertain if pupils' individually have achieved the stated objective.
2. The pupils will solve three word problems with 100 per cent accuracy. After instruction, the teacher measures if pupils have achieved the objective. Learning activities provided for pupils to attain the stated objective need to align, not be separated from what is stated in the objective.

The teacher in using CRTs may announce prior to instruction what pupils are to learn. It is only wise for the teacher to prepare pupils for achieving each new objective with readiness experiences. Thus, pupils need to have had adequate learning opportunities prior to the teacher stressing each new objective in mathematics. Pedagogical readiness would indicate that the teacher has quality learning activities listed in the daily lesson plan so that pupils may be successful in achieving objectives. Adequate and good preparation is necessary on the teachers part to motivate pupils to achieve an objective. Unsuccessful learners in achieving an objective might well need a different teaching strategy. Pupils need to be ready in terms of maturation to achieve each objective. Piaget stressed the following levels of pupil maturation on the elementary school levels;

1. Sensorimotor intelligence—birth to two years. These are the preschool years.

2. Preoperational intelligence—ages two through seven. This includes the kindergarten and first grade levels whereby pupils generally perceive one variable at a time only in a mathematical situation.
3. Concrete operations—ages seven through eleven. These age levels include grades two through grade five, in general. Pupils need many concrete objects in teaching as was true at the previous stage, but now may perceive numerous variables at a time in mathematics.
4. Formal operations—ages eleven and up. This includes pupils in grades six and higher. Here, pupils notice many variables at a time and concrete materials of instruction in mathematics are generally not as necessary as compared to the stage of concrete operations.

Piaget did research on pupils for over fifty years in Switzerland when developing the above four levels of maturation. We suggest studying these levels thoroughly and noticing if the pupils you teach are on these approximate levels of maturation for their age level. Teachers need to be students of research to notice what is recommended in education and what can be done to assist pupils to achieve more optimally. To be sure, there are different levels of readiness for pupils and the teacher may be wasting much time in teaching by attempting to hasten a child being ready to add, subtract, multiply, and divide at different levels of complexity. For example, it would be ridiculous to teach a first grade pupil to divide a seven digit dividend and a three place divison with renaming and having a remainder, unless the learner is extremely precacious. With ample readiness and quality sequence, the pupil can be successful and succeed in achieving objectives in mathematics instruction (Ediger, 1988).

## USING TEACHER OBSERVATION

The teacher needs to be a good observer of pupils in contextual situations when pupils are actively engaged in ongoing lessons and units of study. It takes practice and effort to focus on specifics that pupils are learning in mathematics. Also to be a good observer, the teacher needs to be current and updated in trends in mathematics to know what is being advocated in a modern program of mathematics instruction. What might a teacher be looking for when observing pupils in daily activities in the mathematics curriculum?

1. The quality of attitudes possessed by learners individually toward mathematics. If pupils possess negative attitudes, the teacher needs to be very observant here and assist learners to be successful in each specific step of learning. Failure to learn makes for uncomfortable feelings. No one likes to fail!

Pupils need to experience challenge in the mathematics curriculum and yet the expectations are reasonable in that learners can be successful in achieving objectives. For work well done, pupils should be praised for actual accomplishments. What has not be done well by a pupil needs diagnosis and remediation. If a pupil, for example, makes the following error in subtraction: 42–25 = 27, the teacher needs to assist the pupil to determine reasons for the wrong answer. The pupil might not have understood the concept of renaming/regrouping or borrowing in subtraction. The pupil might have been careless in subtracting the subtrahend from the minuend. The pupil might not have looked at the numerals carefully to notice the processes involved in arriving at the correct answer. What might the mathematics teacher notice when observing pupils being engaged in learning activities?

2. Background information understood by the pupil involving facts, concepts, and generalizations needed in the new lesson. For example, does the pupil understand the addition fact of a set of four objects and a set of five objects combined make a new set of nine objects so that 4 + 5 = 9. Manipulative materials need to be used to make learnings meaningful to pupils.

Pertaining to concepts, does the pupil understand the concept of regrouping and renaming or carrying in addition such as in 36 + 47= 83? Six plus seven in the ones column requires regrouping in terms of thirteen ones is equal to one ten and three ones as well as three tens plus four tens is equal to seven tens. One ten from the ones column needs to be joined to the seven tens to make for eight tens. Place value is also a very valuable concept for pupils understand here, such as the ones, tens, hundreds, and thousands columns for whole numbers. Generalizations that pupils may need here involve, "Changing the order of addends does not affect the sum." This is also the commutative property of addition whereby this generalization may be used on any level of instruction from kindergarten through graduate study. Thus 4 + 5=5 + 4 or 1,967,453 + 3,265,923 = 3,265, 923 = 1,967,453. By emphasizing the commutative property of addition and multiplication, it cuts down on the number of facts to be learned by 50 per cent.

Thus, if pupils miss the understanding of a generalization, might it be that pupils do not attach meaning to a concept within the generalization? Or it a concept lacks understanding, might it be that the pupil does not attach meaning to selected facts therein? It is then very important to have quality sequence or order in pupils engaged within ongoing learning activities. Adequate background information or readiness for learning in the new lesson or unit of study is very important.

3. The style of learning possessed by the pupil. Questions involving style of learning deal with under what conditions pupils learn best. The teacher needs to observe the pupil carefully to ascertain which kinds of leaning opportunities to provide pupils. Does a learner achieve more optimally with concrete, semiconcrete, and/or abstract materials of instruction? Should pupils have more of individual or co-operative class work in mathematics. It might even be that pupil like to work in dyads, two pupils working together on a task in mathematics. The teacher modelling instruction to the class as a whole may be adequate for selected pupils to go ahead on their own on assignments or self selected learning opportunities. Thus, there are selected methods of instruction that pupils like best in terms of activities and experiences.
4. Ways of showing what has been learned. there are numerous approaches whereby pupils individually as well as in groups may reveal what has been achieved. The mathematics teacher needs to be knowledgeable about and informed on how learners might indicate what has been learned. Generally, paper/pencil tests have been used to test pupil learning in any lesson or unit of study. These tests have included standardized, criterion referenced, and teacher written tests. These approaches can be used along with others, such as Howard Gardner's theory of multiple intelligences (Gardner, 1993). Too frequently when testing pupil achievement, linguistic intelligences is used by

the learner, such as in reading and writing. There are other intelligences which pupils may use such as logical/ mathematical to indicate what has been learned. Here, the world of mathematics may be used to show progress and achievement. The following are additional intelligences as determined by Howard Gardner (1993):

1. Space such as is stressed in geometry and in the art curriculum. Many geometrical drawings may be made by pupils to indicate what has been learned.
2. Kinesthetic such as in athletic endeavours and dance with body movement in general.
3. Objective pursuits such as in science.
4. Social interests such as in pursuing learnings of people in time and place.
5. Musical intelligence.
6. Interpersonal (achieving in group endeavours) and interpersonal (accomplishing in individual work) intelligences.

Individual differences might well be provided for when using multiple intelligences theory to permit pupils to show in diverse ways what has been learned. Again, the range of experiences in indicating what has been learned needs to be expanded beyond that of verbal intelligence.

## CONFERENCES WITH PUPILS

The teacher needs to have conferences with pupils individually as well as collectively to appraise achievement in mathematics. These conferences may zero in on what pupils liked best about the mathematics curriculum. The questions may become more specific by noticing and discussing the following with pupils:

1. Determining why assignments are not completed on time. If the assigned work is not completed as the deadline is there, what causes this to happen?
2. Having pupils say what is not understood in a lesson or unit of study.
3. Let pupils explain a new process in mathematics being emphasized by revealing how this is to be done.

4. Obtaining data from learners as to the kinds of learning activities that are most beneficial.
5. Asking pupils which topics they wish to pursue in mathematics.
6. Finding out how pupils wish to be appraised in mathematics in addition to or in place of paper\pencil tests.
7. Plan with pupils an enrichment center or in depth learning station to extend the mathematics curriculum, beyond that of the daily lesson and unit teaching plan being stressed.
8. Ascertain how many pupils would be interested in an after school mathematics club where topics may be studied intensively. The discussion may also center upon developing a mathematics club before school and during the school day. The teacher needs to consult with pupils on ways to improve achievement in mathematics and involve pupils wherever possible in having higher quality objectives, learning opportunities, and evaluation procedures (Ediger, 1995).

## PARENT/TEACHER CONFERENCES IN MATHEMATICS

A very valuable procedure to use in the evaluation of pupil progress in mathematics is to use parent/teacher conferences (Ediger, 1996). Teachers may learn much about pupils by listening to comments made by parents. Generally, parents have the interests of their child in mind when interacting with the mathematics teacher. In these conferences, parents may wish to share information about their child with the teacher so that an improved curriculum is an end result. Parents might also wish to discuss with the teacher what interests the child in mathematics. Further discussions may zero in on what makes for problems by the child in learning mathematics. Politeness is always important in a parent/teacher conference. Careful listening also needs to be stressed. The mathematics teacher wants to learn as much as possible about each pupil so that the best curriculum possible may be in the offing. As an elementary school teacher, the most successful conference Ediger had with a parent involved discussing the following problems faced by the involved fifth grade pupil:

1. Multiplying a two digit by two digit number whereby regrouping and and renaming was involved. The parents even

gave a specific set of factors in multiplication that the child had experienced difficulty with. When specifics such as these are discussed, the mathematics teacher receives very valuable information on what assistance that child needs in school as well as in the home setting.

2. Being distracted from learning by the best friend of the child. The parents requested I change where these two were seated so that disturbing each other was much less likely. This request was easy to comply with.
3. Providing enrichment work for the child, beyond that being assigned. A mathematics teacher should certainly be happy to comply here.
4. Making certain the child is working on the task at hand in mathematics so that as much is being learned as possible. I replied to the parents that the child tended to work hard, but I would continually observe to see that the pupil learned as much as possible.

It was quite obvious that the above named parents took their roles in life very seriously and wanted their child to achieve as much as possible. The child was doing very well in mathematics achievement and had a good attitude toward mathematics as well as all curriculum areas in school. We have always believed that if all parents, optimal achievement in mathematics would definitely be possible. It indeed was a joy to have that pupil in the classroom. The role model presented by this learner was an inspiration to many other pupils in class.

## DIAGNOSING PUPIL DIFFICULTIES IN MATHEMATICS

There are commercial diagnostic tests available to notice pupil weaknesses in mathematics. We believe the mathematics teacher can do a better job of diagnosing pupil difficulties as compared to commercial tests. Why? within a contextual situation, the teacher may notice the kinds of errors pupils make and offer assistance at that moment to remedy the exhibited deficiencies. With commercial tests, the items thereon are outside the framework of what pupils are presently studying in mathematics. When observing pupil problems at a given time in mathematics, what pupils are not doing correctly can be noticed and assistance provided to overcome identified errors. We will describe a few errors on different grade levels which one of us have observed as university supervisors of student teachers.

A first grade pupil continually added 5+2 = 6. The teacher noticed this error and assisted the pupil to overcome the difficulty by showing five fingers on one hand and two fingers on the second hand. These two sets were then combined to make for a sum of 7. The pupil counted the total number of fingers involved. Once the pupil had reviewed that 5+2=7, the addition fact was written into her small notebook for reference. There are times, after meaning has been established, to have pupils put into long term memory the sum of an addition fact.

A second grade pupil continually subtracted in the following manner: 8 - 2=10; 7 - 4=11and 6 - 3=9, among others. The pattern of error here is quite obvious. The pupil was adding instead of subtracting. The pupil was carefully taught to notice the operation sign and to differentiate the minus from the plus sign. To the best of my knowledge, the pupil never made the same error again. The errors exhibited by this pupil may have involved carelessness. Habits of carelessness need to be overcome with assisting the learner to becoming a responsible person.

A third grade pupil completed a set of word problems in which unnecessary information was inherent, such as a family drove three hundred miles each day for five days and spent during that time $200 for food. How many miles did the family drive? The pupil added the 200 on to the 1,500 miles driven. Here, the teacher assisted the pupil to be a critical thinker and analyse what is asked for in the word problem. The question asked in the problem pertained to how many miles the family drove in five days. Nothing was asked about the amount of money spent of food.

A fourth grade pupil copied numerals incorrectly from the basal textbook and therefore came up with several incorrect answers to word or story problems. The teacher assisted the pupil by having the latter read aloud the story problem, especially to notice the numerals therein. Rereading was necessary in several situations.

The pupil had to read the story problems with the numerals accurately until mastery was in evidence. The carryover or transfer values seemingly were noticeable. However, additional assistance in this area at different intervals had to be given.

Selected fifth grade pupils had severe problems in reading and did not comprehend several word problems in mathematics. These pupils, in an atmosphere of respect, were taken aside and given needed help. The word problems were read orally by a good reader to these pupils. A cardinal rule in this classroom was to assist others, but never ridicule or minimize anyone.

Two sixth grade pupils had to be given assistance to work on the task at hand, after an assignment had been made involving the basal mathematics textbook.

The mathematics teacher needs to notice the kinds of errors pupils make specifically and then provide needed guidance. We will briefly outline other kinds of errors we have observed that pupils make.

1. Subtracting a smaller value from a larger one even though the numerals there do not call for this such as 520 - 218=318, *e.g.* 8–0 in the one's column is considered rather than regrouping and renaming from the two tens in the minuend which is necessary when subtracting 218 from 520. The teacher needs to be a good listener when pupils explain the processes following in arriving at an answer.
2. Adding two values whereby regrouping and renaming are involved but not being used such as in 36+25 = 51. Here, the pupil added 6+5 to come up with eleven as the sum, but did not carry the one ten from the ones column to the tens column.
3. Checking division problems by having memorized that the divisor times the quotient is equal to the dividend without doing the actual multiplying of the divisor times the quotient to see if the work is done correctly and is equal to the dividend. To be sure once the understanding is there of how to check a division problem, the pupil should use a calculator to make the mathematics curriculum more enjoyable and of interest.
4. Lacking skills in reading whereby misunderstandings occur in working word problems. Pupils sometimes need assistance in

identifying unknown words. Word recognition skills that should be stressed include using context clues, phonics, syllabication, structural analysis, and picture clues. Independence needs to be developed in reading involving mathematics content.

5. Not noticing operation signs carefully such as +, –, ×, and their inverse operations.
6. Misunderstandings pertaining to the commutative, associative, and closure properties.
7. Attempting to memorize without understanding what has been learned, such as the formula for finding the volume of a cylinder, pyramid, and cone.
8. Inadequate attention paid to ongoing discussions involving a new process such as dividing fractions which was preceded in sequence by multiplication of fractions.
9. Being in a hurry to complete an assignment so that recreational pursuits may be followed. Pupils need to be taught to pay careful attention to what is being pursued and to do the best possible in achievement. If something is not understood, the pupil needs to ask for help.
10. Refraining from enjoying and appreciating mathematics. Here, the teacher needs to determine where the learner is presently and then provide sequential experiences in which the pupil may be successful. Learning activities need to capture the interests of learners.

## USING CHECKLISTS

Many teachers find that using checklists are helpful in remembering what pupils have misunderstood in ongoing lessons and units of study. Behaviours are listed on a paper in which a learner's name may be written in. The following is an example of a checklist:

Name of pupil ------------------ Date-------------------

1. Understands place value of ones, tens, and hundreds. (Encircle which needs more emphasis , if any)
2. Can regroup and rename in addition.
3. Reads numerals accurately.

4. Stays on task.
5. Asks for assistance when needed.
6. Writes legibly.
7. Reads words with meaning and understanding.
8. Has a good attitude toward mathematics.
10. Listens carefully during discussions.
11. Takes an engaged role in learning opportunities.
12. Solves problems using an effective approach.

In the above checklist, the teacher may place a check mark in front of the behaviour that a pupil needs more help in. By dating and keeping a running record of pupil progress, the mathematics teacher is better able to maintain a careful perspective of where a learner is achieving presently in each objective. Growth in the above behaviours should be continuous with each pupil achieving as best possible.

A slight variation of the check list is to use the rating scale. Thus, no one pupil will ever achieve the above behaviours perfectly once and for all, but rather in degrees the pupil will achieve, grow, and develop. For example, in behaviour number twelve above, "Solves problems using an effective approach", the pupil will continuously achieve at a more optimal rate and not achieve the objective as an absolute. Ratings may then be given each pupil on a five point basis. A rating of 5 indicates outstanding work for the pupil at his/her present achievement level, whereas a rating of 1 indicates the pupil is very weak in this area. In between ratings of 4.3 and 2, may be given based on a teacher's observations.

The teacher may save the pupil's checklist results as well as the completed rating scale, for filing, and make comparisons with future observations. It is easy to forget or become hazy on a pupil's achievement unless records are preserved in a folder for each pupil.

## COMPUTER MANAGED EVALUATION

An increased number of teachers and administrators are recording pupil achievement results using computer services. Thus, for each pupil, a running record may be kept on pupil's test scores from teacher written tests, results from CRTs and norm referenced tests, observations made on pupil work habits by the teacher, records of conferences with pupils and with parents, diagnostic information, as well as check lists and rating scales. Journal writing by the teacher pertaining to pupil achievement in mathematics may also be entered into the computer. Student teachers and co-operating teachers provide a good testimony as to the effectiveness of looking at a single child's achievement on the monitor with a wide variety of information to guide in making curricular decisions in mathematics for the involved learner. Teachers need to possess much information pertaining to each pupil in order to make better decisions in terms of sequence in learning for any one pupil. Modern technology then has made it so that

1. little effort is put forth by the teacher into storing information in the computer.
2. information may be quickly recalled for any one learner and analyzed on the monitor.
3. information retrieved may be used by the teacher to increase and improve sequence in learning for each pupil.
4. diagnosis is possible when using information on the monitor for any one pupil to assist the learner to overcome weaknesses in the mathematics curriculum.
5. objectives for a single pupil or the class as a whole may be secured from an overview of learner progress, as presented on the monitor.
6. learning opportunities may be chosen by the teacher according to needs as revealed by pupils.
7. new procedures may be arrived at to further determine needs of pupils in ongoing lessons and units of study in mathematics.
8. machine scored tests provide teachers opportunities to work with pupils on instructional problems in mathematics, rather than working with the mundane in hand scoring tests.

## PORTFOLIOS TO APPRAISE MATHEMATICS ACHIEVEMENT

Portfolios have become increasingly popular as a way of evaluating pupil progress. Portfolios stress the importance of having pupil records preserved in everyday work performed in mathematics. Results from teacher written tests, teacher diagnostic observations, journal writing by the teacher of pupils' achievement, anecdotal records and diary entries kept by the teacher to record specific achievements in ongoing lessons and units of study, purposeful worksheet pages completed by pupils, written work of learners such as from a basal textbook, and log entries kept on attitudes of pupils toward diverse learning opportunities in mathematics are important in the evaluative program. The emphasis here is upon contextual work of pupils in mathematics. Within context, pupils and the teacher appraise the former's specific progress made on a daily and unit basis. The evaluations are made internally to the experiences of pupils, not externally. External evaluations consist of standardized test and criterion referenced test results. Both of these tests are written by educators removed from the local teaching situation. Standardized and criterion referenced tests are given very infrequently such as each being given once a year. Pupil achievement needs to be evaluated more frequently than that. Evaluation of pupil achievement in mathematics needs to be continuous so that the teacher receives feedback on how well a pupil is achieving in mathematics. Diagnosis stresses noticing the kinds of errors pupils individually make and giving assistance to learners in overcoming these deficiencies. Both pupils and teachers need to be actively involved in appraising individual progress of learners in mathematics. What items of pupil products and processes might go into a portfolio for a pupil?

1. A representative sampling of daily work of pupils in mathematics, such as problem solving activities.
2. Snapshots of models made such as model cubes, cylinders, pyramids, and cones in ongoing lessons and units of study.
3. Videotapes of committee and collaborative work by pupils in committee settings.
4. Pupil self evaluation statements as to goals accomplished and those that remain to be achieved within a given period of time.
5. Cassette recordings of discussions and book reports involving the owner of the protfolio.
6. Art work as it relates to mathematics, such as geometry art.
7. Pupil administered self evaluation containing checklists, rating scales, and journal entries.
8. Pupil test results from teacher written tests in mathematics.

9. Construction items as it is feasible to store these items due to size and places of storage.
10. Uses made of technology such as calculators and computer in the mathematics curriculum.

Portfolios and their using internally contextual experiences of pupils to evaluate each learner's progress. Thus, pupils and the teacher are heavily involved in protfolio development. Authentic assessment is then in evidence (Valencia, Hiebert, and Afflerback, 1994).

## CONCLUSION

A modern mathematics curriculum emphasizes using a variety of evaluation techniques to ascertain pupil achievement. Too frequently in the past, standardized norm referenced tests and their results provided major acceptable information pertaining to pupil achievement. These tests have no accompanying objectives for teachers to use in teaching mathematics. Then too, norm referenced tests spread pupils out from high to low in terms of test results, such as from the 99th to the first percentile. Spreading pupils out from high to low is one of the functions of a norm referenced test. Pupils might then be compared from results of the test as to who the high, middle, and low scorers are. Today, the emphasis is placed upon pupils be evaluated in terms of having achieved stated objectives in mathematics in ongoing lessons and units of study, not making comparisons among learners. A variety of approaches are used to ascertain pupil achievement in mathematics.

These approaches include:

1. Criterion referenced tests.
2. Teacher observation of an individual's progress in mathematics.
3. Conferences with pupils.
4. Parent and teacher conferences.
5. Diagnostic testing and their results.
6. Check lists and rating scales.
7. Computer managed evaluation.
8. Portfolio approaches in ascertaining pupil achievement.

## REFERENCES

Ediger, Marlow (1997), *Teaching Mathematics in the Elementary School,* Kirksville, Missouri; Simpson Publishing Company, 302-17.

Ediger, Marlow (1988), *The Elementary Curriculum, Second Edition,* Kirksville, Missouri : Simpson Publishing Company, 141-48.

Ediger, Marlow (1995), "Current Concepts in Teaching Mathematics, *Philippine Education Quarterly,* 7-10.

Ediger, Marlow (1996), *Elementary Education,* Kirksville, Missouri; Simpson Publishing Company, 193-208.

Ediger, Marlow (1998), "Listening and Reading in the Elementary School," *Experiements in Education,* May, 1998, Gardner, Howard (1993), *Multiple Intelligences; Theory Into Practice,* New York : Basic Books.

Valencia, Sheila W., Elfrieda H. Hiebert, and Peter P. Afflerbach (1994). *Authentic Reading Assessment; Practices and Possibilities,* Newark, Delaware; International Reading Association.

# Chapter 10

# USING CALCULATORS VERSUS PAPER AND PENCIL IN MATHEMATICS

How much emphasis should be placed by mathematics teachers in having pupils use calculators only/largely in ongoing mathematics lessons and units of study? Toward the opposite end of the continuum, how much stress should the use of paper and pencil computations have in sequential learnings in mathematics? There are advocates of pupils using calculators in working toward achieving all mathematics objectives. More traditional mathematics teachers advocate rather heavy use of paper and pencil in having pupils achieve objectives in mathematics. Later on, in sequence, calculators are brought into the ongoing lessons and units of study in mathematics.

This paper is divided into two parts. The first part discusses advantages of the rather immediate use of calculators by pupils as compared to more of paper and pencil approaches initially, followed by calculators, when learners are engaged in problem solving experiences in mathematics. The second part steers away from this issue to discussing the uses of principles of learning from educational psychology in focusing largely upon developing meaning within pupils for all learning activities in the mathematics curriculum.

## CALCULATORS IN THE MATHEMATICS CURRICULUM

Calculators have become inexpensive so that most pupils have these instruments to use in achieving mathematics objectives. Schools also, in many cases, can provide pupils with a calculator to use should he/she not have any. We will not go into the details here in terms of capabilities possessed by a calculator that are functional to the task at hand, but will assume that calculators used have those necessary capabilities.

We must caution here that pupils have meanings attached to operations prior to using a calculator. Whatever operation is being performed by the learner, he/she must understand the inherent facts, concepts, and generalizations. For example, in finding the area of a circle, the pupil needs to comprehend the meaning of A = *pi* times radius squared.

Thus, the learner needs to understand the following in determining the area of a circle:

1. the value of ***pi***
2. the meaning of the *radius* of a circle
3. comprehension of the concept *squared*
4. knowledge of why the formula for finding the area of a circle fulfills its functions. A hands on approach needs to be used with models to show how the formula works.

Meaning theory always be stressed by mathematics teachers in ongoing lessons and units of study. Concrete materials of instruction such as real objects and items as well as semiconcrete materials need to be used in teaching pupils. Semi-concrete items consist of pictures, video-tapes, drawings, filmstrips, slides, CD ROMS, programmed materials, and video disks.

Once pupils have attached meaning to inherent subject matter in finding the area of a circle, they should be able to perform operations in finding these areas through the use of the calculator. I would suggest that the problems to be solved with calculator use be as life-like as possible. In society, there are realistic problems which can be used for problem solving activities in the mathematics curriculum. The school buildings, grounds, and classrooms have items circular in shape which pupils may use to determine area.

It is very important to provide for individual differences among pupils in the mathematics curriculum. There are diverse ways to provide diverse achievement levels in the mathematics curriculum:

The following, among others, are ways to provide for diverse achievement levels in the mathematics curriculum:

1. Use the mathematics laboratory concept in teaching-learning situations. Thus, pupils on an individual basis sequence their own progress through the actual weighing of select objects, measuring of surfaces, as well as finding the volume of selected containers.
2. Utilize learning centers in the school-class setting. Learners sequentially choose the task to work on at a particular center. Ideally, the task or learning activity provides for new challenging experiences.
3. Utilize problem solving methods. Pupil with teacher guidance may select realistic problems solving methods. Pupils with teacher guidance may select realistic problems to solve on an individual basis. These problems must be on the present achievement levels of individual learners.
4. Pretest pupils using a reputable series of mathematics textbooks. Each learner is then at a different place within the confines of the textbook in terms of achievement. Pupils individually progress as rapidly as possible in satisfactorily completing sequential learnings in the textbook. The teacher gives explanations and guidance to learners as the need arises. Continual help is also given to diagnose errors made by learners in specific problematic situations. Remedial aid is given to learners to overcome identified deficiencies.
5. Use contracts in the mathematics curriculum. Pupils with teacher guidance write up in contract form what the former are to achieve within a given period of time, such as a few days or a week. The level of accuracy of completed work desired may also be spelled out in the contract. Both pupil and teacher sign the contract or agreement. If the contents on the contract are too difficult for the learner to achieve, needed modifications can then be made.
6. Have pupils individually achieve objectives of diverse levels of achievement. Thus, for example, pupils who achieve at a less complex level as compared to fast achievers, may be guided in attaining objective suitable to their optimal level of development.

## USE OF PAPER AND PENCIL TO SOLVE PROBLEMS

There is much to be said in pupils doing considerable paper/ pencil computations before a calculator is used. As these problems are being solved using paper and pencil, pupils need to go over each step of learning in a much slower manner than using a calculator, immediately or rather soon, after meaning has been established. There is much deliberation involved here. For example, in referring to the previously named problem on finding the area of a circle, the pupil also needs to see and understand the meaning of each concept such as *pi, radius, squared*, and the entire formula fitting together. However, as a pupil works on the problem, he/ she has more time to think about the sequential steps involved in determining area. We have observed pupils who when using paper/ pencil in initial problem solving have more opportunities to analyze, synthesize, and evaluate the why of progressing on the problem being solved. Using a calculator immediately after establishing meaning obtains an answer quickly for pupils. Due to the quickness of punching numerical values, the learning becomes too mechanical. There is a procedure to follow in pressing keys. One can find the square root of a number in a split second using a calculator. The mechanics of doing the work is rapid and accurate. Being too concerned with the mechanics of calculator use might well rob a pupil of establishing understanding. When understanding is lacking, it becomes more complicated to use what been learned. There are problems here also with thinking critically such as in making comparisons between, for example, finding the area of a circle as compared to a square. With rapidity of computations, pupils are used to having answers provided immediately. Problem solving generally requires deliberation and thought. In problem solving, there needs to be a pupil with teacher assistance initiative in choosing one or more problems. Adequate sources need to be used to gather data in answer to the problem. The answer is tentative and subject to testing in practical situations. Critical thinking is necessary here. Thus, there is a need to separate what is salient from what is not needed in data gathered to solve the problem. Also, from the data acquired, it is necessary to place values on the more important as compared to that which is less important as information sources. All information gathered needs to fit into a system that solves the problem, in whole or in part. Creative thought may be more possible in an initial paper/pencil procedure in problem solving. The pupil needs to be creative in determining ways of gathering information and means of solving the problem. Too frequently, the tried and true do not work in problem solving; thus, a new procedure needs to be found. We have observed many pupils in schools, where we supervise student teachers and co-operating teachers, who do better in experimenting using paper and pencil as compared to calculator use as rather immediate ways of solving problems.

## ADVANTAGES OF CALCULATOR VERSUS PAPER AND PENCIL USE

There were diverse opinions pertaining to which procedure is better in teaching.

Advocates of rather immediate pupil use of calculators in problem solving gave the following advantages:

1. It took the drudgery out of pupils' school work in mathematics in that routine operations of addition, multiplication, and division could be performed quickly and accurately. Checking one's work with a calculator could be done just as easily and accurately.
2. It is more enjoyable working with a calculator as compared to the use of paper and pencil.
3. It is good to see the rapidity with which different mathematical operations can be completed.
4. It is excellent to notice fewer errors made in computation.
5. It becomes apparent selected pupils feel that calculators involve having more fun in the mathematics curriculum than would otherwise be the case.

There is an ease and comfort with which calculators are used and yet for the pupil, is it really that easy? The pupil needs to touch the right keys on the calculator for a sum to come out right in column addition. In totaling the items I (Ediger) have purchased from a Master Card printout, I find that so often the wrong keys are pressed. I have started using paper and pencil approaches in checking these totals from a master Card printout. I believe the monthly bank statement can be checked for accuracy just as readily by using paper and pencil.

We think this boils down to individual differences among people. as to which is easier to use calculators or paper/pencil to check bank card and bank printout statements. But when more complex mathematics is involved then the calculator certainly comes in handy such as working problems pertaining to finding standard deviation, quartile deviation, standard scores, percentiles, and correlations. There are too many errors that can be made at different steps along the way when using paper and pencil for these computations. And when many complex computations are being made in experimental studies such as in a doctoral dissertation, the rapidity with which this can be done with accuracy is amazing.

Advocates for using paper and pencil for immediate practice on computations, again these were my student and co-operating teachers whom I supervised, believed the following:

1. Pupils have more time to deliberate with paper and pencil in problem solving as compared to the immediacy of results obtained from calculators. Calculators only provide the correct results if the user touches the proper keys in performing an operation in mathematics. Rote learning rather than thinking could be involved here.
2. Pupils do feel frustration if correct answers are too long in forthcoming when using paper and pencil in problem solving.
3. Selected pupils work more rapidly using paper and pencil when performing the less complex computations as compared to calculator use.

## MEANING THEORY IN TEACHING MATHEMATICS

From the above discussion, it is quite obvious that principles of learning incorporating educational psychology must be implemented in teaching and learning. A Task Force from the American Psychological Association (APA, 1993), after a three year study, came out with twelve Learner Centered Psychological Principles; four of which are in the cognitive and metacognitive domain and are stated as follows:

*Principal 1* . The nature of the learning process. Learning is a natural process of pursuing meaningful goals, and it is active, volitional, and internally mediated; it is a process of discovering and constructing meaning from information and experience, filtered through the learner's unique perceptions, thoughts, and feelings.

*Principle* 2. Goals of the learning process. The learner seeks to create meaningful, coherent representations of the quality and quantity of data available.

*Principle* 3. The construction of knowledge. the learner links new knowledge with existing and future orientated knowledge in uniquely meaningful ways.

*Principle* 4. Higher order strategies for "thinking about thinking"-- for overseeing and monitoring mental operations-- facilitate creative and critical thinking and the development of expertise.

Pupils like to make sense out of what has been learned in mathematics. Otherwise nonsense learning takes place. the mathematics teacher then has wasted the pupil's and his/her own time in the classroom. The pupil needs to be actively involved in each lesson and unit of study to develop understanding of facts, concepts, and generalizations. Thus, within a given learning opportunity, the pupil constructs knowledge. It is the pupil who develops knowledge, not the teacher nor the textbook. The pupil thinks about new content acquired with that previously obtained. Good sequence in learning is a must ! The pupil relates the 'new' with the 'old' content being emphasized in ongoing presentations in mathematics. Sequence resides within the pupil, either in a psychological or a logical order. With a psychological sequence, the pupil orders his/her own subject matter acquired from sequential lessons and units of study. The teacher is a guide and stimulator and encourages through diverse learning opportunities optimal learner achievement. In a logical sequence, the mathematics teacher arranges objectives for pupils to achieve from those which are easier to those being more complex in ascending order of difficulty.

Thinking about thinking, or metacognition, is done when the pupil monitors his/her own progress in goal attainment. The pupil then reasons as to which goals are being achieved and which objectives will necessitate teacher assistance to attain. Higher order thinking skills such as critical and creative thinking come about as a result of pupils' becoming increasingly more proficient in monitoring their very own progress in mathematics.

Critical thought is needed if pupils are to be able to differentiate in finding the areas, for example, of circles, trapezoids, parallelograms, and triangles. Analyzing or separating one from the other in determining area is a necessity in critical thought. When reading word problems, the pupil must separate the relevant from the irrelevant in order to secure an answer to the problem. The order of sequencing the steps in working toward a solution in the word problem also requires critical thought. The pupil needs to establish habits of desiring to monitor himself/herself in ascertaining if logic is being used in finding solutions to problems. Metacognition or thinking about thinking stresses maturity in the pupil when pursuing objectives in the mathematics curriculum. Thus the pupil needs to appraise his/her own logic and thought in ongoing lessons and units of study.

Creativity in the mathematics curriculum is stressed when the pupil uses unique solutions in finding answers to problems. Novel ways of using diverse algorithms to solve problems requires creative endeavours. The pupil has then discovered means of securing answers to problem areas. The teacher stimulates pupil curiosity to experiment with materials and equipment available to arrive at solutions to problems. Meaning theory is of utmost importance to teachers in implementing a quality mathematics curriculum. Pupils using calculators or using paper/pencil approaches in ongoing lessons and units of study must seek meaning and understanding of subject matter being acquired.

Pertaining to four psychologies of learning, we recommend that teachers of mathematics should:

1. implement tenets of behaviourism with its measurably stated objectives. Higher levels of cognition must not be hindered with the use of behaviourism in teaching-learning situations,

2. provide ample opportunities for students to engage in decision making. Learners need to have chances to select sequential learning opportunities as advocated by humanists.
3. stress the structure of knowledge so that students may perceive that subject matter in mathematics is related. In the structure of mathematics, there are definite key ideas that learners meet up with again and again as they progress through the public school years. These structural ideas include the commutative, associative, inverse, and distributive properties.
4. adequately diagnose and remediate students' problems in ongoing lessons and units. Students need to perceive mathematics as being holistic and not isolated specifics in diagnostic/remediation situations.
5. implement problem solving procedures in teaching in learning situations.

## USING AIDES TO ASSIST PUPILS IN MATHEMATICS

There are numerous mathematics educators who recommend strongly that aides be secured to guide more optimal pupil achievement in mathematics. Sometimes, there are too many pupils in a classroom to teach and the regular teacher cannot give the assistance he/she would wish to provide learners in ongoing lessons and units of study. Then too, there are pupils who have behavioural problems and waste much time in the classroom when teaching and learning is occurring. These pupils miss out on important instruction. When the range of pupil achievement in mathematics in very large, it becomes difficult to provide for individual pupils. Thus, it becomes increasingly necessary to have aide service in teaching mathematics.

Bogan (1997) describes three practical approaches in providing aide service to pupils so that the latter may achieve more optimally. One approach is to secure adult help through newsletter notices of the need for volunteers. These aides should be given information on how to proceed with giving pupil help in mathematics. These aides meet with individual pupils once a week for a thirty/forty five minute session. A second approach was to use cross age tutoring. Here seventh graders were able to assist pupils as a part of a school service project. These once a week tutoring sessions for each seventh grader were short in length and focused on specific problems that a pupil might have in mathematics. A third approach was to use peer tutors. A peer, for example, would give assistance to a main streamed pupil. Bogan (1997) gives high praise for aide service provided in helping pupils to achieve at a higher level.

I (Ediger) would like to add a unique program of aide service for a school in which I supervised student teachers in the public schools. At a meeting of the Area Retired Teachers Association, a team of teachers explained the need for retired teachers to help out with tutoring pupils in mathematics. The retired teachers showed much interest in tutoring. Many times, retired teachers feel they are no longer wanted or needed in the public schools. They have much to offer children in teaching and learning. Many retired teachers volunteered their services. The aides provided by these retired teachers consisted of the following, as examples:

1. Listening to pupils read story problems in mathematics orally and helping with word identification.
2. Reading library books to young pupils that contain mathematics content.
3. Assisting pupils with areas diagnosed as causing problems in mathematics such as adding fractions with unlike denominators.
4. Providing more practice for pupils such as in take away problems in subtraction.
5. Working one on one to assist pupils with attention deficits.
6. Helping pupils who have difficulties in making reversals when reading and writing numerals.
7. Giving help to pupils on calculator use.

Area retired teachers need little inservice education in order to teach pupils with regular teacher guidance. They appear to believe that much help can be given as aides to help children achieve at a higher level. This was exemplified by higher standardized test scores as well as increased achievement on district wide tests. At the end of each semester, an appreciation dinner was given to all retired teachers who assisted pupils in mathematics. Comments on an anonymous questionnaire indicated the following feelings from area retired teachers who served as teacher aids:

1. I really enjoyed pupils in mathematics.
2. I feel rewarded in helping pupils with needs in mathematics.
3. I was very much needed in the classroom as indicated by what several pupils told me.
4. I like to use my talents and abilities. Assisting pupils give me just such an opportunity.
5. This reminded me of the pleasant days when I was a regular teacher; I determined what pupils needed and gave each learner the necessary help.
6. I did not know that time could go so rapidly when giving assistance to pupils.

At a different place where one of the authors supervised student and co-operating teachers in the public schools, aide service came from high school students who were taking an elective course in helping younger public school pupils or who were meeting requirements in doing community service. These students needed more inservice education as compared to the retired teachers. Thus, high school students could only serve as aides to younger pupils if they had demonstrated proficiency in mathematics. High school students could only serve as aides to younger pupils if they had demonstrated proficiency in mathematics. High school mathematics teachers made the judgment here as to the fitness of a student to assist pupils. These students needed to possess characteristics of being patient, kind, and good at explaining content to learners. The mathematics teacher held a conference with each student prior to their working with younger pupils. One high school students knew what their roles were in tutoring pupils, elementary and middle school teachers supervised aide service. The program of aide service went along very well due in part to having been carefully selected and having received inservice education. These aides worked with pupils individually on diagnosed weaknesses or taught small groups of learners in mathematics. It is remarkable how pupils individually on diagnosed weaknesses or taught small groups of learners in mathematics. It is remarkable how pupils with aide service did much better in the classroom due to keeping up as well as possible with other learners.

Generally, there are guiding principles for all aides to follow in working with pupils such as the following:

1. The mathematics curriculum is designed to meet personal needs of each pupil. Pupils differ form each other in many ways and the role of the aide is to find what works bests for pupils in solving problems and working on tasks at hand.
2. Pupils have equal access to technology in the classroom to solve problems.
3. Teachers and aids need to assist each pupil to realize his/her highest potential possible.
4. Multicultural philosophy is stressed in the classroom whereby pupils learn from each other and accept/respect others.
5. Teachers and aides need to be enthusiastic about teaching mathematics and desire to assist others in achieving needed knowledge, skills, and attitudes.
6. Pupils are guided to perceive purpose in learning and apply what has been learned.

## MATERIALS OF INSTRUCTION

Most pupils experience a mathematics curriculum whereby a hands on learning approach is emphasized. This means that pupils experience concrete materials in learning. Pertaining to determining the area of a square using either a calculator or paper and pencil approaches initially, additionally commercial as well as teacher made materials are needed. We will list first commercially prepared materials of instruction to guide pupils to find the area of a circle:

1. A videotape which specifically showed the steps involved in determining the area of a circle.
2. A video disk which compared finding the areas of a circle, square, and rectangle. Each step was clearly presented for pupils to follow. Meaning was stressed throughout the presentation for pupils to find these areas.
3. A CD ROM presentation which gave uses for finding the areas of different geometrical figures, including circles.
4. A filmstrip which showed an overlay of a circle on a square to indicate comparisons between the two geometrical

figures, such as radius squared makes for a square. The resulting square is then taken times 3.1417 or pi, to indicate a ratio or relationship between the square and the circle.

5. A programmed package in which pupils individually and in groups moved forward in a step by step process to find the area of a circle.
6. Commercially made cut outs showing a ratio of a square (side squared) and a circle (radius squared) when the former and the latter have the same area, not including multiplying times pi.
7. Textbook and workbook materials of instruction, among others. Ediger (1996) wrote:

Word problems, also called story problems, in textbooks may provide selected difficulties to pupils. In solving word problems, a first step is that pupils comprehend the abstract symbols which made fo words and sentences. Being able to read with meaning is a very first step in solving word problems. Second, pupils need to possess background experiences in solving these word problems. Background experiences provide readiness for problem solving in mathematics. Third, pupils need to understand what is being asked for in the word problem so that problem solving can come about. Fourth, learners need to view the problem in a holistic manner in that salient ideas are needed from the entire word problem in order that solutions may be found. Fifth, mathematical operations need to be performed to arrive at an answer. The answer should be perceived as being tentative, not an absolute. Sixth, the pupil needs to reflect upon the tentative solutions(s). Thus, the learner looks at the weaknesses that might be inherent in the solution. Peer study of the tentative answer has many benefits. Pupils must be able to explain why they did what was done in securing the necessary answer.

Teacher made materials can be effectively used to assist pupils to achieve relevant objectives in mathematics. At workshops and at their own convenience, teachers may make the following to guide pupils in determining areas of selected geometrical figures:

1. A series of cut outs made from construction paper or cardboard pertaining to different geometrical figures.

Pupils may also make these figures in a hands on approach to learning.

2. Formulas for finding areas of geometrical figures with each formula on a separate sheet of paper. The formula can be matched with the geometrical figure for finding the area. These formulas may be posted in the classroom for pupil use as the need arises.
3. A filmstrip may be made pertaining to illustrations of different geometrical figures being taught with the related area formulas for each.
4. Overlays made for depth learning using the overhead projector.
5. A video-type made by teachers indicating sequential steps to be followed in determining areas of diverse geometrical figures.
6. Programmed materials made by teachers which sequence highly specific steps for pupils in determining areas of geometrical figures.
7. Diagnostic and remedial materials made to determine which specific problems a pupil has in mathematics.

## ASSESSING ACHIEVEMENT

The mathematics teacher needs to be a good appraiser of pupils in mathematics achievement. Only then might the results of achievement be used for improved teaching and learning. We find that teachers too frequently do not diagnose pupils adequately to ascertain what is not understood and what needs to come next sequentially. Evaluation should be ongoing and continuous to determine the sequence of experiences for pupils. Evaluation should be done to determine if pupils are achieving objectives. Thus there is a purpose in evaluating and that purpose is to notice learner progress toward goal attainment. Something is done with pupil results from the evaluation process. The products and processes evaluated provide information to the mathematics teacher what it is that should be taught so that pupil progress is continuous. Sometimes the objectives are written at too complex a level and a pupil fails to achieve the intent. The opposite extreme may also occur whereby objectives are excessively easy to attain. The learner then might become bored and lose interest in learning. The teacher certainly has a difficult task in setting challenging objectives for pupils and yet each objective is attainable. A pupil may work on attainable objectives, but the order or sequence is not appropriate. Thus, there is within the set of objectives where the sequence is too complex or too easy. The teacher then must ascertain what to do in teaching wherein the arranged sequence of objectives has not been the best possible. The concept of 'diagnosis' is salient here in that the teacher needs to provide learning activities whereby the learner may experience success and continued progress.

There is a teacher determined sequence in which he/she decides upon what comes first, second, third, and so on in guiding pupils in goal attainment. Within each objective, there are also is a sequence in arranging learning opportunities so that the pupil experiences what is easier to that which is gradually more complex. Pupils need to be successful learners so that an adequate self concept results. Without that adequate self concept, pupils cannot achieve in an optimal manner.

There are numerous procedures for teachers to use in writing test items in mathematics to ascertain learner achievement. These include the following:

1. true-false test items
2. multiple choice
3. essay
4. completion
5. matching

Further ways of evaluating learner progress in mathematics is to use teacher observation, checklists, rating scales, standardized tests, criterion referenced tests, pupil diary entries, log entries by pupils, learner journal writing, and diagnostic tests. Portfolios have become quite popular in use to evaluate pupil achievement; we suggest the following items to be placed in a teacher portfolio:

1. Snapshots of bulletin board displays which have been used in initiating, developing, and culminating ongoing units of study.
2. Videotapes of pupil/teacher planning of the curriculum.

3. Displays of learner products for other pupils and teachers to observe in the classroom setting. These have been made in slide form, but may appear in other media for the portfolio.
4. Cassette recordings of pupil oral reports given within an ongoing unit of study or lesson.
5. Samples of pupil writing involving diverse purposes. These can be in manuscript/cursive style or software packages.
6. Journal entries written by the teacher covering excursions taken into the community.
7. Anecdotal records on diagnosis and remediation of pupil difficulties in learning.
8. Test scores of pupils taught.
9. Diary entries and logs written by pupils pertaining to what was achieved in ongoing lessons and units of study.
10. Summaries of parent-teacher conferences.

There are numerous factors too that are involved in that quality teaching alone is not adequate in order that pupils achieve more optimally. We believe strongly in schools evaluating their noon lunch menu so that quality nutrition is in evidence. Then too, pupils need to have an adequate amount of food. With more and more children living on the poverty level, it behooves schools to provide wholesome breakfasts to learners so that food needs are being met. We recommend too that schools furnish an evening meal to those pupils who do not receive adequate nutrition at home.

Pupils who need assistance should be able to receive this help from teachers either by telephone or in once a week evening sessions. There could be definite days and evenings when pupils individually can ask for guidance in mathematics. Teachers too have their own private lives to live and should not be on call continuously. They may, of course, trade off with others teachers when being available for giving pupil assistance in mathematics. Successful learners develop a better self concept as compared to those who experience much failure. Parents need guidance to assist their offspring to achieve more optimally in mathematics. Too frequently parents do not know how to assist their children in mathematics or they do not wish to take the time for this. During parent/teacher conferences, the teacher needs to take time to help parents guide more optimal pupil achievement. Then too, parental attitudes toward the mathematics curriculum needs improvement. They should perceive the importance of pupils achieving well in knowledge, skills, and attitudes. Parents can set a good model for pupils.

Cognitive objectives are important to emphasize in the mathematics curriculum. Thus, being able to apply what has been learned is salient. Thinking critically and creatively is necessary when determining answers to problems in mathematics. The cognitive domain tends to receive major attention when students attain objectives in mathematics.

Another dimension of teaching stresses students achieving affective objectives. Affective or attitudinal objectives complement the cognitive dimension. A student then who has positive attitudes toward mathematics should achieve at a more optimal rate in that curriculum area. Positive attitudes influence the self concept as well as feelings towards others in ongoing lessons and units in mathematics..

## CONCLUSION

To guide pupils to attain more optimally in the mathematics curriculum, the teacher needs to tend to the following:

1. view and evaluate the quality of objectives for pupils achievement.
2. improve the quality of sequence for learner objectives, learning opportunities, and appraisal procedures.
3. establish challenging and yet attainable goals for pupil attainment.
4. provide for diverse levels of pupil achievement in mathematics.
5. work with parents to improve the mathematics curriculum for pupils.
6. give pupils adequate assistance in mathematics to achieve as well as individual abilities permit.
7. use appraisal results to guide pupils to achieve well in mathematics.

8. Establish a stimulating learning environment for pupils in mathematics.
9. Show care and appreciation for each pupil.
10. Study new trends and implement quality ideas in and for teaching and pupil learning in mathematics.

## REFERENCES

APA Task Force on Psychology in Education (1993), *The learner Centered Psychological Principles: Guidelines for School Redesign and Reform.* Washington, DC, American Psychological Association and the Mid-continent Regional Education Laboratory.

Bhaskara Rao, Digumarti (1987). *Audio Visual Teaching Aids,* Guntur; Nagarjuna Publishers (in Telugu language).

Bogan, Eileen (1997), "Three Equations for an Equitable Mathematics Program," Educational Leadership, Vol. 54, No. 7, pages 46-47.

Ediger, Marlow (1996), "Principles of Learning and the Mathematics Curriculum," *Experiments in Education,* Vol. 24, Nos. 10 and 11, pages 155-59, published in India by the S.I.T.U. Council of Educational Research.

Ediger, Marlow (1996), "Problems in Reading in Mathematics," *School Science,* Vol. 34, No. 1, pages 7-14.

Ediger, Marlow (1989), "Psychology in Teaching Mathematics, *Delta K,* Vol. 27, No. 4, pages 20-23.

Ediger, Marlow (1994), "Mathematics and the Affective Domain, TAMS JOURNAL, Vol. 21, No.1, pages, 41-44.

Ediger, Marlow (1996), "Portfolios, Pupils, and the Teacher," *Philippine Education Quarterly,* Vol. 25, No.1, pages, 41-45.

# Chapter 11

## ISSUES IN THE TEACHING OF MATHEMATICS

There are numerous issues in the teaching of mathematics. These issues need to be clarified and understood meaningfully by teachers, supervisors, and administrators. Too frequently, issues are vague and lack clarity and therefore are not meaningful to educators. Which issues need to be studied and synthesized, if possible?

### THE INTEGRATED VERSUS THE SEPARATE SUBJECTS CURRICULUM

How much of integration of subject matter should there be in the mathematics curriculum? Toward one end of the spectrum, there are educators advocating a separate subjects approach. Here, mathematics has its very own scope (what should be taught) as well as its own sequence (when should the content identified be taught)? Perhaps, mathematics has a more readily identifiable scope and sequence as compared to other academic areas. We believe that in the arithmetic curriculum all educators agree, with degrees of correlation and integration, that addition should be taught first, followed by subtraction, then multiplication, and followed by division in the primary grade sequence. Increasingly more complex as learners indicate readiness is in evidence. No educator would say that for primary grade pupils the sequence should be division, multiplication, subtraction, and then addition. Within the concept of addition beyond single digit addends, subject matter may well increase in complexity, such as having more than two single digits to add, having regrouping and renaming, and having more than one place value to add numerals.

Pupils may well work on correlated mathematics programs whereby addition and multiplication are involved in determining the perimeter of a geometrical figure, such as a rectangle (P = 2L+2W). A fused mathematics curriculum is involved when pupils related arithmetic, algebra, and statistics. Thus, in statistics, pupils at a young age with teacher guidance may make a picture graph from everyday experiences such as birthdays that occur on each of the days of the month. Thus, for example, there may be three pictures for January, two for February, one for March, and so on, depending on when each pupil in the class had his/her birthday.

We believe problems arise in the integrated curriculum in mathematics when social studies, science, and reading/language arts are brought in heavily. Mathematics, however, has always been brought into the curriculum for other academic areas.

In social studies, the following are examples of ways of integration that we have observed when supervising student teachers and co-operating teachers in the schools:

1. Determining how many years have elapsed since a certain event occurred such as the beginning of the Civil War in 1861.
2. Learning about the Egyptian system of numeration when studying a unit on Egypt in the Middle East.
3. Studying the abacus when a unit is being taught on the Philippines.

In science, much use is and can be made of mathematics including the following:

1. The number of electrons, neutrons, and protons in an atom of a particular element.
2. The number of elements that go into the making of particular compounds.
3. The velocity of objects falling from different heights.

The language arts permeate all curriculum areas including mathematics, including the following mathematics/language arts correlations:

1. Reading of word problems in mathematics.
2. Listening to and speaking in committee or collaborative endeavours.

3. Writing solutions to mathematics problems.

In the language arts/mathematics correlation, the listening, speaking, reading, and writing vocabularies are an inherent part of mathematics. One of five major objectives stressed by the National Council Teachers of Mathematics (NCTM, 1989) emphasizes learning to communicate ideas mathematically. Certainly, each pupil needs to become highly effective in communicating ideas to others.

An extreme case of the integrated mathematics curriculum might be the following when studying a thematic unit on fish:

1. Pupils solving mathematics word problems on fish.
2. Pupils studying fish in terms of scientific classification.
3. Pupils singing songs of fish in music classes.
4. Pupils doing art work about fish such as murals, dioramas, pencil sketching, water coloring, and model making.
5. Pupils reading about fish using a variety of reference sources.
6. Pupils engaging in physical education activities by doing motions and movements of diverse kinds of fish.

From the above, we believe we can all see that integration of content can go overboard. One does not want to lose sight of the scope and sequence inherent in mathematics. Mathematics is highly exacting and precise. It is good to relate ideas from other academic disciples if it assists pupils to understand mathematics better in terms of what is being studied. This goes back to the statement of objectives. These objectives need to be carefully chosen so that pupils achieve what is essential and basic in mathematics.

## THE LEVEL OF APPLICATION VERSUS KNOWLEDGE FOR ITS OWN SAKE

John Dewey (1917) was an early advocate of knowledge being practical in that it can be used in society. His beliefs emphasized that knowledge which is used will be remembered better than knowledge acquired for its own sake. Also, if pupils can see how something is to be used, they will find purpose in learning. Reasons are then inherent in pupils wanting to learn. Aristotle (388-322 BC) was an early advocate of knowledge being learned for its own sake. Presently, Mortimer Adler (1902) is an advocate of knowledge being valuable for its own sake. Thus, knowledge has its own value in and of itself (Ediger, 1995).

First, we will discuss knowledge that is learned and used in problem solving situations. Higher levels of cognition is necessary presently for pupils to function well, as possible as in the future workplace/society. Then to the level of application needs adequate emphasis since mathematics permeates our lives in everyday situations. A sixth grade class was asked by the student teacher and co-operating teacher, working as a team whom supervised in the public schools, how one of the authors mathematics is used in the daily lives of individuals. The length of the list was quite long, with thirty five different ways cited. We will mention ten of these ways:

1. Writing checks,
2. keeping a checkbook balance,
3. paying from an invoice from Master Card,
4. counting change in one's pocket or billfold,
5. paying cash for items purchased,
6. giving money to charities,
7. writing diary entrees and listing the dates pertaining thereto,
8. using numerals to find a page in a book,
9. crossing dates off on a calendar,
10. keeping track of allowance money on hand as well as of that spent.

From the above, it is quite obvious that mathematics is very functional and important in the lives of individuals. Solving problems of living are generally involved in applying what has been learned since a new situation is involved each time that mathematics is used. In problem solving, pupils with teacher guidance identify one or more problems. Each problem needs to be adequately delimited so that clarity is involved. Information may then be gathered in answer to the problem. Higher levels of cognition need to be stressed such as critical and creative thinking. Pupils then appraise the content in terms of its worth and in terms of being valuable for the problem to be solved. Creative thinking also involves higher levels of cognition in that novel, new ways may need to be sought to solve problems in mathematics. Next, the information gathered may be used in developing an hypothesis or tentative answer to the identified problem(s). The hypothesis may be tested in a lifelike situation to determine its quality. If evidence warrants, a new hypothesis may need to be developed. There are, indeed, many practical situations to test an hypothesis. Testing here does not mean a paper pencil test, be it norm referenced or criterion referenced, but rather reality is a societal kind of use (Meyer, 1949).

Second, knowledge for its own sake will be discussed. Those educators advocating knowledge for its own sake believe that content is learned for the sake of doing so (O'Neill, 1981). Knowledge then has the following inherent characteristics:

1. possesses its own intrinsic goals and values,
2. is appreciated or its form (structural ideas and patterns),
3. contains beauty in the many designs that may be drawn and created (geometric patterns),
4. provides a foundation or readiness to understand other more complex leanings in mathematics as well as perceive relationships with other academic disciplines,
5. may provide enjoyment for participants,
6. can be taught in an exciting and challenging way so all may benefit from instruction,
7. uses inductive procedures in learning,
8. makes for interest in learning due to fascinating topics discussed in mathematics,
9. stresses rational thinking due to humans being rational creatures,
10. emphasizes logical thinking as a major goal of instruction,

The above are excellent goals that do need to be incorporated into mathematics lessons and units of study. A major objective that may come about here is the level of application and problem solving. We believe that pupils would find many uses for mathematics when working toward achieving the above named objectives. However separate objectives stressing the solving of problems, lifelike and realistic, need to be pinpointed.

## STATE MANDATED VERSUS LOCALLY DETERMINED OBJECTIVES

Testing certainly is emphasized much in today's mathematics curriculum. Certainly, too much testing takes away instructional time in teaching and learning. State mandated testing may take the form of tests developed under the supervision of the stated department of education. Those involved in developing these tests are external to the local classroom; they are not involved in teaching or even knowing the pupils who will be taking the test. Most state mandated tests are called Criterion Referenced Tests (CRTs) since they relate directly to objectives also written on the state level. Teachers then have access to these objectives for use in guiding instruction. At selected intervals, pupils are measured, as prescribed by the state, to determine how well these objectives have been achieved. The tests are usually offered once a year on the second, fourth, and eight grades, although this will vary from state to state. Sometimes, a state will require a norm referenced test to be given to pupils within a state. Norm referenced tests contain no objectives for teachers to use in gauging their instruction. Thus, norm referenced tests lack the validity that CRTs can possess. In either case, these tests are a one shot affair whereby pupils need to reveal when the tests are given how well they are doing in instruction. There are definite weaknesses here:

1. A one shot case does not allow for several variables such as not showing over a period of time how well the pupil is achieving.
2. The one shot situation does not permit observing how well pupils do on a daily basis in each curriculum area.
3. The one shot case may completely determine how the lay public feels schools are doing in pupil achievement.
4. The one shot case stress verbal learnings only, such as reading and responding to multiple choice items. What about pupil achievement being revealed in other ways such as in music, art, drama, and committee work, among others?
5. The one shot case stresses reporting pupil progress numerically, such as the percentile rating or grade equivalent. What about qualitative information on pupils'

progress such as in attitudes and in creative writing activities?
6. The one shot case does not permit pupils to show how they would use or apply knowledge acquired in a lifelike situation.
7. The one shot situation does not permit input from pupils in terms of how they wish to be appraised.

Evaluation specialists need to work on improving the quality of measurement and appraisal instruments so that more effective appraisal of pupil progress is in evidence. Weaknesses of testing need to be identified and overhauled.

Locally determined objectives and evaluation procedures have been emphasized for years in the public schools. When (Ediger) started teaching in 1951, there were no state mandated tests. Each teacher devised his/her own tests to ascertain pupil achievement.

Presently, selected educators stress constructivism as a philosophy of instruction (Rowen and Bourne, 1994). Here, pupils and the teacher may select objectives for the former to achieve. Leaning opportunity to achieve the chosen objectives are also decided upon in the classroom. Appraisal procedures to ascertain what pupils have learned are chosen within the classroom setting. There are then no outside groups, such as state mandated tests and their supporters, who evaluate pupil achievement. Local determination in the classroom or with a team of teachers, decides upon objectives, learning activities, and evaluation approaches. What is missed by pupils is identified when using diverse appraisal procedures, and remedied through a variety of learning opportunities. Reasons provided to have curriculum development, including appraisal procedures, implemented on the local or classroom level are the following:

1. Pupils and teachers are in the best position to know what has been taught and evaluation procedures are valid when alignment is there with the objectives of instruction.
2. Tests written by outsiders, such as on the state level, may not harmonize with what has been taught in a specific classroom. Even more so, there are advocates of multiple intelligences whereby pupils individually possess unique talents in

responding to additional ways in evaluation than paper/pencil tests. Verbal intelligence is used in responding to paper/pencil tests. Musical, artistic, kinesthetic, among others, are additional ways for pupils to indicate what has been learned in mathematics.

3. Teachers on the local level has the best opportunities to study and learn about characteristics of children taught in mathematics. Educators on the state level do not know the children within any classroom; they are externally positioned to the teaching of pupils locally.
4. Mathematics teachers should possess the knowledge and skills to sequence learning opportunities appropriately for pupils so that more optimal achievement is possible. Objectives determined on the state level provide no information on how to sequence these stated objectives.
5. It becomes a problem to align learning activities to be chosen by the teacher with the objectives selected by the state in the latters' mandated objectives.

Perhaps, the state mandated objectives versus locally determined objectives might be harmonized by having rational balance between the two approaches. There still is a problem in using state mandated objectives in that they are externally selected by those outside the classroom setting. Validity is then lacking in testing in that the evaluation procedures do not align properly with the objectives of instruction. An exception would be if the teacher follows very carefully in choosing learning opportunities that assist pupils to achieve the state mandated objectives.

## TRADITIONAL VERSUS PORTFOLIO APPROACHES IN APPRAISING ACHIEVEMENT

Traditional procedures used in evaluating pupil achievement in mathematics have consisted of the use of norm referenced standardized tests as well as teacher written test items. Teacher written test items have consisted of solving word problems, testing on basic addition, subtraction, multiplication, and division facts, as well as using multiple choice, true/false, essay, matching, and completion items. These tests may measure pupil achievement in arithmetic, algebra, calculus, and statistics. Using teacher observation in daily work performed by pupils in mathematics will always be important. Here, the mathematics teacher needs to use updated criteria to appraise, diagnose, and remedy pupil errors and deficiencies.

A relatively recent innovation in appraising pupil achievement in mathematics emphasizes protfolio use (Isele, Frederick, 1995). With portfolios, pupils are heavily involved in appraising their very own achievement. Ownership in evaluation, in large part, resides within the pupil. The teacher of mathematics is a guide and helper in the evaluation process. The portfolio in mathematics is a purposeful collection of pupil products and processes to show imporvement over previous performances. The pupil with teacher guidance might then place the following of his work into the protfolio:

1. Written daily work of pupils including problem solving activities, drill, and practice experiences. Test results of teacher written tests, including the written test items.
2. Diagrams drawn to illustrate concepts understood in mathematics.
3. Snapshots o: construction objects completed in mathematics such as models of geometrical figures.
4. Videotapes of collaboration in mathematics, such as committee endeavours and large group work.
5. Individual activities completed by the learner involving projects.
6. Journal entries written by the pupil in ongoing lessons and units of study in mathematics.
7. Sequential daily diary entries to indicate what was learned on a specific day in an ongoing lesson.
8. Logs written to combine diary entries and develop major generalizations and conclusions.
9. Oral book reports in mathematics on a cassette.
10. Justification for placing the above items in the mathematics portfolio.

The portfolio needs to be well organized with a preface and a table of contents. The portfolio is an excellent device to use in part/ teacher conferences, as well as to indicate achievement in mathematics to interested, responsible persons such as the school administrator, supervisor, and curriculum director. In the portfolio, it is good to include items which show multiple intelligences in mathematics by revealing mathematics achievement of pupils through additional approach than verbal intelligence.

## TRADITIONAL MATERIALS OF TEACHING VERSUS MULTIMEDIA PROCEDURES

Traditional methods of instruction have included use of basal textbooks, workbooks, worksheets, and some audio-visual materials. One problem inherent in using traditional approaches has been how these materials were used in teaching. The same materials used over and over again may make for boredom in teaching mathematics. Thus, if a mathematics text is used each day in teaching mathematics, with no other activities, it may make for a curriculum which lacks interest and challenge. A carefully chosen basal text, used with other materials of instruction, can develop increased interest in learning mathematics on the pupil's part. The mathematics teacher needs to study the pupil and his/her style of learning to notice what assists an individual pupil to achieve more optimally. In supervising student teachers and co-operating teachers in the public schools, we have noticed pupils who seemingly like a textbook centered mathematics curriculum, whereas others needed more semiconcrete or concrete set of experiences to achieve objectives in mathematics. Much, too, depends upon how the basal is used in teaching. A well selected textbook can definitely be used to have pupils think creatively and critically in solving word problems. Even in computations performed, mathematics teachers may guide pupils to think creatively and critically in solving word problems. Even in computations performed, mathematics teachers may guide pupils to think creatively by asking for different ways (algorithms) of computation, such as changing the order of addends or factors when using the commutative and associative properties of addition and multiplication respectively.

A textbook is a guide and can provide many quality learning opportunities for pupils. The basal then needs to have practical applications to every day life situations which the teacher needs to provide pupils. Whatever is learned must have use and application tendencies. If knowledge is not used, it is soon forgotten. To assist pupils in retention of mathematics knowledge and skills, content needs to be used in the many ways possible.

That brings up the problem of mathematics workbooks. Again with everyday use, pupils certainly can be turned of from these kinds of activities. We have noticed pupils working in workbooks with considerable interest. No doubt, there are pupils who prefer abstract sequential experiences as compared to the semiconcrete and the concrete. Teachers who use mathematics workbooks in teaching pupils and have considerable success in doing so have a purpose in mind and they assist pupils to accept these purposes or reasons for the learning activity. Workbook activity needs to possess reasons for their use and these reasons (purposes) pupils need to accept intrinsically in order that achievement in mathematics is possible. It is always important to take a little time when initiating an activity in mathematics to discuss the reasons for these activities. The use of manipulative materials, illustrations, and aduio visual materials directly related to the ongoing lesson/unit can do much to guide more optimal achievement among pupils. Traditional procedures of instructions should:

1. guide pupils to establish interest in the ongoing activities.
2. assist pupils to understand why the content is important to learn.
3. provide for quality sequence in the mathematics curriculum.
4. emphasize providing for individual learning styles and intelligences.
5. help pupils to achieve worthwhile objectives and omit trivia.
6. emphasize balance among cognitive, affective, and psychomotor objectives of instruction.
7. establish meaning and understanding of mathematical content among learners.
8. make provision for individual as well as collaborative learning activities.
9. keep pupils on task in a reasonable way.
10. secure pupil input into the mathematics curriculum.

Toward the other end of the continuum, a multimedia approach in teaching mathematics is advocated. Computer programs, videotapes, slides, filmstrips, films, internet, E-mail, and CD ROMS, among other technology, would provide a variety of activities for pupils. The state of the art technology might then be available to learners in a modern mathematics curriculum. Pupils with teacher guidance may then select and identify problems, gather data or answers to the mathematical problems, evaluate the acquired content critically and creatively, achive an hypothesis or answer which is tentative, test the hypothesis in a virtual reality or lifelike situation, and make necessary modifications if necessary.

A multimedia approach in teaching mathematics provides opportunities for pupils to experience learning activities harmonizing with criteria such as the following:

1. Emphasize diverse activities to develop and maintain interest in mathematics.
2. Have pupils experience activities which harmonize with talents and abilities possessed.
3. Provide a hands on approach to learning in mathematics.
4. Guide pupils to attain vital objectives.
5. Stress empowerment of pupils in mathematics.
6. Assist pupils to reflect upon mathematical content acquired.
7. Facilitate pupil ownership in the mathematics curriculum.
8. Indicate deficiencies possessed by pupils with numerous opportunities to take care of these as necessary.
9. Teach so that success in learning is in evidence.
10. Teaching as facilitating learning in ongoing lessons and units in mathematics.

There needs to be room for both traditional and multimedia approaches in teaching and learning. Certainly, a carefully chosen basal has much to offer in providing relevancy, quality scope, and proper sequence in the mathematics curriculum. The teacher must assist pupil learning in mathematics by using recommended criteria from the psychology of education. Updating the mathematics curriculum strongly stresses a multimedia approach in learning. New procedures should not be accepted in teaching for the sake of doing so, but rather to help each pupil reach his/her potential in the mathematics curriculum. The state of the art technology must assist teachers to plan the best objectives. Learning opportunities, and evaluation procedures possible. Presently, mathematics is vital for each pupil as he/she progresses through the diverse levels of schooling as well as later on in the work place.

## LOGICAL VERSUS PSYCHOLOGICAL SEQUENCE IN MATHEMATICS

There are mathematics educators who believe in a logical sequence in developing the mathematics curriculum. Here, the objectives need to be stated in measurable terms. The teacher determines which objectives to emphasize, written very precisely.

Leaning opportunities then need to be selected by the teacher and arranged sequentially for pupils to achieve stated objectives in mathematics. Evaluation techniques need to be carefully aligned with the specific objectives. The evaluation procedures are used to determine which objectives have been achieved by each pupil. Ideally those not achieved should receive additional learning activities so that pupils may be successful achievers.

The measurably stated objectives, the learning opportunities, and the evaluation procedures are all carefully arranged so that the learning activities guide pupil to achieve each measurably stated objective in mathematics. The evaluation procedures measure if the learning activities assisted pupils to achieve the stated objectives. The mathematics teacher in a logical manner arranges these three parts of the curriculum so that optimal achievement is possible from each pupil.

Toward the other end of the mathematics curriculum, the pupils with teacher guidance have considerable input into the curriculum. A learning stations approach may be in evidence. Here, there may be seven stations, as an example, for a class of twenty-two pupils. Each stations is labeled as to the title of the topic(s) to be covered. Concrete, semiconcrete, and abstract materials should be located at each station. Pupils individually or in committees may select the station to work at. Each station may have a card listing four to five things for pupils to engage in. The pupil is the chooser as to which tasks to complete. Each learner then sequences his/her own learning activities. The mathematics teacher becomes a guide and stimulates pupils to do well in mathematics. There are more tasks as compared to what any pupil can complete so that the learner may omit those that lack perceived purpose. A psychological sequence is involved when the pupil, basically, sequences his/her own learning activities in mathematics (ediger. 1988).

We believe there is room for both a logical and a psychological sequence in mathematics. Certainly, there are things that are essential for all pupils to learn such as addition, subtraction, multiplication, sand division within a problem solving framework. The essentials will be teacher determined. The mathematics teacher than will sequence or order the arrangement of objectives, learning opportunities, and evaluation procedures for pupils.

We believe too there needs to be input from pupils to increasingly develop a child centered mathematics curriculum. Pupils have questions for which they would like to have answers. These questions may become problems to stress in a problem centered mathematics curriculum. The learning activities to sequence pupil learning may involve enrichment centers for pupil active engagement whereby personal choices may be made as to what to learn and the order of learning.

## CONCLUSION

Mathematics teachers are concerned about having pupils achieve more optimally in mathematics. One problem, among others in teaching mathematics, is how to arrange the order of objectives, learning opportunities, and evaluation techniques. Should these be arranged in ascending order of complexity by the teacher? Or, should there be heavy pupil involvement in sequencing his/her own learning in mathematics?

There are numerous variables inherent in teaching pupils such as learning styles and multiple intelligenc. Needs of pupils should be met to improve the mathematics curriculum. Only then pupils might achive more optimally!

## REFERENCES

Dewey, John (1917), *Democracy and Education.* New York; Macmillan and Company.

Ediger, Marlow (1996), *Elementary Education,* Kirksville, Missouri : Simpson Publishing Company, 15-17.

Ediger, Marlow (1995), *Philosophy in curriculum Development,* Kirksville, Missouri, Simpson Publishing Company, 72-73.

Ediger, Marlow (1997), *Teaching Mathematics in the elementary School,* Kirksville, Missouri, Simpson Publishing Company, 46-49.

Ediger, Marlow (1997), *Teaching Reading and the Language Arts in the Elementary School,* Kirksville, Missouri; Simpson Publishing Company, 237-45.

Ediger, Marlow (1988), *The Elementary Curriculum,* Second Edition, Kirksville, Missouri; Simpson Publishing Company, 53-54.

Isele, Frederick (1995), *Performance Based Portfolios for Effective Social Studies Instruction.* Presentation Paper to the National Council Social Studies Convention, chicago, Illinois, November, 1995.

Meyer Adolph (1949) *The Development of Education in the Twentieth Century,* Englewood Cliffs, New Jersey; Prentice-Hall, Inc., 42-64.

NCTM (1989), *Curriculum and Evaluation Standards for School Mathematics,* Reston, Virginia, 5-6.

O'Neill, John (1981), *Educational Ideologies,* Santa Monica, California; Goodyear Publishing Company, 168.

Rowen, Thomas, and Barbara Bourne (1994), *Thinking Like Mathematicians.* Portsmouth, New Hampshire; Heinemann, 19-22.

# Chapter 12

## TEACHING MATHEMATICS IN THE ELEMENTARY SCHOOL

Pupils need to experience mathematics in an interesting way. The teacher must choose worthwhile objectives for learners to achieve. Each objective should be selected with great care. Learning activities to achieve the objectives need to capture pupil purpose or reasons for learning. Evaluation techniques to determine pupil progress must be valid and reliable. These approaches to evaluate should ascertain if each pupil has attained the stated objectives.

### LEARNING ACTIVITIES TO ACHIEVE OBJECTIVES

The mathematics teacher needs to start with concrete materials in teaching-learning situations. Concrete materials are represented by such items as objects, realia, and things. Concrete materials may then stress a hands on approach in learning. If early primary grade pupils are studying addition of a single digit plus a single digit addend (4+3), they may use four sticks and three sticks to be joined together to make a set of seven. The order of addends may also be changed to show that three sticks and four sticks joined together also be changed to show that three sticks and four sticks joined together also make a set of seven. The commutative property of addition states that a+b=b+a. This property is highly valuable for pupils to understand and use since two addends of any value can be ordered in any direction and the answer will be the same in addition. As learners progress through continually higher levels of schooling, they can use the commutative property of addition. The commutative property also holds true for multiplication in that 4 x 3=3 x 4.

It is good to have pupils perceive quantity using diverse examples such as four pupils and three pupils in the classroom make a total of seven.

The semiconcrete facet of learning should follow sequentially from the concrete. In the previous example, if early primary grade pupils were studying the value of 4+3=, pictures may be shown of four dogs and three dogs joined together to show the concept of seven. Again, the commutative property may be shown with the illustrations in that the order of the addends could be changed to show that 3+4=7. Pictures/illustrations should be changed to cats, boys, girls, toys, among others, so that learners truly understand that 4+3 and 3+4=7, and not that the four dogs and the three dogs alone make a sum of seven. The abstract can be printed next to the concrete and semiconcrete representations, *i.e.*, 4 + 3 and 3 + 4=.

With the abstract phase of learning being the ultimate goal of instruction, the mathematics teacher may revert back to the concrete and the semiconcrete. Thus, if pupils are to reveal that 4+3=7, they may show this understanding with checkers, chess pieces, and other materials. Meaningful learning must occur and become a part of the repertoire of the pupil.

In sequence, the pupil may understand the associative property of addition. The associative property states that a+b+c=c+b+a or any other arrangement of the addends. Three or more addends can be ordered in any direction and the sum will be the same. The associative property also holds true for multiplication.

With appropriate order, pupils may generalize that subtraction undoes addition. Thus, if there are seven dogs and three run away, four will remain. Seven minus three equals four. Pupils should notice the number names such as 'four', 'three', and 'seven' as readiness permits. Concrete and semiconcrete materials may be used in subtraction as was true in addition. Ultimately the abstract becomes salient such as 7—4 = 3. With practice on the concrete and semiconcrete materials, learners can become quite proficient in the use of the abstract. The abstract is used in society and is convenient to use as compared to continual referral to the concrete and semiconcrete. Early primary pupils should not be hurried in using the abstract, but should have quality, ample experiences with concrete and semiconcrete materials.

**METHODS OF TEACHING**

The mathematics teacher must experiment with a variety of methods to understand which approach works best with individual pupils. Pupils differ from each other in so many different ways. Thus, the learning style for one pupil may not be the same or similar as compared too another learner.

Many pupils like an inductive procedure. Here the teacher needs to be a good asker of questions. Responses come from pupils in answer to these questions. Practical questions may be asked of pupils such as the following;

1. How many pupils are in our classroom today?
2. How many are absent?
3. How many pupils are in each reading group? The assumption here is that pupils are in different reading groups for instructional purposes.

Questions may also be asked of pupils pertaining to the following contained in a lesson plan;

1. If I place three sticks next to the four sticks as you can see here, how many sticks do we then have all together?
2. Suppose I have these three sticks and join four sticks to this set, how many are there then?
3. If I take three sticks away from the seven sticks, how many are left?

If a pupils responds incorrectly, a tactful approach is to merely ask for another answer. Pupils should be permitted to hypothesize freely without restraints. Should the classroom become disruptive, the mathematics teacher may then call upon specific pupils for an answer. Learners may also raise their hands and be recognized by the teacher prior to giving an answer. It is important to praise pupils for answering correctly as well as for behaving in a positive manner.

It is always important to diagnose why a response is incorrect. Should a pupil say that five sticks remain when three sticks are taken way from the seven sticks, a pupil or the teacher should count in one to one correspondence the number or remaining sticks.

There are pupils who learn best with the use of a deductive procedure of teaching. With deduction, the teacher needs to explain clearly how to work correctly a given problem such as 4+3=7. Within the explanation, the teacher, for example, shows pupils how 4+3=7 using concrete and semiconcrete materials. The explanations must be clear, concise, and meaningful. The teacher needs to observe that pupils are attentive and listening. After using explanations to present content clearly to pupils, the teacher needs to observe that pupils are attentive and listening. After using explanations to present content clearly to pupils, the teacher needs to determine what each has been learned. Many approaches can be used by pupils to reveal that which has been learned including showing with sticks a set of four and a set of three seeds. The two sets are joined together to show the sum. Pencils, erasers, and pieces of chalk may also be used to represent that which was explained by the teacher.

A third way to teach is to have pupils engage in problem solving. for example, the teacher may show seven cookies and have a pupil take three away. The problem is "How many are left?" Learns may speculate in this life like situation on the number of cookies that are left over. With problem solving, social use is made of what is being learned. It is very important for pupils to see how one can use mathematics in the real world. Perhaps, this is the ultimate test of pupils being able to apply mathematics in a functional situation. Best it is, if pupils are stimulated by the teacher to identify problems. Learners might then perceive purpose or reasons for learning. The number of cookies left in the above example can then be divided among pupils for each to eat.

Mathematics textbooks may have selected excellent addition and substraction number pairs for pupils to work. Working at each of the number pair in addition and subtraction, pupils receive practice in what the teacher had presented in the classroom. Learners have a better chance to retain that which has been learned if meaningful practice is in evidence. Accompanying workbooks contain exercises which provide further practice to pupils. With the use of textbooks and workbooks, the teacher must follow the following guidelines;

1. Use a variety of materials of instruction beyond that of textbooks and workbooks since pupils possess diverse learning styles.
2. Do not over emphasize drill and practice to the point where pupils lose interest in learning.
3. Make content meaningful so that pupils understand what has been learned.
4. Guide learners to perceive reasons for learning.
5. Provide for individual differences so that each pupil learns as much as possible.

## SEQUENCE IN LEARNING

Mathematics teachers need to evaluate where each pupil is presently in achievement. It is important to find this starting point. Otherwise if content taught is too difficult, pupils can not learn the new subject matter being emphasized. Content that is too easy promotes boredom on the part of pupils. Thus, the teacher must attempt to teach that which is new to the learner and at the same time is challenging, not the trivial nor the routine. There are several approaches in sequencing learning opportunities for pupils.

First, a logical sequence may be implemented. With a logical sequence, the teacher writes measurably stated, also called behaviourally stated objectives, for pupil attainment. These objectives are highly precise and leave little or no leeway in interpretation as to what will be taught. Prior to implementation, the mathematics teacher may even announce to pupils what they are to learn from the lesson presentation. Pupils then have security as to what is to be learned. Guesswork here is eliminated. Teachers have developed a teaching strategy with appropriate learning opportunities so that each learner may attain the stated objectives. After instruction, the teacher appraises pupils to notice if objectives have been attained. Objectives not achieved need a differed teaching strategy. In a logically developed mathematics curriculum, the teacher selects and writes the objectives, chooses the learning opportunities, and uses quality evaluation procedures to ascertain pupil progress. Logically then the teacher arranges the order of objectives, activities and experiences, as well as appraisal procedures to the best possible to optimalize learner achievement. Advocates of a logical mathematics curriculum believe that properly educated mathematics teachers are in the best position to choose objectives, learning opportunities, and evaluation procedures due to training, education, and maturity.

A second procedure in sequencing activities is to use a psychological mathematics curriculum. Pupils themselves are heavily involved in degrees, when choosing objectives, learning opportunities, and evaluation procedures. A learning stations approach may well be stressed here. The teacher sets up the learning the stations with appropriate materials of instruction at each station. Again, the materials should consist of the concrete, semiconcrete, and the abstract. Approximately four or five tasks or learning opportunities should be listed on a card at each station. Pupils individually may then choose the order of tasks to be completed. There should be more tasks in total than any one child can complete so that choice is involved as to what to complete and what to omit. Time on task is very important for each pupil. The teacher assists pupils with questions and problems so that pupils individually might attain optimally. A psychological sequence stresses pupils individually being involved in choosing ordered tasks. Advocates of a psychological mathematics curriculum believe that sequence resides within the pupil, not within textbooks, work books, or predetermined measurably stated objectives for learner attainment.

The writer recommends the selection of an appropriate sequence, be it logical or psychological, which assists pupils to learn as much as possible on an individual basis. Mathematics teachers must provide for individual differences so that optimal attainment on the part of each learner is possible.

## CONCLUSION

Rather than stress one procedure only as compared to another in teaching mathematics, the teacher must always keep in mind to select the best methodology possible in teaching-learning situations. That best method should benefit each pupil to attain as much as is possible. Pupils may vary much from each other in terms of possessed learning styles. There is certainty, however, in teaching mathematics in that objectives, learning opportunities and evaluation procedures need to be meaningful and understandable, interesting, challenging, purposeful, as well as provide for individual differences in the classroom.

## REFERENCE

Ediger, Marlow and Digumarti Bhaskara Rao (1996), *Science Curriculum*, New Delhi; Discovery Publishing House.

# Chapter 13

## TEACHING SUGGESTION IN MATHEMATICS

There are numerous teaching suggestions to offer in guiding pupils to achieve more optimally in mathematics. There is a problem involved in writing about the implementation of selected teaching suggestions. Why? There needs to be readiness of learning prior to implementing any teaching suggestion. If pupils cannot benefit from the teaching suggestions, the chances are they are too difficult. These suggestions may also be too easy for some and thus not challenge the involved learner. If anything is important in teaching as a priority in mathematics, the instructor needs to begin where the pupil is presently. From then on the materials used in teaching should guide pupils to be successful in attaining new and challenging objectives. Second, the teacher needs to observe what interests the pupil in learning. There are activities that are more interesting as compared to others. We will suggest activities for teachers to use; these must be on the meaning and understanding level of the pupil to be taught.

### USING BLOCKS IN TEACHING MATHEMATICS

Friedrich Froebel (1782-1852) was an early advocate of using a hands on approach in learning for pupils. One kind of material advocated by Froebel was blocks for children. Here, pupils could manipulate these concrete materials to build model buildings, to count, to add, to subtract, to multiply, and to divide by using the blocks. What additional things might pupils do today with blocks?

1. They might be given a certain number of blocks such as sixteen. Learners then individually or collaboratively might arrange these into many different patterns, designs, and answers to questions as possible. Thus, a four by four arrangement of

blocks in a box makes for sixteen as does a two by eight arrangement. Also, a two by two by four high makes an arrangement of sixteen blocks. Pupils need to experiment with a hands on approach in determining how may arrangements can be made of a given set of blocks. For example, with sixteen blocks, pupils may show a two by eight or an eight by two arrangement to show the commutative property of multiplication. Or, a two by two by four arrangement can indicate the associative property of multiplication in that the factors can be multiplied in any order and the product is still sixteen.

2. It is important for pupils to make discoveries such as in using a two by eight or an eight by two arrangement of blocks making for sixteen blocks as the product. The commutative property of multiplication is consistent here as is the commutative property of addition such as three blocks and five blocks or five blocks and three blocks make for a total of eight blocks. The associative property of addition and multiplication, as a pattern, also needs to be discovered by involved learners. Two blocks and three blocks joined together with four blocks has the same number in value as four blocks and three blocks has the same number in value as four blocks and three blocks joined together with two blocks. Each set has nine blocks. There can be more that three sets of blocks joined together to stress the commutative property. The associative property holds true for multiplication in that two times two. There can be more than three sets of numbers to consider in the associative property, such as 2 times 4 times 5 equals 5 times 4 times 3 times 2. The numbers can be arranged in any order and the property of association holds true in addition and multiplication.

## ATTRIBUTE BLOCKS AND BUTTONS

Attribute blocks may be used at the right stage of pupil development to achieve many objectives in mathematics instruction. Thus, attribute blocks may be used to count add, subtract, multiply, and divide, as well as to sort items with definite criteria in mind. Here, we will focus upon sorting based on observable criteria, such as by color, by size, and by geometrical form. The attribute blocks may be thin such as made of plywood and contain diverse colors such as red, blue, yellow, orange, and purple. A set of learners may then sort all the reds in one pile, all the blues in another, all the yellows in a third pile, and so on.

A less exacting way of sorting is to divide the attributes into large, medium, and small sizes. A third way of sorting is to place all the squares in one pile, the rectangles into a second set, the circles into a third set, and so on.

Many teachers enjoy collecting buttons of divers kinds. when ready, pupils individually or collaboratively, may sort these buttons into those which have four holes, three holes, and two holes. Buttons may also be sorted into categories of color and of size. Children should have ample opportunities to construct their very own knowledge when planning the mathematics curriculum with the teacher.

Letting children construct their own knowledge allows teachers to reach the full range of students. Traditional methods of direct instruction, while appearing to work for some, fails to work for a large per cent of students. Those who benefit little from traditional approaches include children from all achievement groups—from average students to those in special education; both these considered 'slow learners' and those labeled 'gifted or talented,'.

All children are unique. They enter learning situations with different backgrounds. They exhibit different learning styles. They develop in their own unique ways, and at their own pace. Consequently, each child will interpret and connect ideas differently and must construct for himself or herself the connections and relationships among those concepts essential to understanding mathematics (Rowan and Bourne, 1994).

## USING BEADS TO SHOW A PATTERN

Pupils may use beads and buttons to develop a pattern of materials in a design. Thus, stringing a pattern of red, yellow, blue, white, and green beads make for an interesting design and pattern. Pupils need to be encouraged in being creative in design development.

Buttons of different colors may also be used in securing a pattern on a string. Pupils need to explore different patterns when stringing beads and buttons.

There are excellent drawings which may be made showing different patterns. Thus blocks of different colors might be drawn showing the following in sequence, as an example, white, yellow, red, blue, black, and green. These are activities which most pupils find fascinating and engaging. Then too, here are ways and materials for pupils to use to perform the four basic operations on number. The commutative and associative properties of addition and multiplication may be shown to indicate understanding by learners.

## NUMBER PATTERNS

Many pupils are truly interested in working with abstract numbers which indicate a pattern. The following is an example:

| The number of counting numbers | Addition of these counting numbers | Sum |
|---|---|---|
| 1 | 1 | 1 |
| 2 | 1+3 | 4 |
| 3 | 1+3+5 | 9 |
| 4 | 1+3+5+7 | 16 |
| 5 | 1+3+5+7+9 | 25 |
| 6 | 1+3+5+7+9+11 | 36 |
| 7 | Pupil need to complete 7-9. | 36 |
| 8 | | |
| 9 | | |

The background information factor is important to consider when stressing abstract learnings for pupils. Also, the complexity of abstract numbers and numerals needs a thorough consideration. Good mathematics teachers soon realize what their pupils can and cannot achieve, in general. Perhaps, teachers need to use more challenging strategies of teaching whereby pupils may realize new heights in mathematics achievement. However, frustration on the part of pupils should not be a part of making the curriculum more challenging. After all, pupils individually need to be successful learners. Negative feelings accrue from experiencing failure on the learner's part. Quality sequence in learning whereby new learnings are directly related to those previously experienced should be in the offing.

Learning opportunities for pupils should be interesting to capture learner attention. They need to possess purpose so that pupils feel there are values in learning. Individual differences need to be provided for such as pupils of different levels of capacity and achievement must have appropriate learning opportunities. Pupils need to understand that which is taught so that meaningful learning accures (Ediger, 1994).

## ART AND GEOMETRY

Cutouts from different colors of construction paper may emphasize circles, squares, rectangles, semi-circles, triangles, and trapezoids to be used by pupils to make different animal, human, and imaginary figures. Learners tend to enjoy this activity and can be quite creative in their endeavours. They seemingly are on task continuously when engaging in geometry art. Learners need to call each geometrical figure used by name. In this way, many pupils at the early primary grade level have learned to call each figure using the correct name.

A display of each finished product in geometry art may be shown on the classroom bulletin board or on the hallway wall outside the classroom. Pupils from other classrooms observe these exhibits and in some cases have asked their teachers if the same or similar activity could be used in their classroom.

In geometry art, pupils should be able to–

1. know likenesses and differences among the different geometrical figures.
2. determine the perimeter of each when readiness is in evidence.
3. compute the area of each as appropriate sequence is in evidence.
4. find uses for each geometrical figure in society.
5. add additional geometric figures to the repertoire of learning.

## KIT OF MARKERS AND PLACE VALUE CHARTS

Each pupil needs to have a kit of markers in a bag. These markers should include corn seeds, soybean seeds, tooth picks, and short pencil. The teacher can readily determine if a young child understands what 4+5=9 by having the child at his/her desk reproduce with markers this basic addition fact. Or, the teacher may have pupils show at their desks 9–6=3 with the use of markers. 'How many' when counting may also be shown such as the value of ten. The teacher may observe rather quickly if a pupil understands what is called for. If a class size is large, in particular, the teacher may scan each pupil's desk to see if responses made are correct in terms of what is called for.

The markers lend themselves very well to understanding place value when this concept is being taught. Thus, eleven seeds may be regrouped into one ten and one one. In a place value chart with pockets, the pupil may place congruent strips of construction paper in the one's column and in the ten's column. Pupils need to attach meaning to what is meant by ones, tens, hundreds, and thousands, in sequence. A chart with pockets numbered for each place value can be very helpful for pupils to understand ones, tens, and hundreds.

## COUNTING RULES

Pupils enjoy games in mathematics. Games are a way of learning to achieve objectives. Thus, games have educational values as well as in playing for enjoyment. A game that may be played needs to fit in sequence into the ongoing lesson/unit of study pertains to, "What is my rule?" Thus, the teacher may print on the chalkboard or into the word processor the following: 3, 6, 9, 12. Pupils need to identify what the rule is in writing these numbers. More complex rules may be written as the need arises for older pupils as well for the talented/gifted. A calculator may also be used when readiness is in evidence. Modern technology should be experienced by all pupils when the necessary background skills and abilities have been developed. There are excellent software packages such as drill and practice, tutorial, simulation, and games which might benefit all learners depending upon their previous experiences in using personal computers. Schools need to keep up with society in the use of computers. Mathematics, as one curriculum area, can provide pupils with opportunities to use computers flexibly when the need arises in school and in society. Pupils presently as well as in the future at the workplace need to become proficient in using technology fully. Computer use has made it easier for pupils to write word problems as well as to do and check diverse computations, such as in long division (Ediger, 1997).

## EVERYBODY PARTICIPATES

Sometimes, it seems that only a few can participate at a given time in a discussion in mathematics. It is good to have as many participate actively as possible. Mathematics teachers need to think of ways whereby all may participate. They might write on the chalkboard or type into the computer, addition number pairs such as the following: 15=32=47, as an example. If the answer is correct, pupils shown by raised hand or with a thumbs up signal. If incorrect, no response may be made or a thumbs down signal may be shown. In this way, the mathematics teacher may quickly spot which pupils responded correctly or incorrectly as well as those who watch how others will respond.

The same responses may be made if the number of dots shown on the chalkboard is greater than or less than a certain number. For example, if the number of asterisks is the following inside a circle: {* * * * * * * * * * *} with pupils being asked if this is more than eight, a thumbs up approach should be used. If less than eight, a thumbs down signal should be used. The examples given may be more complex or easier, depending on an appropriate achievement level of pupils involved. Place value can be taught here in that pupils may trade ten of the eleven asterisks for a set of ten to be shown on a place value chart with one slip of paper in the tens column and one slip of paper in the ones column.

The flannel board may also be used to show cut-outs thereon of how many members in a set. Thus, if twelve felt cut-outs of bears are shown, pupils are asked to indicate thumbs up or thumbs down if this is more than or less than ten. The twelve felt cut-outs may be represented on the place value chart as having one ten (one strip of paper in the tens column) and two strips in the one's column. When ready, pupils may show the twelve cut-out bears in the following arrays: two by six, six by two, three by four, four by three, one by twelve, and twelve by one. Here, pupils, not only are learning multiplication, but also the commutative property of multiplication, as well as factoring (Ediger, 1996).

## USING TRANSPARENCIES

The teacher may face pupils directly when using the overhead projector with the use of transparencies. With the projection showing on the wall, the teacher may use transparencies that harmonize with the objectives of the ongoing lesson and unit of study. If pupils are studying seven plus five equals twelve, the teacher may place seven transparent circles on the transparency together with another set of five circles. Here, learners may determine the value of 7+5. The set may be rearranged as 5+7= to indicate the commutative property of addition. The sum of twelve might then be shown on the place value chart with one slip of paper in the tens column and two slips of paper in the ones column.

Diverse kinds of materials should be used in teaching to vary experiences for learners. Application needs to be made frequently of what has been learned by pupils. Here, pupils apply what has been acquired by placing strips of paper properly in the ten's and one's columns on the place value chart.

## FILMS, FILMSTRIPS, AND SLIDES

There are educators who might say that these three devices are outdated in teaching and have been replaced by video-tapes. We respond with the idea that the teacher look to see what kind of content is on the film, filmstrip, and set of slides. One of us have been an excellent film, when supervising student teachers in the public schools, that did an outstanding job of having pupils learn to differentiate cubes, rectangular solids, cylinders, spheres, cones, and hemispheres. The objects and drawings of these geometrical solids were clear with a pleasant voice explaining the differences involved.

One of us also observed a student teacher using a filmstrip and accompanying cassette tapes to explain how to find the area of the following:

1. A square and a rectangle
2. A right triangle and a circle

Too much content was covered in the filmstrip, but there was unusual clarity in the discussions pertaining to determining area. We suggest the teacher fill in with additional content and discussions when the quality filmstrip attempts to cover too much content in a short sequence of frames. The teacher then needs to use more examples of finding the area of a square, of a rectangular, of a triangle, and of a circle. To understand finding the area of a circle, for example, takes time with many examples needed to show the value and meaning of 'radius,' 'radius squared,' and '*pi*'

One of us also observed a student teacher use a set of slides to show the concept of equivalent fractions. The student teacher narrated her own slides shown. Several frames showed meaningfully how one/half and two/fourths are equivalent. Thus, to fourths were placed over the one/ half to assist learns in clarity of the concept being taught.

An advantage of using filmstrips and slides in teaching is that the content is still and does not move when teaching from a frame. Also, the teacher may spend as much time as needed to have pupils attach necessary meanings to content taught from one frame before moving on to the next frame. Some of the student teachers and co-operating teachers their won filmstrips and slides to fit into the sequence of content being taught. One filmstrips contained sequential content on adding unit fractions. Here, pupils with teacher explanation understood how the denominators need to be alike before adding unit fractions. For example in adding one/third and one/half, pupils realized the necessity of changing the one/third to two/sixths and the one/half to three/sixths when using "card board *piazzas*." Thus, two/sixths and three/sixths were joined together to make five /sixths of a *piazza*. As readiness, pupils had studied adding one/third plus one/third of the "cardboard *piazza*" making for two/thirds. Another student teacher and co-operating teacher made a series of slides on finding the area of squares and rectangles. Each slide was clear on why the length times the width equaled the area in square units. Concrete materials were also used in showing how to find the area of a square and of a rectangle (Ediger, 134-5).

## USING A GEOBOARD

A geoboard may be made readily and used in teaching geometry. An eight inch square piece of plywood may be obtained. Single nails need to be driven in far enough into the plywood so the nails are solidly stationed. The shingle nails should make for one inch squares when driven into the plywood. Pupils may use a rubber band encircling the necessary nails in making the desired geometrical figure to show a triangle, square or other geomatical figure.

The mathematics teacher may show to pupils a geometrical figure such as a square by stretching a rubber band around four nails. The square may be used, among other material of instruction, to have learners identify a square. Pupils may make a square on the geoboard when asked to by the teacher to show that they can differentiate a square form among other geometrical figures. Learners might also make squares from different colors of construction paper.

## ESTIMATING IN THE MATHEMATICS CURRICULUM

Being able to estimate well is very important to pupils since many things are estimated by individuals in society. Pupils may estimate the distance between the teacher's desk and the end of the room. After estimating, learners collectively or individually may check their estimations. There are so many things that pupils may estimate in the classroom and then check the estimation:

1. how many peas go into a bottle.
2. how many cupfuls are in a pint.
3. how many eggs go into a carton which has room for a dozen.
4. how many teaspoons make for a tablespoon.
5. how many ounces make for a pound.
6. how many square feet in the classroom.
7. how many square inches on a desktop.
8. how many quarts in a gallon.
9. how many pecks in a bushel.
10. how many objects make a gross.

The use of real objects is important in each of the ten above named items for example, in number two above, pupils may measure using water showing the number of cupfuls that make for a pint. It is important to make an educated guess first and then measure to determine the correct answer.

## USING MONEY

Pupils need to become proficient in the use of counting money. Practical application needs to be made of money when possible. Thus, a model grocery store may have empty containers of wrappers from cereal, soap, sugar, candy, and fruits/vegetables. On each item a price needs to be listed. We would suggest using the prices of values being studied presently in mathematics. If pupils are studying addition facts such as 5+3=8, 6+2=8, 9+3=12, and 8+4=12, among others in addition families, then related prices may be put on each container of wrapper, such as eight cents on a container of fruit. The teacher may explain to pupils that this is not the actual price presently in grocery stores, but these values are used by pupils now in the mathematics curriculum. Each pupil may then shop for two items and add the cost. Actual money such as a dime may be used to pay for two items costing 7+3 cents respectively. Pupils may also learn to make change if this is needed from the purchase of two items. Calculators and computers may be used in developing the total for items purchased.

When pupils are ready, they may estimate and 'buy' items from a sales catalog displayed in the classroom. Estimating costs may be very valuable here if a coat costs $53.95 and a pair of shoes cost $55.19, the first value may be rounded to the nearest dollar as could the second value. Thus, $53.95 would rounded off to $54 and $55. 19 would round off to $55. Now $54 plus $55 is much easier to total in an estimation. Pupils need to learn the rules for rounding off. If any one place value column has a value of five or higher, the rounding off is made to the nearest next higher value such as $53.95 to the nearest dollar is $54 since nine in the tenths column is 5 or higher in value and the next highest value is 4 in $54. Rounding off is very useful in making many estimations.

One of the student teachers together with the co-operating teachers whom one of us supervised in the public schools had pupils use an order form to 'order' $200 of merchandise from the above named catalog. The order had to come as close as possible to $200 in value. Pupils individually or in committees, as they desired, discussed items of merchandise carefully and worked hard to come up with a final order. Check blanks were duplicated. Pupils could then fill in the correct amount of the purchase on the duplicated check blank.

## FLASH CARDS AND DRILL/PRACTICE SOFTWARE

As much as possible, pupils should apply what has been learned and thus receive practice on these experiences. However, there are times when pupils just do not remember or recall basic addition, subtraction, multiplication, and division facts without drill and practice. There is time then for pupils to engage in drill and practice activities. These can be quite interesting, especially if a pupil works with another learner. Two to three pupils may check the accuracy of each other when using flash cards to notice achievement on these basic operations on number. Those facts missed can be taken over again by using the flash cards. A variation in using flash cards is to emphasize software in drill and practice. The software, as is true of flash card use, stresses what pupils have been studying in an ongoing lesson or unit of study and yet the basic facts had not been mastered to the point of automatic recall. After drill and practice activities, pupils should have opportunities to use what has been learned. The level of application is very important in the mathematics curriculum. Prior to any drill/practice activity, pupils need to understand content being emphasized. Thus, if drill/practice activities stress 5+4=9 using flash cards or software/computer, pupils should have ample opportunities to use the subject matter acquired (Ediger, 1996).

Learning opportunities in drill and practice, as is true of all activities, should be interesting, purposeful, and provide for individual differences. Never should it be dull and boring. Pupils will not achieve much if activities are uninteresting and uninspiring. The mathematics teacher should work out sequential strategies whereby pupils individually learn as much as possible and learning is encouraged, not stifled.

Drill and practice activities should be—

1. purposeful in that there are reasons for pupils to engage in these kinds of activities.
2. use is made of content learned and not drill/practice emphasized for its own sake.
3. subject matter is understood and meaning attached to what is being experienced.
4. learning opportunities are varied and not the same activity stressed over and over again.
5. retention of content learned is in evidence.

## ADDITION BINGO

Addition bingo can be a fascinating way to learn for many pupils. A bingo card needs to have the answers to a card from a pile drawn by the learner of the game. The bingo card may be drawn having one inch squares with five answers in each row lengthwise/ widthwise. Each square then contains an answer to a basic addition fact. Thus, the leader draws a 5+6= — card. A pupil covers the answer '11' if it appears on his/her bingo board. The first pupil that has five answers covered in a row lengthwise/widthwise or diagonally is the winner of the game of addition bingo. The game also lends itself well to using subtraction, multiplication, and division facts.

With the use of games in teaching mathematics, the teacher should use the following guidelines:

1. Pupils should achieve vital objectives in mathematics when playing games.
2. Entertainment should not be emphasized, except if it emphasizes vital mathematics content to be learned.
3. Proper sequence in learning opportunities should be in the offing for all pupils.
4. Success in learning is a must for each pupil.
5. Individual differences among learners needs provision so each may attain optimally.

## FINDING MISSING DIGITS

When readiness is in evidence with adequate past experiences, pupils may find the missing digits in a carefully prepared exercise. For example, the pupil may determine what number is missing in each of the following:

52+15=6..., 28+34=6..., ...7+23=...0.

Pupils then fill in the correct number where the dotted line is located. Understanding place value is orderly, significant, and salient for all pupils. Performing the four basic operations is important in becoming proficient in calculation and attaching meaning to what has been learned.

The following are additional addition problems:

1. Name two numbers whose sum is 56.
2. Name two numbers whose sum is greater than 60.
3. Name two numbers whose sum ends in 6.
4. Name three numbers whose sum is 82.
5. Name three number whose sum is 24.

In finding missing numbers, pupils should—

1. feel challenge, but not frustration.
2. work together well with others when working collaboratively.
3. be responsible in governing their very own behaviour so that continuous progress is possible in mathematics.
4. appraise personal habits of learning to encourage achieving, growing, and developing.
5. engage positively in problem solving situations.

## MULTIPLICATION BY NINE

Pupils may discover an interesting pattern when multiplying by 9 in drill/practice or problem solving situations. They may answer the following:

9 x 1 = ... 9 x 2= ... 9 x 4= ... 9 x 5= ... 9 x 6= ... 9 x 7= ...

The correct answer to each of the above may be checked by adding the separate digits which then gives a sum of 9. This would be true for each of the above named multiplication facts in that the separate digits for the answer, when added together, would equal 9. Also, if two or more digits, where a number '9' is used as multiplier and/ or multiplicand, are multiplied, the sum of the separate digits in the answer is divisible by 9 with no remainder. Then too, there are many interesting patterns for pupils to observe in mathematics, such as the following, when considering the counting numbers:

| | | | | | | | | | |
|---|---|---|---|---|---|---|---|---|---|
| 1 | 2 | 3 | 4 | 5 | 6 | 7 | 8 | 9 | 10 |
| 2 | 4 | 6 | 8 | 10 | 12 | 14 | 16 | 18 | 20 |
| 3 | 6 | 9 | 12 | 15 | 18 | 21 | 24 | 27 | 30 |
| 4 | 8 | 12 | 16 | 20 | 24 | 28 | 32 | 36 | 40 |
| 5 | 10 | 15 | 20 | 25 | 30 | 35 | 40 | 45 | 50 |
| 6 | 12 | 18 | 24 | 30 | 36 | 42 | 48 | 54 | 60 |
| 7 | 14 | 21 | 28 | 35 | 42 | 49 | 56 | 63 | 70 |
| 8 | 16 | 24 | 32 | 40 | 48 | 56 | 64 | 72 | 80 |
| 9 | 18 | 27 | 36 | 45 | 54 | 63 | 72 | 81 | 90 |
| 10 | 20 | 30 | 40 | 50 | 60 | 70 | 80 | 90 | 100 |

When readiness is in evidence, pupils, collaboratively or individually, may make many discoveries by studying the above table. Pupils may then discover how to multiply, and divide, among other things, when using the table. Learning can indeed be very exciting when pupils notice patterns in the mathematics curriculum. We have noticed teachers who, when having pupils perceive patterns, notice things that had not been observed previously in pupil achievement.

The great philosopher Rene Descartes based his philosophy of idealism on the certainty of mathematics with its order and consistency.It does not possess complete order and consistent, but it comes close to doing so. One of us have put on the chalkboard the following problem for the graduate students to solve: 4+3 x 6+8=×.

Approximately half the class came up with the answer '50', whereas the remainder came up with '30'. Those who came up with '50' followed thorough with moving consistently from left to right when computing; the rest knew the correct rule of performing the multiplication operation first and then adding the rest of the numbers in any order. There is consistency and order when following rules of which operation to perform first here, such as multiplication:

In looking for patterns, pupils should –

1. enjoy looking for patterns in mathematics.
2. make discoveries which are relevant.
3. apply what has been learned in a new situation.
4. use critical and creative thought in discovery learning.
5. show accuracy in work completed in mathematics.

## DETERMINING RATIOS

Learning about ratios is very useful to pupils in school and in society. If a table is set with one knife, one fork, and one spoon for each of two people. The ratio is one to one for the number of knives, forks, and spoons when comparing the two persons. There is a one to one ratio. If person A being twenty years older than person B, a six year old child, receives three cookies as compared to person B receiving one cookie, the ratio is three to one. When comparing person B to person A, the ratio is one to three. Thus person B receives one/third as many cookies as person A. If person A eats two slices of bread and person B eats one slice of bread, the ratio is two to one.

Pupils enjoy determining ratios with lifelike situations, in particular. There are numerous questions that pupils like to raise such as the following:

1. If person A eats one and one/half slices of bread and person B eats two/thirds of a slice, what is the ratio?
2. If person A eats one/half of a pizza and person B eats one/fourth of the same pizza, what is the ratio?

Proportion is closely related to ratio, as a topic of study. Many pupils have asked what the height of the flagpole is on the local school building. The mathematics teacher, for example, may have pupils speculate on how to determine the height of the flag pole without climbing to the top, an unsafe procedure. Each pupil may estimate the height before proportion is taught to pupils. The mathematics teacher might begin teaching/reviewing ratio when referring to the flagpole. First, pupils may speculate on how this is to be done when thinking of ratio, a previous learning. Pupils might measure the height of a small shed nearby and its corresponding shadow. The height of the flagpole is not known, but the length of the shadow can be measured rather accurately. Now then, the ratio of the height of the shed to its shadow is five feet to three feet, and the length of the flagpole shadow is nine feet. Thus, 5/3 is equal to the unknown 'x/9'. How can we determine the unknown which is the height of the flagpole must be three times higher than the height of the shed. The height of the flagpole then is 15 feet (Harel and Confrey, 1994). Pupils should have many experiences with ratio and proportion using practical learning opportunities. These learning opportunities should:

1. assist pupils to achieve relevant objectives in mathematics.
2. guide pupils to apply what has been learned.
3. help pupils to work co-operatively with others.
4. develop skills of reasoning and thinking.
5. encourage problem identification and solving.

**PER CENT AND ITS USE**

There are many times when pupils will read about the concept of per cent. In store windows, sales are mentioned with a certain per cent to be taken off each item to be sold. Or the sale stresses the selling price indicating a certain per cent has already been taken off. Thus, pupils should desire to know the original price of the item to be sold. Learning about fractions will always be a prerequisite. For example, a circle divided equally into four parts will indicate each part to be one/fourth of the entire circle. One out of four is equal to twenty-five out of one hundred. In congruent circles, one could put one fourth of one circle over 25 hundredths of another circle to show the two values are congruent. Another way of saying this is 25%. Twenty-five per cent means 25 parts considered out of 100. A prerequisite in studying per cents is decimals whereby in the above example 1/4=25. One of four parts is equal to 25 out of 100 parts. Thus, 0.25 means twenty-five out of one-hundred. Thus, a suit selling originally for $100 and a 25% discount would involve taking off one/fourth or 0.25 of that original price. The discount then is $25 which, of course, is found by multiplying $100 times. 25. Why multiply the per cent of discount times the original price? The discount is 25% of $100. The word 'of' means times or multiply the selling price of the suit is $100-$25 or $75.

To encourage interest in per cent, the following may be done:

1. Pupils and the teacher may bring in newspaper and news magazine articles on sales where per cent is mentioned. These articles need to be discussed and the content understood.
2. Pupils individually or collectively may work on simulated items, written by learners themselves, whereby discounts are mentioned in the advertisements. Pupils may then determine the selling price when the original price is stated as well as the listed per cent of discount is included in the ad.
3. Pupils need to attach meaning to each problem involving per cent and be able to explain processes inherent in solving discount and selling prices.
4. pupils need to understand why there are sales of items with the involved discounts.
5. pupils need to understand what is involved in advertising such as to develop desires of people to buy, whether the item is needed or not. Later on, pupils will need to learn to live within their budgets or amount of money available for making purchases, involving the use of credit cards.

## DRAWING TO SCALE

Pupils need to be able to read information from maps and globes. Information, involving mathematics, to be read includes degrees North and South of the Equator, degrees East and West of the Prime Meridian, the International Date Line, Time Zones, the Tropic of Cancer, and the Tropic of Capricorn, among others. Meaning needs to be attached to each of these concepts. Memorization is not adequate when writing and depth is important speaking about equinoxes or latitudes/longitudes. Understudying in depth is important when emphasizing map and globe concepts. Here, the mathematics curriculum and social studies with its map and globe learnings intersect. An integrated curriculum is an end result whereby pupils experience subject matter as being related, not isolated (Ediger, 1997).

The concept of scale is very important for pupils to attach meaning to, since maps and globes are used frequently by adults as well as increasingly so by children. Real experiences may be brought in for children to pursue in making drawings where a scale is being emphasized. A teacher and her student teacher whom I supervised in the public schools showed pupils a scale drawing of the living room of the former's house. The drawing was neatly done and much effort had gone into making this drawing. Pupils were very curious in the drawing and asked many questions, such as the following;

1. How large is the living room?
2. Why did you make this scale drawing?
3. Might it have been drawn smaller or larger?
4. What scale did you use in doing the drawing?
5. Could we also make a scale drawing, such as of this classroom?

The teacher had the fourth grade pupils measure the length and width of the classroom. The next problem was how do we get the size of the classroom on an eight by eleven inch sheet of paper? Different scales were tried out and each was too large to get the drawing of the classroom on a sheet of paper. The classroom was thirty feet long by thirty feet wide. One inch should equal five feet seemed reasonable to most pupils. Thus, the size of the drawing on the 8 x 11 inch paper would be six inches by six inches. Some pupils worked individually while others worked collaboratively in doing the scale drawing. One learner worked on a drawing whereby one inch would equal seven feet. A different committee worked separately on a scale drawing in which one inch would equal six feet. The latter made for difficulties in making the drawing since unusual sized fractions needed to be used. Pupils then realized how important it is to use a convenient scale to make the drawing. The scale also has to be large enough so that it covers the entire page.

The National Council Teachers of Mathematics (NCTM, 1989) in their volume *Curriculum Standards for School Mathematics* listed the following broad objectives for pupils to achieve:

1. Learning to value mathematics.
2. Becoming confident in their ability to do mathematics.

3. Becoming mathematical problem solvers.
4. Learning to communicate mathematically.
5. Learning to reason mathematically.

## DRAWING GRAPHS

Pupils in the early primary grades may experience success in making picture graphs. Thus, the teaching of statistics may begin on the kindergarten level and then progress may be made sequentially throughout the different levels of schooling, including graduate school. Statistics is useful in society when reading diverse kinds of graphs.

What kind of graph should make for beginning leanings for pupils? We suggest making a picture graph. The different months of the calendar year might be listed on the chalkboard vertically. A picture of each child having a birthday during that month may be placed next to the month of the birthday. The following is an example with x's used instead of the picture of a child who had the birthday:

| | |
|---|---|
| January ----- | x x |
| February---- | x x x |
| March-------- | x |
| April--------- | x x x x |
| May----------- | x |
| June---------- | x x x x x |
| July--------- | x |
| August------- | x x x x x x |
| September-- | |
| October ------ | x x |
| November ---- | x |
| December ------ | x x x x x x x |

When glancing at the above graph, pupils can make many observations including:

1. Which month had the most birthdays?
2. Which month had the fewest or no birthdays?
3. Which months tied for having the same number of birthdays?

In sequence, pupils then may experience making bar graphs, line graphs, pie or circle graphs. Statistical figures and tables may also be made by pupils when readiness is in evidence.

The NCTM (1989) lists the following standards for kindergarten grade four elementary school mathematics:

1. The understandings that children already have when they enter school should be valued and built on.
2. The K–4 curriculum should be developmentally appropriate.
3. The quality of content and instruction is far more important then the quantity.
4. Children should build confidence in themselves as mathematics learners.
5. Children should be actively involved in doing mathematics.
6. children should see how mathematics is applied to other subjects and in daily activities.
7. A broad range of content should be taught.
8. Calculators and computers should be used appropriately as both computational and instructional tools.

## CONCLUSION

There are numerous learning opportunities for pupils in the elementary school. Teachers need to grow and achieve in using diversity of leaning opportunities developmentally appropriate for pupils. The following are ways for teachers of mathematics to learn about new and different learning opportunities for children to achieve vital objectives:

1. Talk with other teachers on your grade level or other grade levels about what is done to improve mathematics instruction.
2. Attend grade level meetings of teachers and discuss problems in teaching mathematics.
3. Read current literature in teaching mathematics in the elementary school and implement those ideas that would assist pupils to do better in mathematics achievement.
4. Participate in state and national conventions on mathematics instruction. Secure new ideas in instruction pertaining to mathematics.

5. Survey catalogs on materials for teaching mathematics. Talk to the principal about ordering selected materials, necessary in teaching mathematics.

## REFERENCES


Ediger, Marlow (1994), "Early Field Experiences in Teacher Education," *College Student Journal*, 28(3), 302-03.

Ediger, Marlow (1997), *Teaching Mathematics in the Elementary School*. Kirksville, Missouri; Simpson Publishing Company, 187-207.

Ediger, Marlow (1996), *Elementary Education* Kirksville, Missouri; Simpson Publishing Company, 156-65.

Ediger, Marlow (1988), *The Elementary Curriculum*, Second Edition, Kirksville, Missouri; Simpson Publishing company, 134-35.

Ediger, Marlow (1996), *Essays in School Administration*, Kirksville, Missouri; Simpson Publishing Company, 142-47.

Ediger, Marlow (1997), *Social Studies Curriculum in the Elementary School*, Fourth Edition, Kirksville, Missouri; Simpson Publishing Company, 120-41.

Harel, Guershon, and Jere Confrey, Editors, (1994). *The Development of Multiplicative Reasoning in the Learning of Mathematics*, Albany, New York; State University of New York Press, 62-89.

National Council Teachers of Mathematics (1989), *Curriculum and Evaluation Standards for School Mathematics*, Reston, Virginia, NCTM, 5-6.

National Council Teachers of Mathematics (1989), *Curriculum and Evaluation Standards for School Mathematics*, Reston, Virginia; NCTM, 7.

Rowan, Thomas E., and Barbara Bourne, (1994), *Thinking Like Mathematicians*. Portsmith, New Hampshire; Heinemann, 25.

# Chapter 14

# COMPUTERS IN THE MATHEMATICS CURRICULUM

Computers have certainly made their inroads into the mathematics curriculum. The home setting, too, has an increasing number of computers to which pupils have much access to. There are numerous questions and problems that teachers and supervisors have pertaining to computer use. Continual improvement is made on computers and their capabilities. The cost of computers has gone down as the years have progressed. What can mathematics teachers and supervisors do to make for a quality curriculum in the school setting?

## SOFTWARE, THE COMPUTER, AND MATHEMATICS

There are numerous software packages available for pupil use. Quality is very important in software/computer use. Then too, these programs must fit into the ongoing learning opportunities being emphasized in mathematics. Thus, the sequence or order of learning opportunities continues when computer use follows other kinds of stimulating learning opportunities. With good sequence, each pupil may continue to achieve as much as possible. The mathematics teacher also needs to stress the interests of pupils in teaching and learning situations. Appropriate introductions whereby pupils receive and possess the prerequisite knowledge to use a new software program needs to be in the offing. Pupils do need the background information to benefit more optimally from the software program. For example, if pupils need drill and practice exercises in multiplication with regrouping, the software contents should provide ample opportunities for the pupil to receive the drill and practice necessary. The drill and practice learning opportunities relate directly to the objectives of the ongoing unit of study. Use must be made by the learner of what has been learned in the drill and practice program. With use, content acquired will be remembered longer than otherwise would be the case (Ediger, 1997).

Second, a tutorial program in software may be needed to initiate new learings in the mathematics curriculum. Thus, pupils may experience subtraction involving a three digit minuend and a one place divisor with no remainder. Readiness factors need to be taken care of so that the pupil can engage meaningfully in the new program of instruction. Necessary facts, concepts, and generalizations for prior knowledge have been taken care of so that pupils with teacher guidance may make continuous progress in computer use. The mathematics teacher can do much to encourage pupil interest by recognizing the latter's achievement. If the sequence in the program is not optimal, the mathematics teacher may fill in the void with quality teaching and instruction.

Third, if diagnosis is necessary to determine specifically where a person is experiencing one or more difficulties in an ongoing lesson in mathematics, a software program designed for remediation may be used. The diagnosis/remediation program may pinpoint difficulties, for example in place value, involving ones, tens, and hundreds. Once the error is spotted, the teacher is in a better position to provide learning opportunities that assist pupils to understand place value. Learners then need to apply what has been learned to a new situation so that optimal progress is possible (Ediger, 1996, 209-14).

Fourth, simulation software stresses reality in a virtual environment. Reality in learning opportunities is needed so that pupils realize mathematics as being functional and not learned for its own sake. Software programs stressing simulation need to be chosen carefully in that pupils need to experience success in learning as well as feel its functional values. Simulations will stress problem solving activities and these kinds of experiences should be at the heart of a quality mathematics curriculum (National Council Teachers of Mathematics, 1989, p. 32). The identified problems need to be clarified and made meaningful. Data needs gathering in order to secure information for the chosen problem. An hypothesis or answer should be forthcoming for the problem. The hypothesis is tentative and needs to be tested in a lifelike situation, if possible. Revisions to the original hypothesis might well be an end result.

Simulations can stress the importance of pupils developing communication skills effectively in collaborative situations. It is vital that pupils learn to communicate well orally and in written work. The mathematics teacher needs to have communication skills as major objectives in the mathematics curriculum. In school and later at the work place, individuals need to use language effectively. These skills might well be correlated with simulations as well as in all facets of work in the mathematics curriculum.

Games, another kind of software, may motivate pupils to learn more. Here, teacher may plan for healthy competition among two or three sets of learners. A team may win if they outdo the other two or single side in playing a game. Pupils may learn much in playing games and at the same time enjoy each game. We have observed number of pupils being involved in games and the excitement was great with satisfying results. Games can be another way of learning. Pupils do desire variety in learning activities in mathematics. The fames may involve teams responding to basic addition, subtraction, multiplication, and division number pairs. Higher levels of cognition may also be inherent in that pupils respond to complex problems that need solving.

The type of software used by the mathematics teacher in teaching pupils depends upon the following:

1. The purpose involved such as is there a need for drill and practice or should more of virtual reality be emphasized in simulations.
2. Readiness factors on the part of pupils such as content being too complex or too easy. The contents in the software should be on the instructional level of pupils whereby new subject matter is learned and individuals may be successful in achievement.
3. User friendly work that can be done by pupils. The software then should be on the user level of proficiency. Thus, the goal

here is for pupils to achieve vital objectives in mathematics and not be hindered by complexities in using the computer.

4. Sequence in that the software fits into the lesson presently being stressed in an appropriate order.
5. Meaningful learnings which accrue on the learner's part.
6. Interest factors in learning that promote achievement in mathematics.
7. Individual needs met in mathematics when computers are used.
8. Items which are clear in the software program. Hazy, vague content does not assist pupils to learn effectively in mathematics.
9. Appropriate feedback provided to pupils based on responses made as to correctness or lack thereof.
10. Responses to software programs increased achievement in mathematics more so as compared to other kinds of instructional materials (Ediger, 1995, pp.161-88).

## TECHNOLOGY AND MATHEMATICS IN INSERVICE EDUCATION

Which are relevant problems faced by teachers in using modern technology? Teachers need assistance and guidance to use modern technology effectively in the mathematics curriculum.

I (Ediger) devoted several days to teaching the functions of graphic calculators. These tools enable students to convert equations to graphic representations, thus helping them make connections between mathematics concepts. Students can also use these devices to make predictions based on a statistical analysis of prior records — for example, the world record time for running a mile.

When I introduced graphing calculators into our algebra classes, the students did not buy into them immediately. Using them seemed like more work than not using them. (Indeed two months passed before the students felt comfortable using the calculators.) To motivate them, I begin offering incentives. Each day I challenged them to earn extra credits by being the first to learn a new function or to discover functions that I had not yet taught. These positive incentives allowed them to risk trying something new because if they failed, they stood to lose nothing (Davis, 1997).

The teacher in the above named two paragraphs did an excellent job of teaching. For other teachers, the above uses of a calculator to achieve objectives in the mathematics curriculum might be quite new. Perhaps readiness is lacking for these teachers to make good use of calculators. Here then is an important role for inservice education. The kind of inservice approach in using technology should be decided largely by teachers. Principals and supervisors should provide leadership in implementing the agreed upon inservice program. The problems of teachers in using technology need to be surveyed and assistance given where needed. Our feelings and experiences have been that is best to provide individual assistance as needed to teachers in technology use. In context then, teachers may receive the quality of assistance necessary. When several teachers on a team face similar problems, the computer specialist may provide needed help. With a one to one basis or a committee setting, teachers can pinpoint what is wanted from the specialist in terms of becoming more effective in computer use. There might be a need also for an entire faculty of a school to have instruction in computer use if the contents are salient in a workshop. The workshop must lend itself to some general knowledge that participants need to improve the mathematics curriculum. All faculty members need to have input as to what to cover in the general session. Practical use of the computer should be stressed as to needs indicated by the teachers. The presenter in this general session must be very knowledgeable pertaining to using technology in the mathematics curriculum.

Once the problems have been identified in the general session, committees may be formed to work on the identified problems. Teachers individually should choose the committee that will benefit them most in becoming more skillful in computer use. The focal point here should be for teachers to do a better job with technology use in teaching pupils. Each committee's progress should be shared with other committees in the room setting.

There are also individual needs in assisting teachers to use technology more effectively in ongoing units of study in mathematics. Each teacher in the workshop needs to work on problems of his/her very own choosing. Consultant and library sources need to be available to help teachers on an individual basis.

What has been emphasized in committee and individual endeavours may be used in teaching and learning situations. Feedback from the teacher using the new approaches might be given to others in the workshop as to the successful use of the innovation in the classroom.

We have attended faculty meetings where problems pertaining to computer use in the classroom were listed on the agenda. These problems were then discussed in the faculty meeting. There is no reason why faculty meetings may not become an important place for inservice education (Ediger, 1996, pp. 126-35). The school curriculum should not lag behind that of society in technology use. Then too, computer use should capture learner interest as much as or more than other materials of instruction. The newness and the novelty of computer use does capture pupil interests in mathematics. Pupils do not learn will unless their interests are aroused. We have noticed pupils attend to the computer carefully whereas other learning opportunities might not be as fascinating. Reasons for learning have been more forthcoming when computer technology is used in mathematics as compared to more traditional procedures used in teaching and learning. Seemingly, pupils are well aware of living in a computerized world and the importance of becoming skillful therein. With reasons involved for leaning, pupil purpose increases in desiring to achieve in mathematics. Computer use is another way of learning and assisting pupils to achieve more optimally. Understanding of new subject matter increases when another avenue of learning is open to assist pupils to understand, achieve, and grow. Perhaps, computer use in being another avenue of learning and being widely represented in society makes for more purpose and reasons for attainment on the part of pupils in the mathematics curriculum. A software presentation that truly inspired pupils when studying the history of numeration dealt with the Egyptian system. The following learnings were acquired by pupils:

1. Each heel bone of an ox, shaped like an arch, represented a value of ten. None heel bones represented a value of ninety.
2. Each coiled rope represented a value of 100. There could be as many as nine coiled ropes representing a value of 900.

3. Each lotus flower represented 1,000. Nine lotus flowers represented 9,000.
4. Each bent finger represented a value of 10,000. Nine bent fingers represented 90,000.
5. Each tadpole represented 100,000. Nine tadpoles represented 900,000 (Ediger, 1997, p.70).

The contents of the software program portraying the above was clear, sequential, and captured pupil interest. It also indicated how different academic disciplines become related such as in this case mathematics and history. It is good teaching procedure to relate information for pupils when teaching. If pupils perceive knowledge as being related, they will be able to emphasize more holism in their thinking. Also, one idea might trigger off other ideas when relating subject matter from several disciplines. The mathematics teacher needs to be aware of not integrating content for the sake of doing so. Relating of content needs to have a purpose for doing so and at the same time pupils will be achieving objectives more readily in ongoing units of study in mathematics.

## USING THE WORD PROCESSOR IN MATHEMATICS

For all practical purposes, the word processor has completely replaced the typewriter. Typewriters are indeed difficult to locate and even to see. Pupils, when ready, should learn to use the word processor effectively in mathematics. The word processor can be used profitably in any curriculum area as well as in society. Keyboarding skills should be learned by pupils when readiness is in evidence. There is no exact school level when pupils may possess these readiness factors. To be sure, a pupil on the early primary grade levels might not have the eye/hand coordination to learn key boarding skills. Learning these skills should not be forced upon a child, but rather teachers need to observe when pupils display an interest in keyboarding skills and provide sequential assistance.

There are certainly many advantages of using a word processor with great skill. Thus, the user does not need to possess thorough skills in spelling words correctly. Spell checkers will take care of many spelling errors. The pupil, however, needs to be fairly close in correct spelling of each word to have spell checkers work effectively. Learning to spell words correctly is not an outdated procedure of teaching. Words, sentences, and paragraphs may be changed easily in location by using cut and paste approaches. Deletions and additions might be readily made with word processor use. How might a word processor be used effectively by pupils in mathematics?

1. Pupils individually or collaboratively may type word problems to be exchanged with others to solve. Pupils then realize the inherent problems involved in writing these problems. They also become increasingly proficient in the composing and determining of what should go into a word problem. Feedback from the pupils working on these problems in terms of finding solutions assist the writer(s) to communicate clearly and accurately.
2. Drill and practice activities may also be written by pupils to be exchanged with others for answering. We believe in having pupils being actively involved in writing basic number pairs that are being studied in class as well as write story problems.
3. Mathematics journal writing may be emphasized whereby a pupil or a committee write-up what was leaned in mathematics and what is left to learn. Here, pupils reflect upon what has been taught and learned in mathematics. Reflecting upon previous learnings acquired assists pupils to remember subject matter achieved. Journal writings may be shared with others and with the mathematics teacher.
4. Pupils may compose on a daily basis of what transpired in a single lesson. Each entry is dated and becomes a part of a diary. By looking back at what was taught and learned, the pupil may reflect upon facts, concepts, and generalizations achieved.
5. The word processor may be used to relate daily diary entrees to develop a log. The log covers a longer period of time as compared to diary entries. Thus, logs summarize the diary entrees within a time interval such as two weeks or a month. Critical and creative thinking are involved in developing logs in mathematics.
6. Much of a portfolio to appraise pupil achievement may be developed by using a word processor. Thus, scores from tests as well as from daily work completed in mathematics may be entered into the computer. Objectives for the portfolio also may

be entered into the computer. The portfolio is a representative sampling of what a pupil has achieved in mathematics covering a definite interval of time. Projects may well be to large to put into a portfolio. All written work of a pupil may be typed into the computer such as a book report pertaining to mathematics. A printout then provides data of a pupil's achievement in mathematics. Pupils then will have snapshots, video tapes, cassettes, art work, and other artifacts, covering class work, in the portfolio. Snapshots may be taken of a pupil's construction project emphasizing a game to be played in mathematics. Video tapes to show the quality of committee work in an ongoing lesson or unit of study might well become a part of the portfolio. A cassette tape may contain an oral book report on mathematics given by the learner. The art work may pertain to drawing diverse geometrical figures, as an example.

As the reader can see, there are many uses for a word processor in the mathematics curriculum. A creative mathematics teacher continues to fined new uses for the word processor. He/she types the following into the computer:

1. Anecdotal records, rating scales, checklists, journal writing entries, among other written reports of individual and committee endeavours of pupils in mathematics.
2. Teacher written tests such as multiple choice, essay, true/false, matching, and completion.

## MATHEMATICS AS A LANGUAGE

There are numerous opportunities for pupils to communicate orally to other learners in the classroom such as in a group discussion. There need to be flexible standards developed co-operatively involving pupils with teacher guidance. These may be the following:

1. All should participate, but no one dominating the discussion.
2. Ideas should be presented clearly and accurately.
3. Respect for the thinking of others must be respected.
4. Each person needs to be accepted in collaborative endeavours.

5. Individuals talents and skills should be recognized.
6. Pupils individually need to feel successful in learning so that a better self concept results.

Within committee endeavours and large group instruction, pupils may reveal and realize mathematics as a language. The following are concepts and terms that are peculiar to mathematics: squares, rectangles, circles, semicircles, rhombuses, triangles, commutative, associative, additive identity, multiplicative identity, among others. Mathematics then needs to be conceived as a language to be used in communicating accurately to and with others. When communicating with others, the following should be emphasized for effective communication:

1. *Stress.* to be effective, a word may need to have more stress or be said louder than other words; otherwise a monotone voice will be in evidence. Pupils may practice saying a sentence where at times each word is stated at a softer or louder stress. Here is a mathematical sentence that might be used: "The area of a right triangle is found by multiplying base times the height and then divide by two." Pupils may take turns in critiquing each other in a positive manner the degree of stress which needs to be in the offing. Each of the words in this sentence may be said louder in sequence than the others. Pupils may then discuss how meanings change when different words are stressed more heavily that others. Which word in the above sentence then should be said louder that the others for effective communication? Should it be *area, triangle, multiplying, base, height,* and/or *divide*. Pupils always need to attach meaning to what has been learned, but appropriate stress in oral communication also needs to be in the pupil's repertoire.
2. *Pitch.* Some word are said with a higher pitch than others for effective communication. A speaker who presents all content on the same/similar level of pitch might well lose his/her audience in the oral communication process. When using the cassette recorder, pupils individually may experiment with pitching words higher and lower so that effective communication may be an ultimate end result. The content for the exercise should come from content presently being studied. Thus, in the following sentence, pupils may practice different levels of pitch: "Subtraction is the inverse operation of

addition." We would suggest taking the first word and pitching it higher than the others in the sentence.

Then go on to word number two and notice how the meaning of a sentence changes with higher and lower levels of pitch. The goal here is to communicate well with learners and the teacher..

**3. Juncture**

There are pupils who disregard punctuation marks and the meaning of a sentence becomes vague and hazy. Juncture refers to pauses at appropriate places when oral communication is ongoing. Meanings of a sentence change much when punctuation is minimized in speaking activities (Ediger, 1997, pp. 197-206).

With its own vocabulary and language, it is important for pupils individually to convey subject matter effectively to teachers in the classroom and in society. The National Council Teachers of Mathematics (1989, p. 84) lists the following standards for grades five through eight in oral communication:

*Standard two: Mathematics as Communication*. The study of mathematics should included opportunities to communicate so that students can:

* model situations using oral, written, concrete, pictorial, graphical, and algebraic methods.
* reflect on and clarify their own thinking about mathematical ideas and situations.
* develop common understandings of mathematical ideas, including the role of definitions.
* use the skills of reading, listening, and viewing to interpret and evaluate mathematical ideas.
* discuss mathematical ideas and make conjectures and convincing arguments.
* appreciate the value of mathematical notation and its role in the development of mathematical ideas.The word processor may be used in any of the above named starred situations where writing is involved. Thus, when reflecting upon mathematical ideas (the second starred item), we

recommend journal writing which may be typed into the computer. Journal writing emphasizes that pupils individually write about what was learned and what is left to learn from an ongoing lesson in mathematics (a diagnostic and remediation software package may be of help here). For the third starred item above, pupils may make a mathematics dictionary covering necessary words and their related definitions. These, words and definitions might also be typed into the computer in making for a personalized mathematics dictionary. Starred item number four above, pupils may secure subject matter from CD ROMS as well as from internet. Starred item number five above lends itself well to videotaping pupils in a discussion working on a solution to a problem in mathematics. The discussion might well be evaluated in terms of desired criteria.

Stared item number one above may be emphasized with a videotape presentation whereby the presenter's provide models in writing for pupils to follow. Starred item number one also stress additional ways to present information such as using pictures and graphs, as well as concrete materials to indicate what had been learned. A source for illustrations as models may come from CD ROM printouts. Graphs may be typed into the computer as needed information for a program to indicate line, bar, and circle graphs.

The last starred item which deals with the attitudinal dimension may receive its model from technology in the form of a videotape. Adequate readiness needs to be present so that pupils may benefit more optimally from each technological approach to learning, such as benefiting from pupils in the videotape showing quality attitudes toward mathematics in the classroom setting.

## CONCLUSION

Teachers and supervisors continually need to appraise the present mathematics curriculum to notice necessary changes that should be made. A modern mathematics curriculum makes much use of technology. Society emphasizes heavy use of technology in the business world and schools should not lag behind in using technological approaches to assist pupils to learn more optimally. Thus, teachers and supervisors need to evaluate the mathematics curriculum to ascertain needs that must be fulfilled. Thus, the following questions need to be answered by mathematics teachers and supervisors pertaining to including technology more fully into the mathematics curriculum:

1. Which objectives should be added and which deleted so that pupils achieve more optimally in mathematics?
2. What can be done to stress rational balance among knowledge, skills, and attitudinal objectives?
3. How can objectives and learning opportunities be sequenced so that pupils benefit more so than formerly from instruction in mathematics.?
4. Should pupils have more opportunities to select what to learn and the order of these learning activities or should the objectives and learning opportunities be determined by teachers and/or by the state with mandated objectives?
5. How should technology and other materials of instruction be appraised to ascertain under which conditions pupils learn best?

## REFERENCES

Davis, Sara Jeanne Holster, "How Mastering Technology Can Transform Math Class, *Educational Leadership*, 65 (3), 50.

Ediger, Marlow (1997), *Teaching Mathematics in the Elementary School*, Kirksville, Missouri; Simpson Publishing Company, 187- 206.

Ediger, Marlow (1996), *Elementary Education*, Kirksville, Missouri, Simpson Publishing Company, 209-14.

Ediger, Marlow (1995), *Philosophy in curriculum Development*, Kirksville, Missouri; Simpson Publishing company, 161—88.

Ediger, Marlow (1996), *Essays in School Administration*. Kirksville, Missouri; Simpson Publishing Company, 126-35.

Ediger, Marlow (1997), *Social Studies Curriculum in the Elementary School*, Kirksville, Missouri; Simpson Publishing Company, 70.

Ediger, Marlow (1997) *Teaching Reading and the Language Arts in the Elementary School,* Kirksville, Missouri; Simpson Publishing Company, 197-206.

Ediger, Marlow and Digumarti Bhaskara Rao (2000), Teaching Reading Successfully. New Delhi : Discovery Publishing House.

National Council Teachers of Mathematics *(1989), Curriculum and Evaluation Standards for School Mathematics,* Reston, Virginia; NCTM, 32.

National Council Teachers of Mathematics, *Curriculum and Evaluation Standards for School Mathematics,* Reston, Virginia; NCTM, 84.

# Chapter 15

# CO-OPERATIVE LEARNING VERSUS COMPETITION: WHICH IS BETTER?

Most educators appear to advocate co-operative learning in the curriculum. Pupils then are to work together harmoniously to achieve objectives in the curriculum. Heterogeneous grouping is also recommended so that mixed achievement levels of pupil work in a committee setting. These educators emphasize democratic living in the classroom when pupils are grouped heterogeneously as compared to homogeneously. Co-operative endeavours stresses democracy as a way of life, according to may educators, as compared to competition among pupils in the classroom. If full inclusion is emphasized, then a committee in co-operative learning may truly be heterogeneous with increased diversity in terms of pupil abilities. Let us examine the philosophy of co-operative learning and heterogeneous grouping more fully.

## CO-OPERATIVE LEARNING

As we read journal articles and other teacher education materials we feel that most educators advocate co-operative learning throughout much of the school day. There is a distinctive kind of reasoning emphasized by advocates. Pupils may then learn from each other. Perhaps, more can be learned from peers as compared to the teacher. Learners are co-operative beings and like to work together with other pupils. Co-operative learning can be emphasized in all curriculum areas and throughout most or all of the school day. Pupils are serious achievers when working together with peers. Each one desires to do his/her fair share of work within a committee. Fast learners can assist the slower pupils to achieve well. They can learn from the slow learners in return. Pupils need to learn to get along with each other and to respect the abilities of others. Diversity in the curriculum is to be stressed.

We believe there are numerous loopholes in the reasoning of co-operative learning advocates. We emphasize that not all pupils by any means are co-operative. There is rivalry, hostility, and aggression among pupils. To be sure, there are many pupils who are co-operative beings in wishing to work well together with others in an harmonious manner. One has only to observe pupil behaviour to notice that pupils are both co-operative and nonco-operative beings. We thoroughly agree that pupils should learn to work well with others in school and later in the work place. But to what degree in terms of the total length of the school day should pupils work on co-operative endeavours? Our thinking is that pupils should work in committees effectively since life itself consists of working well with others. However, there are many times when individuals need to work by the self. All of us find ourselves working on tasks and responsibilities by the oneself, without involvement of others. Thus, there needs to be rational balance in the school curriculum between working with others as well as working individually on tasks and activities.

There is seemingly a learning style which pupils possess that prefers working with others on lessons, projects, and activities. These pupils, no doubt, might well prefer a committee or co-operative learning experience. Together, the pupil may achieve more than working individually. These pupils might be motivated more so with other learners than working by the self. Learners may motivate and challenge each other in a committee setting and yet efforts are harmonized to attain a togetherness in an educational endeavour. Pupils need to be highly accepting of each other in co-operative learning. They must respect diversity among pupils and ideas. The use of ridicule and sarcasm is to be frowned upon. Rather, the pupil needs to encourage broad participation by members of the team. Group cohesion is necessary so that the goals of co-operative learning are being attained. The committee may be evaluated together as well as individually in their team contributions. All need to participate actively and achieve maximally. Failure for one or two to achieve in co-operative learning hinders optimal attainment for these pupils. Each must be serious in persevering and working toward objectives. The individual needs to blend his/her efforts with those of others on the team. All on the team must participate optimally, no one dominate the committee endeavours. Learners should stay on the task at hand, not digrees from agreed upon goals. Tasks need to become clear through interacting with each other. Achievement toward goals must be reviewed periodically in order to notice how much progress has been made and how much further the committee needs to go in order to achieve agreed upon goals.

The teacher in co-operative learning becomes a guide, a stimulator, and one who encourages, but not one who lectures nor dispenses information. He/she is a resource person who has much knowledge of keeping pupils on task. The teacher as resource person has numerous materials and necessary information from which pupils in co-operative learning may gather what is needed to achieve objectives. As a helper and facilitator, the teacher is motivated to assist pupils to be creative, to engage in critical thought, and to identify and solve problems. Higher levels of cognition are necessary here. The t ̀acher knows how to relate to learners in order that higher levels of cognition on the pupil's part in teaching and learning is in evidence.

There are selected questions that need to be raised pertaining to co-operative learning. These are the following:

1. How much time in the school day should be given to co-operative learning?
2. How should committees be formed for co-operative learning?
3. Who selects members of a committee?
4. How permanent should committee membership be?
5. How flexible should committee membership be if a pupil wishes to change to a different committee?

Frequently, we have received the impression that writers/speakers in education recommend continuous co-operative endeavours in a classroom. Certainly, learning opportunities need to be varied. Little is mentioned as to who should choose committee members. The teacher may make the choices. Pupils could also volunteer to serve on a committee. Random selection could be used to determine committee membership. Committee membership could be very short indeed for a particular group, perhaps a day or several days. Membership could be rather enduring also, such as planned tasks that last six weeks or so. There are different types of tasks such as those that are short in duration, such as planning refreshments for an end of the school year party. Co-operative learning members could also be together for an entire thematic unit of six weeks such as planning and making a model bedouin village in a unit on The Middle East. There will be pupils who do not like the project or a selected pupil on the committee. What is the answer here? This happens even if members have been chosen carefully using desired criteria.

## COMPETITION IN THE SCHOOL CURRICULUM

There are a few educators, not many, who advocate a competitive curriculum. Many reasons are given for the competitive philosophy. Generally, it is based upon the free enterprise system. The US is not keeping up with Japan and Germany in world trade. US pupils need to be more competitive and be first in the nation in mathematics and science as advocated by the National Governors Conference in 1989 with Education 2000. Warnings are given by news reprorters.as to low achievement in mathematics and science of US pupils as compared to those of other industrialized nations. Goals have been established on the state and local levels in order that learners may measure up to these levels in terms of what is deemed necessary to be first in the work in mathematics and science. Competition here rather than cooperation is emphasized.

The voucher system has many supporters in the US. Parents receiving the voucher money may redeem it at an other school which they deem to be better than the local school. The voucher money, if it becomes law, stresses that per pupil costs of education for a school year at the local school would equal the voucher that may then be used at the receiving school. There are advocates of parents being able to use the voucher money in either pubic or parochial schools. Advocates believe with competition, bad schools and teachers will have no clients and therefore not be in existence. The better schools with more clients than ever will serve as models for other teachers to emulate. Competition for numbers of pupils in a school under the voucher system is strictly competitive. Poor schools will go out of business.

Merit pay has numerous advocates in the US. With merit pay teachers rated as being superior or excellent receive additional pay for their quality services. Those supporting merit pay believe that teachers individually will work harder and do a better job of teaching once they are rewarded for doing outstanding work. Differentiated pay is then desired among teachers. No longer would the single salary schedule then be in operation. The latter is based on the number of years of teaching experience and the level of attained education at colleges/ universities as being sole determines of salary to be obtained by a teacher. Critics state that mediocrity is rewarded in teaching with the single salary schedule. If merit pay is implemented, competition for the higher salaries would then definitely be in evidence.

Open enrollment also emphasizes the free enterprise system. Here, parents choose for their sons and daughters which kind of a school the latter are to attend. The chosen school may bypass many local schools and school systems. Parents and the child do the choosing not the local school or the locally assigned teacher. The purpose is competition in parents choosing which school and teacher is best for their offspring. Teachers and schools not selected may need statewide superintendents and newly retrained and re-educated teachers.

In a few states, *e.g.*, Kentucky and New Jersey, schools must measure up to a definite standard in terms of standardized test results, or the state will take over deficient schools. There is competition here in a school not being delinquent as to pupil achievement revealed by test results.

The US Secretary of Education may list state by state how well pupils are achieving in different curriculum areas. This is called the wall chart. States are compared against each other in terms of pupil achievement, money spent on education per pupil, and average daily attendance of pupils. With competition among the different states in terms of wall chart figures, personal pride of each state to improve in education might be an end result when making these comparisons, according to selected educators and many lay people.

There are schools that have arranged contracts with commercial companies to teach their children. Educational Alternatives Incorporated (EAI) from Minneapolis, Minnesota is an example. EAI agrees with the school district how much achievement and the cost of services will be involved in a given school year. EAI then assumes responsibility for administration and instruction of the involved schools. There is competition here between the public schools and commercial companies in terms of who can provide the best education for pupils. It might well be true that school administrators and teachers remain the same with EAI as compared to earlier arrangements. EAI still does the training of teachers to use methodology as they deem to be good and profitable.

Additional means of competing with the public schools in terms of teaching pupils is to have charter schools and magnet schools.

When supervising student and co-operating teachers in the schools, we have observed the following to encourage competition among pupils in the classroom setting:

1. A chart on the wall showing the names of each pupil in class indicating how many words were spelled correctly for each week using the basal spelling text. Gold stars were received by the top spellers, followed by silver stars for the next best set of spellers. Other colors of stars were situated next to the name of the pupil indicating his/her spelling achievement.
2. The teacher announcing to the entire class how many problems each pupil solved correctly from one lesson from the basal text in mathematics. The announcements were made for each day of pupil practice in mathematics using the basal textbook.
3. Pupil test results in social studies were posted on the bulletin board ranking learners from high to low in achievement. The teacher commented on how well or how poorly individual pupil here had achieved.
4. Prizes announced prior to beginning a new unit in science. These prizes were to be awarded to pupils depending upon

how many total points each received a result of participating in different projects and tasks.

5. The pupil of the day selected by the teacher being presented with the wearing "the king's or queen's hat. There was much competition among pupils in class in being able to wear this hat for a day.

There are many additional examples which can be given whereby competition can and is being emphasized in the classroom setting. Pupils are compared with each other as to term projects, daily assignments, oral reports, oral reading, and test results, among other items. A major purpose of standardized tests is to compare one pupil against another. A parent, after receiving information of test results from his/ her offspring, may, during informal conversation, compare test results with parents of other children. We have heard parents reprimand their children for not doing better on a standardized test. Generally, the reprimand emphasizes why the child did not do better than so and so. Many parents are highly competitive in wanting their offspring to be a cheer leader, member of the first team in football or basketball, have a leading role in the school play, and/or being a class officer.

Competition can be healthy; it can also be destructive. Co-operative learning can be positive as well as negative. It all depends upon what transpires in either competitive or co-operative situations.

We will first discuss healthy competition. Here, pupils respect each other even though one or more persons in a given situation do not experience victory. Healthy competition can bring out the best within the person. Effort and perseverance is involved! There can be much interest on the part of all in competition be it between individuals or within a committee competing against another committee. We recommend the following guidelines for stressing competitive events:

1. Those competing should be somewhat equivalent in talents, skills, and abilities.
2. Those competing should have positive attitudes toward each other.

3. Those competing should have a desire to participate and learn.
4. Those competing should have definite goals to achieve in the competitive event.
5. Those competing should realize that not all individuals can be winners. Best it is if all pupils can be winners. This is definitely possible.

Questions that might be raised about competitive behaviour in the classroom setting include the following:

1. Does competition increase hostility among pupils toward each other?
2. Does competition hinder pupils in achieving affective objectives?
3. Does competition work against the learning style of selected pupils?
4. Does competition compare involved pupils unfavorable due to differences in abilities, interests, and capabilities?
5. Does competition increase achievement of pupils?

Teachers might wish to encourage positive competition among individuals in the classroom setting. Competition is neither good nor bad, but it depends upon how it affects individuals.

We all need to realize that as adults, we compete in numerous ways such as for jobs and occupations, promotions, marriage partners, good grades in classes taken, and for leadership responsibilities in society, among others.

Co-operative learning has its advantages and disadvantages. The advantages are the following:

1. Pupils do have opportunities here in learning to work together with others.
2. Selected pupils have as their favourite learning style the working together with peers, rather than working individually.
3. Goals in life can be achieved in co-operating with each other, rather than through dog eat dog approaches.
4. Learners can realize that school and learning may be enjoyable through co-operative learning.

5. **Pupils need to learn to assist each other in the school and classroom setting. We human beings, are dependent upon each other for survival.**

**Questions which need to be raised about co-operative learning include the following:**

1. **might pupils become highly competitive in a negative way within a committee setting?**
2. **might personality clashes hinder pupil achievement in committee settings?**
3. **might there be learning styles whereby selected pupils do not do well in group work, but would achieve better in more competitive settings? We would like to emphasize here that pupils individually may compete against their past performance with intent of making continuous progress.**
4. **might there be a rational balance between individual and committee endeavours in the curriculum which could benefit most pupils?**
5. **might there be leaders who do their best in co-operative learning?**

There are no clear cut answers to these questions. Even well designed research studies have their many weakness. Human beings write test items for the measurement device, ensuring much subjectivity in a research study. Objectivity occurs when all conditions are kept similar in giving the tests to the experimental and the control groups. Or can they be similar/same? No, they are not. Pupils feel differently from one time to the next. Not all pupils find that revealing what has been learned occurs best through testing. There are pupils who like authentic means of revealing what has been learned better as compared to being tested.

## CONCLUSION

Educators need to re- examine the cooperation versus competition philosophies in teaching pupils. Which approach is better of the two? It is hard to say. Neither approach in and and of itself is good. There can be negative teaching in either approach. We have seen bad teaching as well as good teaching in either case. Merely having co-operative learning or saying that one has co-operative learning does not make for goodness or badness. What truly matters is how each approach affects learners in the school and classroom setting. We would recommend having rational balance among the two approaches. Pupils need to learn to work harmoniously with others as well as work well on an individual basis. Each pupil should strive to achieve optimally when working individually. After all, life in school and in society consists of both!

## REFERENCES

Ediger, Marlow and Digumarti Bhaskara Rao (1996), *Science Curriculum*, New Delhi; Discovery Publishing House.

Ediger, Marlow and Digumarti Bhaskara RAo (2000). *Teaching Reading Successfully*, New Delhi: Discovery Publishing House.

Marja, Talwi and Digumarti Bhaskara Rao, eds. (1996), *Educational Leadership and Social Changes*, New Delhi; Discovery Publishing House.

# Chapter 16

## WHEN PUPILS FAIL, THEN WHAT?

Much is written about avoiding pupil failure in school and having an increased number graduate from high school, than the present seventy-five per cent rate. There probably is no other institution, other than the public schools, whereby so many pupils are to attend the same institution and go through a similar curriculum, especially the elementary and middle school years of schooling. The high school level provides more opportunities for pupils to differentiate in terms of courses taken, such as electives in the curriculum as compared to the elementary school. Or a pupil on the secondary level may go the vocational rather than the academic route. It appears, however, that the academic route is considered much superior as compared to the vocation route. We do not believe that it should be perceived this way. Rather, individuals are different from each other in many ways and selected pupils will feel more empowered in vocational as compared to academic classes. Society certainly does need its vocational people to do carpenter work, repair automobiles, prepare food in restaurants, do plumbing, and the myriads of needed employment in society.

### VOUCHER SYSTEMS

There are educators and people from the business world who advocate that schools which fail pupils should provide vouchers to parents to choose a receiving school for their child. Here, Parents need to be very receptive in studying what different schools have to offer meeting individual needs of pupils. Receiving schools need to publish brochures to indicate what they have to offer incoming pupils. They should make known what it is that would assist pupils to do well in school. Dissatisfied parents may have behaviourally disordered children and need a school for their children that can offer necessary curriculum. We would venture to speculate that pupils who do not do well in school, according to parental expectations, may have special needs. These pupils have not done well in the sending schools and now are looking for greener pastures where all is well. This may or may not follow when a pupils have not done well in the sending schools and now are looking for greener pastures where all is well. This may or may not follow when a pupil under the voucher system changes schools. Then too, if there are many vouchers available, will receiving schools be able to provide for pupils whose needs were not met in the sending school? If there truly is an outstanding teacher, known to many that he/she can help many pupils to be successful, how many new pupils can he/she take from receiving schools? Will the receiving school have adequate assistance for this excellent teacher to handle the new pupils? Or will the new pupils provide a burden to the outstanding teacher so that he/she can no longer do an excellent job of teaching. It takes one child who has many emotional problems to disrupt an entire classroom continuously. Then too, if the parents of this child are highly verbal in voicing dissatisfactions in the receiving school, what is the next alternative? A highly vocal parent can do much to hinder teachers in providing for individual pupils. If pupils do not achieve up to what news reporters or the lay public wants in terms of test results, teachers are to blame in whole. It almost appears as if pupils have no responsibilities for achieving unless they have an inward desire to do so.

What if parents do not have money to pay for differences between what the receiving school asks for in terms of money and what the sending school offers? There can be quite a gap between the two in dollars. Then too, transportation can be a real problem in sending a pupil to a different school. Will parents have the money and time to take their child to a different school? Schools also need to be chosen on the basis of what will truly assist a child to do better. This can be a major problem in selecting a new school for a pupil to attend under the voucher system. This opens the doors to a touchy situation in that some parents would choose parochial schools for their children. Would it be constitutional to send a child to a parochial school from voucher moneys? If too many pupils with parental approval decide to attend parochial schools and if this were legal, the parochial system of instruction would change much.

Special services for the handicapped would need to be provided. All pupils who wished to do so may have to be admitted to the chosen parochial school. The role of the state might involve supervising parochial schools in term of teachers hired and the quality of the curriculum offered. Parochial schools might then need to be need to be enlarged with a problem arising as to who would pay for these costs.

We have the following questions to ask about the voucher system of parental choice of schools for their children, in addition to the problems raised above:

1. Will the quality of education really improve for the pupil with the voucher system?
2. Why not spend the voucher money, instead, in improving all public schools in the US?
3. How are brochures developed by receiving schools presenting their data in terms of honesty, objectivity, and integrity?
4. What happens to receiving schools when receiving vouchers to admit pupils in terms of school size, and quality of instruction?
5. What happens to a pupil who no longer attends the neighborhood school in terms of feelings and friendships left behind?

## OPEN ENROLLMENT

There are several states in US, such as Minnesota and Lowa in USA that have open enrollment. With open enrollment, parents may choose which school in the state their child is to attend. The neighborhood school might, of course, then be bypassed. The local school is not as certain how many pupils they will have at the beginning of the school year since the option is open in terms of which school the pupil will be attending. Parents may then select a school based on the kind of curriculum which will be offered to their child. There is no money available in terms of vouchers to pay for changing from one public school to another. Parents need to find out then which school might offer a curriculum that would be of benefit to their children.

Feelings of insecurity may be there when a public school does not know how many pupils will be at the beginning of a school year. The same would be true of any receiving school. A problem then of space for pupils and adequate teachers need to be considered by the receiving schools. Many times, educators and the lay public argue that poor quality schools will be eliminated with open enrollment plans. Thus, schools offering poor quality education may eventually have too few pupils to operate an educational system.

We have the following questions to raise about open enrollment:

1. Do parents select schools based on quality or rather on slogans presented? In other words are there ulterior motives in making choices of schools such as a boy or girl desiring to play on a basketball/football team which is known for its winning record and possible scholarships? Perhaps, there is nothing wrong in wanting to be on a top team in competitive athletics in order to obtain a scholarship. For example, we do have the theory of multiple intelligences which includes bodily/kinesthetic intelligence.
2. Why not attempt to improve all public schools so that diverse curricula are offered within each school to provide for individual differences among pupils?
3. How can parents know which school will meet the needs of their children best?
4. Does a receiving school with a good track record want to accept numerous other pupils and perhaps ruin their good reputation due to having too many pupils or to many disruptive pupils?
5. Is it best for a local district to know approximately how many pupils there will be at the beginning of a school year in order to make quality plans for instruction?

## MEASURING PUPIL ACHIEVEMENT

There are many ways to measure pupil achievement including standardized norm referenced tests, criterion referenced tests, districtwide tests, state mandated tests, tests which accompany a basal reading or mathematics series, Education 2000 goals with diverse states developing tests to measure pupil achievement in attainment of stated objectives, national tests such as the National

Assessment of Educational progress (NAEP), and international tests which makes comparisons of pupil achievement among nations on the planet earth. We do not think educators and the lay public understand how each test is devised any why there is so much controversy about how to measure pupil achievement and progress.

A. *Standardized Tests*. There are many rules which need to be followed before a test is standardized. A standardized test has the same directions to follow for all taking the test. The time limits are the same for all regardless of ability and achievement levels of pupils involved, scoring procedures of the results are the same, among other standardizations. The results of our pupils having taken the test are compared with those of the group the test was standardized on in numerous pilot studies. The manual section of the standardized test will state which categories of pupils were included in the standardization group.

We see the following as major weaknesses of standardized testing to indicate pupil progress:

1. There are no objectives that go along with these kinds of tests. The teacher then cannot teach so that pupils might achieve objectives. Guesswork is involved in terms of what the test is to measure. What the teache teachers is then not valid in terms of content in test items on the standardized test.
2. Pupils lack security in not knowing what they will be tested on. What has been studied might be completely unrelated to content in the test items.
3. A test such as standardized tests may have high reliability and yet validity is difficult to determine. To be valid a test must measure what it purports to measure and that is pupil achievement in the different curriculum or academic areas. What is taught by teachers varies much from school to school. In a national curriculum, pupils could be studying similar things in each of the different curriculum areas. That is something, however, that would not be prized in the us, at least not now. Thus, there are no common objectives in and on standardized tests that teachers should teach for so that pupils might be successful in goal attainment. In addition to validity, reliability is an important term in

testing and evaluation. It is much easier in pilot studies to obtain statistical figures on reliability. Reliability stresses consistency of test results for pupils when a retest or split-half reliability is used. Thus the chances are if a test item is written clearly, the pupil will respond consistently when the same test is being given such as in test-retest reliability. From pilot studies in standardizing a test, weak items can be eliminated or modified so that consistency in terms of pupils' responses is obtained.

B. *Criterion referenced tests*. Here, the teacher has relatively easy access to the objectives that need emphasis in teaching so that he/she may stress selected subject matter in teaching learners. The test items then might be quite valid for pupils if the teacher has aligned instruction with the stated objectives. The content taught may then be valid since it aligns with the objectives. Reliability might also be good if the results from the CRT are the same/similar from pupils in a test/retest situation.

Our reservations about CRTs include the following:

1. The developers of the CRTs did not run pilot studies on test results of pupils; thus there is no data to show the validity and reliability of the CRT. In fact, this has happened in selected states in the US. The governor of a state then wished to hurry with implementing a new CRT and did not have educators do statistical analysis of pupil test results.
2. CRTs tend to have too many factual test items rather than stressing pupils engaging in critical and creative thinking as well as problem solving. Generally with multiple choice test items, the trend would be for factual knowledge to dominate content in and on the test.

C. *Districtwide Tests*. These tests are developed in the same way as is true of CRTs. Districtwide tests, however, are written by teachers and administrators on the local school district level as compared to the state level as was true of CRTs. Unless carefully developed districtwide tests might have the same weaknesses as do CRTs. It costs money and takes time to run tests of validity and reliability in pilot studies. However unless these pilot studies are run, the tests might well have weak and unclear test items. There are ample opportunities in districtwide tests to align with content taught by teachers within that district.

D. Test which Accompany a Basal Mathematics Textbook Series or other Academic Area. Here, I will discuss mathematics only and accompanying tests with the basal text. There are several series that have tests inside the basal which the teacher can give to pupils. The tests seem to be well aligned, in most cases, with content covered for each unit of study in the basal. Authors of the text and the accompanying tests advocate pupils be given the test prior to teaching the first unit, for example. If a pupil obtains a score of eighty per cent or higher on the unit being pretested, he/she need not study that unit, but can take the pretest for the next unit of study in the basal. Again, if a score of eighty per cent or higher is secured by the pupil taking the pretest, he/she need not study or do the work in that unit of study. This approach of passing out of a unit continues until a pupil does not get eighty per cent or higher of the test items correct on a pretest.

We see the following weaknesses on a basal textbook test to measure pupil achievement:

1. These tests seemingly are not that valid and reliable to have pupils test out of studying and doing the work within a unit of study. We have heard most teachers of mathematics in my graduate classes as well as co-operating teachers whom we supervise in the public schools make statements that doubt the strengths of using these tests to measure if pupils can test out of a unit of study. However, teachers do say pretests such as those related directly to a textbook have their strengths to offer assistance to teachers in teaching pupils. Thus, what pupils miss on these pretests may become a part of objectives to achieve in the mathematics curriculum.
2. Mathematics contains more exact and precise knowledge as compared to such curriculum areas as reading and literature, art, music, physical education, and social studies when ascertaining learner progress. We believe that mathematics tests due to their objective content can do a better job of measuring pupil progress as compared to other academic disciplines. There still as a problem as to what to

emphasize on these tests such as products versus processes, the practical as compared to the theoretical in mathematics.

3. Face validity may be fairly strong in subject matter tests since the writers of the tests look at content taught and then arrange items therefrom for the test. However, predictive validity is desired since the results form a learner in having taken the test is to predict how well he/she will do on the next ensuing unit of study.

E. *Education 2000.* The year 2000 is near and goals need to be looked at continuously for purposes of improving the curriculum as well as new trends are entering into the arena. At the 1989 National Governor's Conference, major broad objectives were identified at this meeting. I (Ediger) will mention two here for comment. I realize the Conference statements are very general in terms of objectives for pupil attainment, namely US pupils are to be first in test results in international comparisons among pupils in science and mathematics. US pupils have not done well in international comparisons on test results. There are and can be numerous reasons for achievement levels of US pupils when comparisons are made. I will raise several questions pertaining to these occurrences:

1. Are the objectives of US schools aligned with the tests of international comparisons?
2. Much stress is placed upon US pupils using what has been learned such as in science and mathematics. Do the test items on international comparisons also stress application of content learned or are more theoretical objectives being emphasized?
3. Do pupils reveal what has been learned through testing or are there better ways such as hands on approaches to indicate achievement in mathematics with the use of real objects?
4. Are there selected countries in the world whose pupils do better on international tests of comparison due to classroom work in mathematics stressing more of what is covered on these tests?
5. Which pupils are tested in the different nations when international comparisons are made? For example, US educates all pupils regardless of handicaps possessed such

as mental retardation and those with behavioural disorders. Are these pupils a part of us pupils being tested and compared with other nations who do not have these kinds of learners in the comparison pool? US pupils stay in school until the senior year of high school when about 80 per cent of this age group graduate. How does this compare with other nations in holding power of schools? If more of the cream of the crop of pupils are tested in a nation, then higher achievement is possible here.

6. Are there too many variables among nations when making comparisons in science and mathematics achievement? For example, it is very difficult to make comparisons among nations as to how money earmarked for school is spent. In the US much of school moneys goes to busing pupils from rural areas into school. A considerable amount of money is spent also on busing for integration of the races purposes. There are nations that do not even have school buses such as Russia.

F. *The National Assessment of Educational Progress (NAEP).* This is a real puzzier to me when viewing test results from NAEP. NAEP tests a sample population of nine, eleven, and thirteen year olds in the US every year. When test result are not what editors and writers of commentaries want, there is much criticism of schools.

Writers of test items can write them at an easier as well as a more complex level. If I (Ediger) want to show that the public schools are failing, I would write very difficult test items so that pupils would indicate low achievement. Should I desire to indicate very high public school achievement, I would write exceedingly easy test items for pupils to respond to. NAESP results do not tell me anything. The most information I can receive from NAESP is what the writers and statisticians declare. One of my sons jokingly says when he has finished glancing at NAEP results— "Ten per cent of seventeen year olds did not know who the first president of the US was," or "Two per cent of the pupils tested could not identify what a verb is." Generally, the statements given here in a humorous way state the very low pupil achievement, never in a way that "Ninety-five per cent of thirteen years old could write a meaningful paragraph." I would like to see the test items on the NAEP and analyze them in term in terms of clarity and relevance. The test items on the NAEP are given outside of context. What worker in society is given a test to indicate how well he/she is doing his/her job? The answer is none. One shows proficiency by doing and applying, not from test results. I cannot become excited about the low test results as shown by NAEP. Constructivism is a philosophy of testing that stresses contextual situations for pupils to reveal what has been learned. People at the work place also indicate how well they are doing within a context, not within a testing framework.

## CONSTRUCTIVISM AND EVALUATION

Constructivism emphasizes pupils being evaluated in terms of the situations they are in. For example, if pupils write a get well card to an ill classmate, there is a need for a writing activity. When the get well card is written, then there should be efforts made to appraise the quality of the card that will be sent to the ill classmate. Or, if a committee of pupils is doing a science experiment that relates directly to the ongoing unit, the quality of the experiment needs appraising in terms of desired criteria. It is very difficult, for example, to write a paper/pencil test item or items covering how well a science experiment was done.

Pertaining to two versions of constructivism, Alrasian and Walsh (1997) wrote:

> *These fundamental agreements among the constructivists are tempered by some important areas of difference about the process of constructing knowledge. These differences are reflected in two versions of cognition: developmental and socio-cultural.*
>
> *Developmental theories, such as Piaget's represent a more traditional constructivist framework. This major emphasis is on the universal forms of structures of knowledge* (e.g., *prelogical, concrete, and abstract operations) that guide the making of meaning. These universal cognitive structures are assumed to be developed and organized, so that prelogical thinking occurs prior to concrete logical thinking in a developmental sequence. Within this framework, the individual student is considered to be the meaning maker, with the development of the individual's*

> *personal knowledge being the main goal of learning. Critics of developmental theories of cognition point out that this perspective does not take into account "how issues such as the cultural and political nature of schooling and the race, class, and gender backgrounds of teachers and students, as well as their prior learning histories, influence the kinds of meaning that are made in the classrooms." Cognitive developmental theories, it is claimed, divorce meaning from affect by focusing on isolating universal forms of knowledge and thus limiting consideration of the socio-cultural and contextual influence on the construction of knowledge.*

Constructivism then stresses the following:

1. pupils being evaluated in terms of how well they perform within a specific ongoing learning activity.
2. pupils indicating they can apply what has been learned within a relevant task.
3. pupils indicating what has been learned in an intrinsic situation such as an experience that is being stressed presently, not in a formal testing situation extrinsic to the tasks being pursued.
4. pupils perceiving the value of the activity being pursued and revealing strengths and weaknesses therein.

## ADDITIONAL TESTS BEING ADVOCATED

It appears that schools and education of pupils is criticized all over the world (The Educational Review, 1997), Kakkar wrote on 'Crisis in Education in India:'

> *What the school, of late, has been doing sometimes makes people talk of deschooling education and foreseeing a future in which there may be no school at all. This will not happen. But there is certainly ahead of us an interval of rethinking fundamentals, and of raising schools different from the ones we have.*

Education is not only in a crisis just because the school is suddenly doing worse. In fact, it has done a terribly poor job all along. But what we have been tolerating in the past we can no longer tolerate today. It is a sheer delusion to think that school has been a place that children loved, that school years are years of happiness, or that students learned a great deal in school. School, in fact, has been a place of misery, of boredom, of suffering, where, as every teacher knows, only one of every fifteen students learned anything, if at all. Even college students around the turn of the century cannot expect to learn much. They go to college because they have nothing else to do, or because it leads to a professional career, or because it is the socially accepted thing to do, to make valuable connections.

There have been very vocal critics of US education over the decades. Illich (1972) came out with his book on *De-Schooling Society*. He recommended a thorough doing away with public education and offered a plan of schooling whereby arrangement would be made between a master in a field of specialization and the pupil wanting to learn what the specialist had to offer. The specialist may offer classes in the following areas: Music, art, drama, literature, geography, history, the sciences, and so on. Illich believed that compulsory school attendance made for mediocrity and dehumanized education. I (Ediger) well remember teaching and doing relief work on the West Bank of the Jordan from 1952-1954 and of the many refugees and bedouins that had very little formal schooling. When riding a bus from Jerusalem to Jericho, the bus would stop along the way to let selected passengers get off. There were several young bedouin boys that got off midway between Jerusalem and Jericho and followed a path to their tent at a distance. I truly felt for these young men and the lack of opportunities they had in life with, perhaps, no formal education. Poverty and the lack of education are two evils that one sees too frequently in societies around the world.

Bedouins living in tents and herding sheep and goats as well as having camels for transportation in a nomadic setting do not have a changing environment to look forward for. I certainly could not buy the idea of deschooling society.

Too frequently, slogans in society are given to justify the thinking of the one presenting the diverse slogans (Ediger, 1997), such as in the following:

"let's have the business world teach pupils; the public schools are not doing the job." Additional slogans here could be, "The private sector has always been able to do things better than the public sector. Thus, performance contracting has been emphasized in selected schools in which a certain level of achievement is guaranteed by the contractor in return for payment on a per pupil basis. Educational Alternatives of Minneapolis, Minnesota is involved in teaching pupils on a business basis. Performance contractors desire to make profits, large profits if possible for their ventures which is teaching in this case. Performance contracting was emphasized in selected school systems in the early 1970s.

Commentaries and reports on education can be quite critical. How accurate are these writings? It is hard to say. We believe a rational question might be raised about how much better other institutions in society are doing as compared to the educational arenas. There are many slogans which abound in American society.

There are groups such as the National Alliance of Business (NAB) who have felt that public school pupils definitely are not achieving adequately. They have offered to write tests which would demonstrate to the lay public what is lacking and needs to be changed in the public schools after viewing the test results. These approaches would involve a tremendous change in American school policy if this were done. Why? The business world of free enterprise might then determine what is of value and should be taught in the public schools. There are other segments of the population such as labor that would not be represented in such a venture. Questions that need to be raised here pertain to the following:

1. How can the business world know which content should appear on tests?
2. Is there more to the education of children other than business interests?
3. What would be the rationale of having the business world be involved in testing pupils in the public schools?

4. How does the business world train their employees at the work place; is there a model for their advocacy in the educational arena?

In addition the business world and their plans of action, there are governmental leases who come up with ideas in education and the public schools. Thus President Bill Clinton in his 1997 State of the Union Address called upon the US to become first in the world in terms of quality education offered for public school age pupils. He advocated testing every fourth grader in reading achievement and every eighth grader in mathematics to ensure that high national standards in education are being met. Results from the tests would indicate what help a child needs to improve in reading and in mathematics. President Clinton advocated having the best teachers in the world if the best schools in the world are to come about. About one million volunteers will be needed in the public schools to provide assistance and ensure that pupils are reading independently by the end of the third grade (Bill Clinton, 1997).

Action by US governmental leaders can be excellent in order to focus on the importance of education and the public schools. There are definite questions that might be raised here pertaining to additional testing and the writing of new tests such as testing fourth grades on reading achievement and eighth graders on mathematics progress:

1. Are sufficient tests available already to measure pupil achievement academically without writing new tests?
2. How will new tests be developed to stress validity in reading? There are many issues involved in reading such as phonics *versus* the whole language approach.
3. How much testing of pupils should be emphasized to determine achievement? Here we come up with the debate of testing versus constructivism to indicate learner progress in teaching and learning situations.
4. How do test results of pupils in a single testing situation differ from learners revealing everyday progress in the classroom, as observed by teachers, in revealing reading achievement?

5. Who will be involved in writing test items so that politics is minimized to indicate pupil achievement in the public schools?

## CONCLUSION

If pupils fail, then what? There are so many alternatives here that may be discussed. First of all, is the result of failure internal in that the pupil does not care, nor put forth effort? Or, do pupils fail due to the numerous variables inherent in the public school system? Numerous approaches are used to assist pupils to do better in a receiving school such as would be true of the voucher system. Here, parents may choose which school their child is to attend, with the money available that would equal to what the sending school spends per pupil. The receiving school may spend more money per child and thus the parent needs to make up the difference plus transportation costs. Sending pupils at public expense to denominational schools is still not in evidence since church and state separation regulations apply in most cases. Open enrollment is available in selected states in the US, such as Iowa and Minnesota, whereby parents may select the school within their state for the child to attend. Parents need to be aware of the curricular offerings in a new school chosen. The objectives, learning opportunities, and evaluation procedures need to harmonize with the pupil's very own style of learning. This would be true of all plans open to parents to assist the pupil to achieve and avoid failure. There may be problems involved when parents select a school away from home base for their child to attend. There may be room and board costs when the pupil is living away from home. Then too, the child may not be close to home when there is such a need to be near to parents/ guardians.

Measuring up to predetermined standards can be difficult for many pupils. Standardized tests do not have these predetermined standards; however, different school districts may be using these kinds of tests to measure learner progress within a given school year. A slow learner may achieve at a low level on a standardized test and yet be achieving as well as can be expected. A gifted/ talented pupil may achieve at a high level on the standardized test but is not really applying himself/herself in teaching and learning situations.

CRTS can be excellent if higher levels of cognition are being measured for pupils to attain. Learners may also progress as rapidly as possible on each of the sequential objectives with provisions then being made for individual differences. Slow learners here need additional assistance to achieve as optimally as possible. Districtwide achievement tests operate in a similar manner as do CRTs. Both need to be valid and measure in terms of what pupils have had opportunities to learn in the school curriculum. If the test items are vague and poorly written, learner achievement will not be indicated in an appropriate way.

Tests based on the basal textbook being used can be one way to appraise learner progress. That is true of all valid and reliable evaluation techniques in that each procedure is an approach to determine what a pupil has learned. There are no perfect ways nor panaceas to appraise pupil achievement. The teacher needs to ways nor panaceas to appraise pupil achievement. The teacher needs to use a variety of techniques to determine what pupils have learned.

The National Assessment of Educational Progress (NAEP) tests a random sampling of pupils in the US to ascertain what has been achieved. This is a complex venture in that the test items can not be valid for pupils to achieve. Thus there is no alignment between objectives of which there are none listed for pupils to achieve on the NAEP and the evaluation items for that test. It would indeed be difficult for test writers in writing items that are to represent that which pupils have learned and achieved. The following questions arise:

1. How difficult or how easy does one write each test item in terms of complexity?
2. What subject matter is to be covered on the test?
3. Which is the most appropriate way for pupils to reveal what has been learned? Different ways of revealing learning may include paper/pencil tests such as is used in the NAEP tests; however, there are numerous additional

ways such as experiment, demonstrations, hands on approaches, and art work, among others.

4. How much emphasis should be placed upon subject matter content in the tests as compared to skills and attitudes?
5. What meanings are to be given to test results of pupils?

If, for example, forty per cent of nine year olds cannot write a meaningful sentence, according to NAEP results, then the teacher needs to assist pupils in writing meaningful sentences. It is difficult to know what is meant by a meaningful sentence, according to NAEP workers and measurement specialists.

Constructivism has the most merit of all approaches in ascertaining what pupils have learned. why? The evaluation is not a one shot approach, but can be ongoing and continuous. Within a learning situation then, the teacher appraises how well a pupil is doing. The results may be obtained from teacher observation as well as test results. Feedback is then given to the pupil on what can be done to achieve sequentially (Ediger, 1996).

Perhaps, all of the approaches mentioned above have some merit. However, the goal is to assist pupils to achieve more optimally, not to obtain test scores for comparisons to be made among pupils nor to minimize human values of individual learners. If pupils fail, teachers need to have information on guiding pupils individually to be successful learners.

## REFERENCE

Alrasian, Peter W., and Mary E, Walsh (1997), "Cautions for Classroom Constructivists," *Education Digest*, vol. 62, No. 8, page 63, (condensed from *Phi Delta Kappa*, Vol. 78, No. 2, pages 444-49.

Bhaskara Rao, Digumarti, ed. (1997). *Education for the 21st Century*, New Delhi ; Discovery Publishing House.

Bhaskara Rao, Digumarti, V. Venkateshwara Rao and V. Vamsi Krishna, eds. (2000). *Distance Education in Different Countries*, New Delhi; Discovery Publishing House.

Clinton, Bill (1997), "President Clinton's Call for Action," *Education Digest*, Vol. 62, No. 8, pages 4-7.

Ediger, Marlow (1977), "Slogans in Education and in Society, *Journal of instructional Psychology,* Vol. 24, No. 1, pages 37-41.

Ediger. Marlow (1996), *Essays in School Administration,* Kirksville, Missouri; Simpson Publishing, pages 93 and 94.

Harshitha, Digumarti, ed. (2000), *Education in India,* New Delhi; Discovery Publishing House.

Kakkar, S.B. (1997), Crisis in Education in India, *The Educational Review,* Vol. 102, No. 1 pages and 2.

Illich, Ivan (1972), *De-Schooling Society,* New York; Harper and Row.

# Chapter 17

## GOALS IN THE MATHEMATICS CURRICULUM

Objectives need to be selected carefully since they provide definite direction in terms of what the mathematics teacher will be teaching. There are states that mandate the objectives for pupils to achieve. Pupils are then tested, based on these objectives, at selected intervals as they progress through the diverse school years. When the objectives are stated in measurable terms, the teacher needs to make certain that learning activities are provided which harmonize with the stated objectives of instruction. The criterion referenced tests will then attempt to measure if learners have been successful in goal attainment. They are generally aligned very carefully with the stated objectives to make for increased validity of instruction. If the state mandated objectives are more broadly stated, the mathematics teacher has more leeway in choosing learning opportunities which harmonize with the general objectives. With these general objectives, it may not be as certain then what pupils will be tested on if state mandated criterion referenced tests are used to ascertain pupil achievement. When the writer started teaching in a rural school in the early 1950's, he chose his own objectives to stress instruction. There were no state mandated objectives to guide instruction. In 1989, the National Council Teachers of Mathematics (NCTM) came out with a carefully designed set of objectivies for teaching and learning situations. The NCTM objectives provide voluntary guidelines for teachers to use in developing instructional strategies. The NCTM Curriculum Standards for School Mathematics: Grades K-4 (1989) emphasized the following, among other objectives of instruction:

1. Mathematics as Problem solving: Students will;
   * use problem solving approaches to investigate and understand mathematical content.

* formulate problems.
* develop and apply strategies to solve a wide variety of problems.
* verify and interpret results.
* acquire confidence in using mathematics meaningfully.

2. Mathematics as Communication: Students will;
    * relate physical materials, pictures, and diagrams to mathematical ideas.
    * reflect on and clarify their thinking about mathematical ideas and situations.
    * relate their every day language to mathematical language and symbols.
    * realize that representing, discussing, reading, writing and listening to mathematics are a vital of learning and using mathematics.

More will be discussed here pertaining to these NCTM standards. it is important to notice that problem solving as an objective is considered to be very import for mathematics teachers in designing the curriculum. In society, people in many of life's situations, are solving problems using mathematics. Thus individuals or groups identify a relevant problem, gather needed information as possible solutions, test the answer or hypothesis, and revise the hypothesis if necessary. Problems in mathematics arise when buying goods and services as well as when selling goods and services. Pupils in class need to think of solving their own personal problems in mathematics such as when items are actually purchased and change is needed from the currency used in the transaction. They might also devise simulated problems to solve in the classroom setting. There are excellent simulations in computer use which pupils might engage in actively in solving problems involving virtual reality. It is important for pupils to try different algorithms in the solving of problems in mathematics. Pupils individually need to discover which algorithm works best in any given situation. Accuracy in working on problems is of utmost importance. Certainly, pupils need to test the accuracy of solutions to problems. Estimating if an answer is reasonable is a recommended procedure here. When being able to provide reasonable estimates, the learner checks his/her response with that which appears to be plausible. It is always good to be able to estimate, for example, the cost of a given set of items purchased even if a calculator has been used in ascertaining the sum. One can, of course, punch in the incorrect values in addition when using a calculator. Hopefully, pupils will ultimately and continuously develop feelings of confidence in doing mathematics. Success in mathematics breeds more success. Quality sequence in mathematics will increase pupil's chances of growth, achievement, and progress in mathematics.

Each person communicates ideas in society pertaining to the world of mathematics. Communication may take the form of being oral, written, and/or pictorial, among other ways. The world of reality presents concrete materials such as goods and services purchased. What is real needs to be communicated in mathematical terms, symbols, and words using numerals, such as the counting or whole numbers. The proper operation symbol needs to be used such as plus, minus, multiply, or divide. Thus, the concrete or real may be expressed in the abstract.

It is always good if pupils think about or reflect upon what has been done or learned in mathematics. If pupils do not reflect upon mathematics used in problem solving, the chances are that forgetting will occur. The reflection can provide review opportunities in which there are opportunities to look for new algorithms to be used or alternative ways of perceiving a problem, as well as rehearsal of that which has been learned previously. Shantha Kumari(1994) found that students differ significantly if taught by the reflective as compared to traditional methods of instruction. There were also significant differences between pupils in attitudes and creative thinking when teachers taught using reflective as compared to traditional methods of instruction. Rational thinking too would say that pupils learn more when reflection upon content is inherent as compared to a lack of reflection. Academic achievement, positive attitudes, and creative thinking increase when learners think upon and ponder upon facts, concepts, and generalizations in the academic arenas, according to the Kumari's study.

Learners need to think of ways of using what has been learned. To frequently, pupils separate what has been learned in the classroom with what is needed in the real world in society in making transactions. This separation should not be made. After all, mathematics teachers need to guide pupils to use and apply the concrete (objects, items, realia), semiconcrete (pictures, illustrations, drawings, diagrams), and the abstract (numerals, numbers, and operational signs) to functional situations in real life. The dichotomy between classroom and society need to be avoided. Rather, school and society become one in learning and applying that which has been and is being learned.

A variety of procedures need to be used in guiding pupil learning so that optimal achievement in mathematics may occur. Reading, discussing, writing, listening, observing, drawing, and dramatizing, are methods of instruction that may be used as learning opportunities in guiding pupils to achieve more optimally in realizing NCTM standards of instruction.

## MATHEMATICS AS GENERAL EDUCATION

Each pupil needs to experience quality in the mathematics curriculum. Mathematics lessons and units of study are for all pupils. Carefully chosen objectives, learning activities, and evaluation procedures need to be in evidence. Ralph Tyler (1949), late professor of the University of Chicago, raised four questions that all teachers need to ask and determine answers for in teaching and learning situations. These questions are the following:

1. Which objectives should pupils achieve?
2. Which learning activities should be chosen so that pupils might achieve the stated objectives?
3. How should the curriculum be organized for pupils?
4. How should pupil achievement be evaluated to notice learner progress?

The above named questions are vital to ask and to plan carefully for their implementation so that each pupil might realize optimal achievement. Thus, each pupil needs the best of objectives, learning activities, organization of the curriculum, as well as evaluation procedures in the mathematics curriculum. In determining objectives of instruction in mathematics, the teacher needs to have pupils engage in higher levels of cognition. The lowest level, rote learning is not to be completely discarded. However, pupils need to attach meaning to what is being taught in ongoing lessons and units of study. Thus, if pupils do not understand what is taught, forgetting may well occur rapidly. Purpose or reasons for learning may be hindered. Motivation to learn is closely related to pupils understanding facts, concepts, and generalizations. The cognitive levels of objectives must go beyond that of rote learning. A higher level pertains to pupils using what has been learned. There are numerous practical activities whereby pupils may use subject matter acquired. Primary grade pupils might use what has been learned by 'buying and selling' in a miniature grocery store with prices marked on the empty food containers. Pupils may then 'shop' for groceries by using toy money to pay for the food items purchased.

Interest in achieving vital goals can go downhill. Certainly, pupil interest in learning in mathematics is also of utmost importance. Interest in learning sustains pupils to attend and persevere in ongoing tasks in mathematics. Learning activities to achieve objectives should be on the pupil's understanding level. Individuals do possess different levels of achievement and interest in a topic in mathematics. Mathematics teachers then need to meet individual needs of pupils. Each activity needs to possess vital subject matter so that relevant objectives might be attained.

## EQUITY IN MATHEMATICS

Pupils need to experience equity in the mathematics curriculum. Individuals then should achieve optimally regardless of race, creed, sex, or national origin. pupils individually should be guided to experience quality in ongoing lessons and units of study. Too frequently pupils of lower socioeconomic levels, for example, have been limited in their experiences with computers. Schools in low income levels do not have the technology that better financed classrooms have. With less financing, the number of computers become more limited. These computers might also be older and possess fewer capability advantages. Lower income level homes certainly will not have the number of computers that higher income levels have. In a rapidly expanding information age, pupils from poverty level homes will certainly be disadvantaged as compared to their counterpoints in sub-urban public schools and higher income level pupils attending private schools. Equity in funding of schools and equity in opportunities to learn must be the lot of all pupils. Money does not solve all problems to be sure, but it does buy a lot of advantages that poverty cannot attain. With twenty-five per cent of United States pupils coming from poverty level homes, it behooves school leaders to see to it that pupils individually experience equity in the mathematics curriculum. If pupils from poverty level homes do not experience equity, they will be further and further behind in mathematics achievement as compared to learners from more favorable levels of home incomes.

A quality mathematics curriculum is needed by all elementary school pupils so that further sequential learning will be their lot on the secondary school levels. If pupils do not experience a quality kindergarten through high school mathematics curriculum, selected pupils will be held back from entering certain fields of science and engineering, among other endeavours. It takes a good mathematics curriculum for all pupils so that each can make the best vocational choices possible. The best objectives, learning opportunities, and evaluation procedures need to be available to all learners. Equity is a salient concept to emphasize in developing the mathematics curriculum.

## MEMORIZATION IN MATHEMATICS

Mathematics teachers need to be careful about pupils memorizing subject matter in the curriculum. Too frequently, pupils have been required to memorize basic addition, subtraction, multiplication, and division facts without understanding what has been learned. To be sure, pupils ultimately need to respond quickly to tese basic facts. However, meaning and understanding always come first. Memorizing is the lowest level of cognition such as being able to recall answers to basic addition, subtraction, multiplication, and division facts. Mathematics educators always state the importance of pupils attaching meaning to what is being learned. Learners first need to comprehend subject matter acquired. For example, a first grade pupil should be able to show comprehension to the value of 3+4 = — when this is being studied in an ongoing lesson or unit of study. How might the pupil be taught as well as how may the learner show meaning and understanding in achieving objectives? Teachers might have pupils discover the answer by showing a set of three sticks and asking how many there are here. If pupils can count rationally, they will respond with 'three'. Next the teacher should show a set of four sticks and ask pupils how many there are in this set. The two sets are then joined together to have pupils respond with what three sticks and four sticks are in number when joined together. using sticks and other manipulatives, the pupil individually should attach meaning to a basic addition fact. Understanding the meaning of 3+4 = - is very important for further sequential learning to occur. It may be necessary for a pupil to memorize later what 3+4=-, if manipulate experiences continually need to be used when responding to answer what this basic number pair equals. However, meaning and understanding come prior to rote learning and memorization. Pupils can apply and use what has been learned much better if meaning is there as compared to committing content to memory without the needed understanding.

## RAPIDITY OF LEARNING

There are teachers who feel that pupils should complete problem solving and computation exercises with great speed. Generally, pupils will work at optimal speed if understanding is there in work performed. If they do not do so, then the mathematics teacher needs to emphasize time on task for individual pupils. There are pupils who waste time in getting to work as well as during the time the mathematics activity is in evidence.

Learners here need assistance to persevere in mathematics. Learners should set high goals for themselves and attempt to achieve them. They need to build confidence in their very own abilities. Pupils tend to develop a good self concept if success is experienced in ongoing lessons and units of study. Teachers should sequence learning opportunities so that pupils individually achieve new challenging, objectives and are successful in doing so. Once pupils are successful learners, they tend to develop an inward desire to learn, grow, and develop in mathematics. Emphasizing speed in computing or solving problems, generally, is not a part of a quality mathematics curriculum.

## CO-OPERATIVE LEARNING

The writer when being an elementary pupil remembers all work and assignments being completed in mathematics on an individual basis. It was considered cheating to work together with others. John Dewey (1959–1952) advocated pupils working in committees or small groups when learning. He believed that pupils achieved more when working co-operatively than individually. Dewey felt that pupils did not like working the self, but preferred to work collaboratively with other learners. Today, much stress is placed upon pupils working harmoniously together to solve problems. When working together, pupils learn form each other, as well as from the teacher. They assist each other as well as challenge the thinking of committee members, leading to higher levels of cognition.

Committee membership should be small such as three to five members so that all can participate freely when interacting with each other. It is good procedure to start with one committee first in order that the teacher can learn to work with a group. If all pupils in a classroom started working on committees immediately, the teacher may not be able to move form committee to committee in order to provide guidance and direction. Once a single initial committee is able to proceed with minimal assistance from the mathematics teacher, a second committee may be formed. The second committee needs to assume more and more responsibilities before additional committees are in evidence. The mathematics teacher is not a lecturer or dispenser of information but one who motivates, encourages, and challenges committee members to stay on task. He/she helps pupils to confront and solve problems within the framework of committee endeavours. The mathematics teacher also guides pupils to use proper procedures in committee work in which:

1. all participate and no one dominates committee endeavours.
2. learners stay on task and not waste valuable time.

3. each respects the thinking of other participants.
4. ideas are presented clearly.
5. pupils discuss and learn from each other, leasing to higher levels of cognition.
6. processes and products of mathematics are equally important.
7. goals and objectives of instruction are being realized.
8. active involvement of learners in a hands on approach is being stressed.
9. emphasis is placed upon critical and creative thinking.
10. application of subject matter is emphasized.

Should committees and co-operative learning be emphasized throughout the day or should there be time also for individual work by pupils in the mathematics curriculum? There needs to be rational balance between the two approaches. In society individuals work collectively as well as individually. People need to use time wisely be it in groups or on an individual basis. Also there needs to be time for the class as a whole be taught together. Thus, there are common learnings in mathematics which all pupils in a classroom can experience. Here, the teacher must be careful that all pupils are attending and achieving when large group instruction is being emphasized. Flexible grouping is necessary so that individual, committee, and large group instruction is emphasized when needed to guide each pupil to achieve adequately in mathematics.

## USING MATHEMATICS TEXTBOOKS EXCESSIVELY

Well selected textbooks in mathematics add much to the mathematics curriculum as learning opportunities. These texts tend to be well written and provide a guide to the teacher in selecting objectives, learning opportunities, and evaluation procedures. Much time is saved by the teacher when using a basal or multiple series of mathematics tests in planning the curriculum. The writer reads in journal articles periodically that a teacher teachers well since he/she is not using a mathematics textbook in teaching pupils. When not using/or using heavily a basal text says nothing about the quality of teaching . One can teach well with or without the use of basal textbooks in mathematics. If content therein is made meaningful, interesting, and purposeful for pupils, it might well be that a good job of teaching mathematics is in evidence when using a quality mathematics textbook.

There are exceptions, however, to the use of mathematics basal texts and teaching effectively. Many pupils do require a hands on approach in learning. Pupils do possess diverse learning styles and stressing the concrete or enactive phase of learning assists many pupils to achieve more optimally. Thus, blocks, seeds, pop bottle caps, sticks, models, toys, and other objects are necessary to engage pupils actively in learning. It is also wise in teaching to stress the iconic or semiconcrete facets of learning such as use of pictures, films, filmstrips, videotapes, video disks, soft ware packages, and other modern technology in teaching and learning situations. These materials are one step removed form real live situations as are indicated in the concrete/enactive materials. Too frequently, textbook content stresses the abstract phase of learning largely. Thus, reading of content in story or word problems as well as strict computation in addition, subtraction, multiplication, and division emphasizes the symbolic and the abstract to the near exclusion of the concrete/enactive and the semiconcrete, iconic materials of instruction. Pupils might then lack meaning and understanding of what is taught. The writer believes very strongly in pupils attaching meaning to what is being learned. Learners also need at attend and pay attention to ongoing lessons and unit objectives as well as learning opportunities. A very of learning opportunities must be provided to pupils so that each may learn as much as possible in mathematics. A teacher must truly provide for individual differences among learners. If content presented is too difficult, pupils cannot achieve and learn. If it is too easy, boredom and a lack of challenge to learn might well be an end result.

The nature of mathematics has helped to determine what is taught and when it is taught in the elementary grades. Whole number are the basis for many mathematical ideas; moreover, experiences with them arise long before children come to school. Thus, whole number work is stressed first. Work with rational numbers logically follows work with whole numbers. Such seemingly 'natural' sequences are the result of long years of curricular evolution. This process has involved much analysis of what constitutes a progression from 'easy' to 'difficult' based in part on what is deemed to be needed at one level for the development of ideas at later levels.

Once a curriculum is in place for a long time, however, people tend to consider it the only 'proper' sequence. Thus, to omit a topic or to change the sequence of topics often involves a struggle for acceptance.

Sometimes the process of change is aided by an event, such as when the Soviet Union sent the first Sputnik into orbit. The shock of this evidence of another country's technological superiority speeded up curricular change in the United States. The "new math" of the 1950s and 1960s was the result, and millions of dollars were channeled into mathematics and science education to strengthen school programs.

The problem remains continually as to what should be taught elementary school pupils in mathematics. Teachers, principals, supervisors, parents, and curriculum directors need to study and appraise continuously what knowledge has most worth for pupils in mathematics. One early statement of objectives on what knowledge has most worth was advocated by Herbert Spencer of whom Brubacher (1966) wrote:

> *In mid-nineteenth century England a somewhat different approach was being made to educational aims by Herbert Spencer (1820–1903), the social philosopher. Perturbed by the confusion in educational aims in his day, Spencer looked about for a standard by which to determine their relative value. This he found in the contemporary emphasis upon utilitarianism and on science, especially evolutionary thought, to which he was quite sympathetic. Answering his own question on how to live completely, he arranged the aims of education in the order of their survival value to the individual and to society. First of all, education should aim to teach the art of self-preservation, second, it should teach one how to earn a living, next, it should ensure survival by teaching about rearing and disciplining children, fourth, education should fit one for social and especially for political duties; and last, though most of Spencer's predecessors put this aim among the first, education should equip one for enjoyment of the refinements of culture- of art, literature, and the like.*

Spencer's objectives stressed the practical and the useful in mathematics, among other utilitarian curriculum areas. Abstract knowledge, theories, and learning for its own sake would not be advocated by Herbert Spencer. The Seven Cardinal Principles of Education were developed by the National Education Association (NEA) and stressed what is useful in society, not self development nor knowledge for the sake of knowledge (1918). These broad goals were the following:

Command of fundamental processes, health, citizenship, worthy home membership, vocations, worthy use of leisure time, and ethical character.

Problems arise when the mathematics curriculum is viewed from either a subject centered or a problem centered approach in teaching and learning. A subject centered mathematics curriculum may not stress what is practical or useful. It might emphasize a textbook/ workbook approach in teaching pupils. Perhaps, a new other materials are involved in learning activities provided to provide for meaning and understanding. The goal is to have pupils learn subject matter, not necessarily application of content acquired. Toward the other end of the curriculum is a more utilitarian centered mathematics curriculum whereby pupils learn to identify and solve lifelike problems. In the subject centered curriculum, the teacher does more direct teaching of content to pupils whereas in a problem solving approach the teacher is a guide and encourages learners to identify and solve problems. Perhaps, the issue may be clarifies further when stressing the basics in mathematics as compared to a practical curriculum in mathematics. The basics have never been identified although there is much talk about its importance. These essential, it is believed, are needed by all pupils regardless of ability and achievement levels of learners. The basics have their very own scope and sequence arranged ahead of time prior to instruction. In contrast, the practical is emphasized in sequence when the problem(s) have been chosen and need solutions. a practical curriculum cannot be determined specifically prior to instruction. Generally, as the need arises, practical learnings will be needed by involved by learners.

## USING A VARIETY OF METHODS OF INSTRUCTION

Too frequently, teachers fail to use diverse methods of teaching mathematics. The same or similar methods are used over and over again. Thus, a teacher may lecture and explain each new lesson to pupils rather continuously for sequential days of instruction. The chalkboard might be the major material of instruction used here. Would pupils in most cases become bored in these situations. Why not change methodology in teaching so that pupils are more attentive and achieve more optimally?

There are numerous methods of teaching that may be used. Learning by discovery has many advantages in its use. Pupils individually or in committees may discover on their own answers and procedures to problem solving in mathematics. The teacher then asks questions and probes so that pupils find out on their own, rather than the teacher lecturing/explaining how to proceed in securing an answer to a problem. Pupils tend to be fascinated in learning by discovery and finding out on their own. Higher levels of cognition are stressed in these types of learning activities.

Much has been written pertaining to mathematics anxiety on the part of women in the public schools as well as in higher education. A hypothesis to examine is if discovery learning assists in minimizing anxiety in mathematics. Each pupil needs to learn as much as possible in terms of knowledge, skills, and positive attitudes in ongoing lessons and units of study in mathematics.

Somewhat toward the other end of the discovery learning continuum is a hierarchical approach in teachers teaching mathematics. In a hierarchical manner, the teacher determines the objectives for pupil achievement which includes state mandated objectives. He/she decides upon the sequence or order of learning opportunities for pupils in mathematics. Additionally, the mathematics teacher here decides upon which evaluation techniques to use to determine pupil progress.

The writer believes strongly that pupils should be involved in determining which objectives to achieve in mathematics. Learners also need to have a voice in which learning opportunities need to be emphasized as well as appraisals procedures to use in the appraising process. Why should pupils be involved in decision-making?

1. Life consists of deciding between and among alternatives. Thus, learners need to have opportunities to make choices from among alternatives.
2. Pupils need to become increasingly independent as they progress through the public school years of schooling. There is no other alternative since parents become older and eventually have to cease having control over their offspring. Pupils continually and gradually need to lean upon themselves for ideas, problem solving, and responsibility.
3. Higher levels of cognition involving critical and creative thinking as well as problem solving very frequently go along with decision - making skills.

There are numerous ways in which pupils can be involved in determining the mathematics curriculum. These include the following:

1. planning with the teacher, what to complete for enrichment/ extra credit work.
2. deciding with teacher guidance what needs to be retaught, reviewed, as well as remediate in terms of subject matter taught previously.
3. working problems using diverse algorithms. The algorithm decided upon works best for the involved learner.
4. choosing sequential tasks to complete when using learning centers in mathematics in the classroom.
5. selecting from among alternatives, for example, as to which problems to complete when the teacher stresses that any five out of eight problems needs to be finished.

Pupils differ from each other in numerous ways such as in interests, abilities, achievement, and learning styles. The mathematics teacher then needs to make provisions so that each pupil learns as much as possible. Thus, selected learners may learn more through a teacher/ pupil planned curriculum than using other approaches.

The interdisciplinary curriculum is receiving much emphasis in printed educational materials a swell as to teacher education conventions. Thus, the teacher may organize the curriculum in terms of teaching arithmetic largely in ongoing lessons and units of study. A separated subjects curriculum is then in evidence. Certainly, higher levels of cognition such as cortical and creative thinking as well as problem solving may be emphasized in a separate subjects curriculum. With higher levels of cognition, the chances are that geometry and algebra will increasingly be included in the mathematics curriculum, resulting in a correlated or fused curriculum. Adding in an integrated manner, probability and statistics, graphing, and trigonometry, among others, goes beyond the correlated mathematics curriculum and may be called the broad fields design for instruction if taught in a related manner, not as separate subjects. The interdisciplinary curriculum goes beyond the broad fields curriculum and might include science, social studies, the fine arts, and physical education. Mathematics may well be the language of science since the latter stresses precision and accuracy of measurement.

Among items, the student teachers and co-operating teachers stressed:

1. Pupils determining the distance around the walled city of Jerusalem in the English as well as the metric system of measurement. This distance was related to some landmark near to the local school.
2. Pupils finding a city or other area eighteen miles form the local school in comparing Jerusalem and Jericho which are the dame distance apart.
3. Pupils comparing elevations among selected cities in the United States. This was compared with the elevation differences between Jerusalem and Jericho, 2,500 feet above sea level and 800 feet below sea level respectively.

Pupils might also study the Roman and Egyptian system of numeration as examples in relating history in the social studies with mathematics. There numerous questions that need to be asked pertaining to the interdisciplinary mathematics curriculum. These are the following:

1. How much of the interdisciplinary/integrated curriculum should one emphasize in mathematics. To be sure the language arts areas of listening, speaking, reading, and writing are an inherent part of the mathematics curriculum. These area of the language arts are musts in mathematics and cannot be omitted. NCTM (1989, page 78) Standards That Pertain to Communication, Reasoning, and Connections emphasize the following, among others, for grades five through eight.

*1. model situations using oral, written, concrete, pictorial, graphical, and algebraic methods;
*2. reflect and clarify their own thinking about mathematical ideas and situations;
*3. develop common understandings of mathematical ideas, including the role of definitions;
*4. use the skills of reading, listening, and viewing to interpret and evaluate mathematical ideas;
*5. discuss mathematical ideas and make conjectures and convincing arguments;
*6. appreciate the value of mathematics notation and role in the development of mathematical ideas.

Teachers should place high priority upon pupil communicating ideas in mathematics. Thus, pupils are able to listen carefully to ongoing expression of ideas in mathematics. Learners need to listen for diverse purposes such as listening for directions, sequence of subject matter presented, facts, concepts, generalizations, main ideas, processes and solutions to problems, as well as critical and creative listening. In the area of oral communication, learners should speak clearly and accurately. They need to be able to explain a process or procedure with meaning and understanding. It is important to convey specifics, conclusions, applications, unique ideas, and analytical content to others in school and in society. The importance of quality oral communication can not be over emphasized. Listening is related directly to oral communication when interacting with others in the mathematics curriculum. In the area of reading mathematical content, pupils should learn to read fluently and independently. The skills of phonics, syllabication, structural analysis, use of picture and context cluses are important in mathematics. Learners need to understand content read so that progress and achievement are continuous and optimal. Reading to obtain knowledge and meaning in mathematics, as well as be able to use information secured are salient goals in mathematics. Also, pupils need to become analytical readers, interpreting content in novel ways. Learners should be able to appraise subject matter read. Realizing the worth and value of subject matter in problem solving is salient. The reading of symbols such as +,–,×, among others presents subject matter that truly is unique to the mathematics curriculum.

Being able to write legibly to communicate ideas clearly is very necessary for achievement in mathematics. Legibility in writing numerals, operation signs, words, and sentences as well as paragraphs are salient goals to achieve for all pupils in mathematics. Proper spacing, alignment, proportion of letters and symbols, and neatness of work must become a part of the repertoire of each pupil. Clarity in communication of ideas in mathematics is important if pupils are to become proficient in critical and creative thinking as well as problem solving.

Pertaining to correlating language arts and mathematics, Kolstad and Briggs (1996) wrote the following:

> *Research on including reading, writing, and oral language in maths is very positive. Not only do the students benefit as mathematicians, they develop as readers, writers, and speakers from the additional opportunities to practice these skills. Practicing language arts skills across the curriculum is in line with the whole language movement, as well as with the integrated curriculum approach. The benefits of including literature and reading experiences throughout the curriculum have been expanded upon by whole language researcher. Research by Grossman, Smith, and Miller (1993) and Evans (1994) strongly supports the benefits of using writing for improving student performance in mathematics. In order to uphold the NCTM recommendations, students must learn to communicate mathematically, in writing and through oral language (Capps and Pickreign, 1993).*

Research supports the benefits of incorporating reading, writing, and oral language into mathematics instruction to help students convey mathematical information in familiar words and to assist them with their thinking processes, as they work through math calculations and problem solving situations. Another reason writing is a valuable asset in mathematics instruction is that the teacher is better able to evaluate students' understanding of math concepts and processes based upon what the children have written. A teacher can also evaluate students by what they say. By including oral language activities in math lessons, students' abilities to communicate mathematically will improve. Thus, a teacher will be better able to evaluate and clarify students; thought processes, while building student's confidence in their own abilities to discuss mathematics. Therefore, based upon the many benefits and the number of emerging strategies for implementing language arts into mathematics, the teacher should begin incorporating reading, writing, and oral language activities into mathematics lessons on a regular basis.

Despite the valuable strategies and teaching techniques now being used, more research needs to be conducted on the benefits of incorporating language arts into the math curriculum and teachers need more suggestions and additional resources to ensure the success of a language-rich math program.

## RESPONSIBILITY OF THE TEACHER

Mathematics teachers have salient responsibilities if pupils are to attain vital objectives of instruction. Pertaining to being model teachers in the classroom, they should stress (Ediger, 1994):

1. meaningful lessons and units of study. With meaning, pupils understand and comprehend that which was contained in ongoing learning opportunities.
2. interesting content and skills in the curriculum. With interest, the pupil and the curriculum become one, not separate entities. Pupils should attend and achieve form ongoing lessons and units of study.
3. purpose in learning. With purpose for learning, pupils accept reasons for attaining relevant facts, concepts, and

generalizations presented. Purpose development by the teacher may take little time indeed. With education, the teacher explains clearly and concisely why pupils should achieve the objectives to be stressed. With inductive approaches, the teacher raises a few questions about the new lesson whereby the pupil responds and perceives purpose and reasons for learning. Extrinsic rewards can be emphasized. Here, the teacher announces prizes and awards that pupils can secure if they attain the objectives of the lesson. Pupils need to know precisely what is to be learned to obtain the rewards.

4. sequence in learning. with quality sequence, pupils relate newly acquired information with that previously achieved. Previous knowledge attained provides readiness for the new objectives to be achieve. Pupils need guidance to perceive relationship of knowledge in teaching- learning situations.
5. balance among objectives stressed. Thus, knowledge, skills, and attitudes—three kinds of objectives need to be achieved by students. These objectives interact and are not in isolation from each other. For example, if pupils possess positive attitudes, they should achieve needed knowledge and skills more readily.

## REFERENCES

Bhaskara Rao, Digumarti, ed. (1996). Encyclopaedia of Education for All, 5 vols. New Delhi; APH Publishing Corporation.

Bhaskara Rao, Digumarti and Digumarti Pushpa Latha, eds. (1998). International Encyclopaedia of Women, 5 Vols., New Discovery Publishing House.

Brubacher, John S. (1966), *A History of the Problems of Education*, New York; McGraw Hill Book Company, Second Edition, 16.

Capps. L.R. and J. Pickreign (1993), Language Connections in Mathematics : A Critical Part of Mathematics Instruction, *Arithmetic Teacher*, 41, 8-12.

Ediger, Marlow (1994), Early Field Experiences in Teacher Education, *College Student Journal*, 28, 302.

Evans, C.S. (1984), Writing to Learn in math, *Language Arts*, 61, 828-35.

Kolstad, Rosemaire, and L.D. Briggs (1996), Incorporating Language Arts Into The Mathematics Curriculum : A Literature Survey, Education, 116:431.

National Education Association (1918), Commission on the Reorganization of Secondary Education, *The cardinal Principles of Secondary Education,* US Bureau of Education Bulletin, 35.

National Council Teachers of Mathematics (1989), *Curriculum and Evaluation Standards for School Mathematics,* Reston, Virginia ; NCTM, NCTM (1989), 78.

Reys, Robert L, Marilyn N. Sudydam, and Mary Montgomery Lindquist (1995), *Helping Children Learn Mathematics,* Fourth edition, Boston; Allyn and Bacon, Page 3.

# Chapter 18

# PSYCHOLOGICAL FOUNDATIONS IN TEACHING MATHEMATICS

Mathematics teachers need to study diverse psychologies of learning for use so that individual learners may be guided to attain as optimally as possible. With a thorough knowledge of the psychology of learning, teachers may do a better job of teaching mathematics to pupils of all ability levels. Individual differences among learners must be provided for in order that each pupil may learn as much mathematics as possible. A quality mathematics teacher emphasizes objectives, learning opportunities, and appraisal procedures that assist pupils individually to perceive meaning in the mathematics curriculum.

## MEANING THEORY IN TEACHING MATHEMATICS

Mathematics teachers need to be certain that each pupil attaches meaning to facts, concepts, and generalizations acquired in the curriculum. With meaningful subject matter, pupils may understand that which was taught. Understanding content presented in mathematics assists the pupil to clarify information. Clarity of understanding stress that pupils comprehend subject matter presented. In deductive teaching, the teacher explains each fact, concept, and generalization so that meaningful learning may accrue. When induction as method of instruction is used, the mathematics teacher asks numerous questions of pupils to receive answers and feedback if they understand what was taught. Teachers must spend adequate time for depth instruction in guiding pupils to perceive meaning, deductively and inductively, through the use of concrete, semiconcrete, and abstract materials of instruction in terms of content taught.

Directly related to pupils attaching meaning to ongoing content presented, leaner must be able to use subject matter acquired. If subject matter acquired is used, the chances are it will be retained better than if it were not used. The teacher should assist pupils to apply facts, concepts, and generalizations acquired. Thus, information can be used in solving word problems from the basal textbook used in the classroom. Pupils may also use previously acquired content when solving life-like problems in mathematics. The teacher might write problems and photocopy then for learners to respond to. These problems are directly related to what has been taught in ongoing lessons and units in mathematics. learners too may write problems and exchange papers with others to solve each problem so that application can be made of what has been learned previously. Discussions led by the teacher can also get pupils wholeheartedly involved in making use of subject matter learned.

The mathematics teacher needs to guide learners to engage in higher levels of cognition when using meaningful materials for learners. Thus, pupils need to have opportunities to engage in critical thinking. In separating the relevant from the irrelevant in working to secure answers to a word problem in mathematics involves critical thought. A separation then of what is salient as compared to that which is not important is necessary in critical thinking. That which is significant is then used to obtain an answer to a word problem contained in the basal or written by the teacher or a learner. Life in society demands that pupils become proficient now and in the future as an adult in the area of critical thought. Separating reality form fantasy and the real from that which is imaginary are necessary ingredients in critical thinking.

Novel solutions are needed to solve numerous problems. Creative thinking then needs adequate emphasis in the mathematics curriculum. For example, to solve a word problem, several algorithms may be used to arrive at an answer. Each algorithm might well provide the correct answer. Learners should become familiar with diversity involved here so that the algorithm that works best for the pupil may be used. Unique solutions to word problems should assist pupils to explore different options to each problem in the societal arena. Hopefully, this transfer from the mathematics curriculum to the real world of society will be in evidence. In society, individuals meet up with unique situations in which solutions are needed that are different from any solution used in the past.

Life-like problems actually faced by learners in mathematics need adequate emphasis in the curriculum. These problems involve buying and selling items, how to stay within one's own budget, as well as an increased use of mathematics in society emphasize problem solving involving reality. A creative mind may be necessary presently for the pupil as well as in the future to solve these problems involving mathematics. Creative thinking must be a definite goal in the mathematics curriculum. Critical thought is also necessary for pupils in solving life-like problems in mathematics. Comparing solutions in answer to a problem certainly stresses critical thought. Further situations involving critical thought emphasizes analyzing a problem in mathematics to study component parts. After comparing and analyzing possible solutions in dealing with problems in mathematics in the real world, a synthesis is needed. To synthesize, creative thinking again is in evidence. Synthesizing emphasizes securing wholeness in coming up with a solution to a problem area. Steps inherent in solving life-like problems (or word problems) in mathematics include the following:

1. defining the problem whereby clarity is in evidence.
2. gathering information in arriving at a tentative solution.
3. developing a hypothesis based on the acquired information.
4. testing the hypothesis in step three above.
5. revising the hypothesis, if needed.

In addition to pupils attaching meaning to what has been learned, applying that which has been learned, and engaging in higher levels of cognition, pupils also need to perceive purpose in learning in ongoing lessons and units off study in mathematics. There are selected approaches which can be used by the mathematics teacher to guide pupils to perceive purpose for achieving. A deductive procedure might be used. With deduction, the mathematics teacher explains to learners why the subject matter to be studied is relevant. I believe that the small amount of time needed to explain to learners why the subject matter to be acquired is salient is time well spent in teaching and learning situations. Instead of a deductive approach in guiding pupils to perceive purpose or reasons for learning, there are teachers who prefer an inductive approach. Here, the mathematics teacher asks questions of pupils as to why they believe the content to be studied is relevant to learn. Inductive procedures are more time consuming as compared to deduction since responses must come form learners when determining the relevance in studying vital facts, concepts, and generalizations in mathematics.

A third approach in guiding pupils to perceive purpose in learning is to use extrinsic rewards. Here, the mathematics teacher needs to announce prior to instruction what pupils are to learn as well as the reward that will accrue to learners if they achieve this goal. Rewards to be given might be inexpensive prizes, tokens to be exchanged for prizes, time given for a self selected activity, or extra recess time. The reward must motivate pupils to achieve more optimally in mathematics. It is given to pupils only if they have attained a goal announced by the teacher prior to lesson presentation. The amount of learning that must be acquired before the pupil secures the reward is a motivator for the learner. Receiving the reward for goal attainment is a reinforcer to encourage similar future behaviour.

Interest is a powerful factor in learning. The mathematics teacher needs to obtain the attention of all learners during teaching-learning situations. To demand attention of pupils does not capture learner interest in mathematics. Rather, the teacher needs to use a variety of materials in teaching mathematics to obtain intrinsic interests of learners. These activities include lifelike problems which need solution, textbook and workbook assignments, films, slides, video tapes, video disks, illustrations, teaching aids, technology, integrated learning systems, teaching units, as well as resource units of study in mathematics. In using a variety of learning activities, the mathematics teacher has a better chance in securing learner interest as compared to a single type of material. The tone of the teacher's voice must have appropriate voice inflection, pitch, and juncture. A monotonous tone of voice will not tend to obtain learner interest and attention. Quality eye contact with pupils should aid in obtaining pupil attention and promote learning in mathematics. Interest of pupils in ongoing lessons and units of study develops effort for achieving.

## THEORIES OF LEARNING IN MATHEMATICS

Selected theories of learning in educational psychology used by the teacher should assist pupils to attain at a more optimal level. Operant conditioning, as developed by B.F. Skinner (1904-1988), has done much as a theory of learning to guide learner progress. Dr. Skinner stressed the use of programmed learning in emphasizing behaviourism as a psychology of learning. Here, a qualified programmer would determine what pupils are to learn in any unit of study in mathematics. The body of knowledge within the unit is broken down into component parts. The steps of attainment are very small when working on a program in mathematics, be it in textbook or software form. The pupil, here, generally reads a sentence or two, depending on the maturity level of the involved learner. He/she then views a related illustration, responds to a test item, and checks the response. If correct, the pupil is rewarded. If incorrect, the pupil now knows the correct answer and is also ready for the next sequential programmed item. The program has been tried out previously in pilot studies with needed modifications made. The content to follow in each program moves from the simple to the increasingly more complex. The same procedure, or a slight modification, may follow in each step of learning such as read a sentence or more, view an illustration, respond to a test item, and check the correctness of the response as provided by the programmer. Answers given by the learner are either correct or incorrect. By being correct approximately 90 per cent of the time in responding, the pupil can make continuous progress with increasingly complex items in programmed learning. A positive self concept could be an end result for pupils if they respond with an approximate 90 per cent correct in terms of accuracy. Tutorial programs using computers tend to stress tenets of programmed instruction. Simulation in computer use may also stress programmed learning, providing it is not too open ended in its subject matter presentation. B.F. Skinner believed strongly in answers being either right or wrong when learners make responses. Shankaranarayana wrote:

> *For Skinner (1969), " teaching is an arrangement of contingencies of reinforcement which expedite learning." Skinner believes that promotion of learning is possible by giving attention to the*

*following factors: the behaviour that is to be learned, the reinforcers that may be used, and the scheduling of reinforcers.*

*Skinner recommends the use of programmed instruction which provides for individual differences by allowing students to achieve at their own rate of speed. In terms of Skinner' operant behaviourism, "a program can be seen as an arrangement of material that will lead students to emit correct responses and will also provide reinforcement for that response. The essential elements of programmed instruction ... are (1) an ordered sequence of stimuli, (2) specific student response, (3) immediate knowledge of results, (4) small steps, (5) minimum errors, (6) gradual shaping of terminal behaviour, and (7) self pacing.*

B.F. Skinner has a well known and popular name in education. His experiments in teaching and education have indeed been numerous. Morris and Pai (1976) wrote the following:

*As Skinner has pointed out several times, the most important task of the teacher is to arrange conditions under which desired learning can occur. Considering the fact that teachers are to bring about changes in extremely complex behaviour, they should be specialists in human behaviour. Effective and efficient manipulation of the multitude of variables affecting children's intellectual and social behaviours cannot be accomplished by trial and error alone, nor should such work be based solely on the personal experiences of the teacher, since this covers only a limited range of circumstances. Consequently, a scientific study of human behaviour is vital in the improvement of teaching, because it provides us with accurate and reliable knowledge about learning and leads to the development of new instructional materials, methods, and techniques. Similarly, an empirical analysis of the teaching process is essential, for it clarifies the teacher's responsibility through a series of small and progressive approximations. This approach makes teaching practices more specific, thereby facilitating a more effective evaluation.*

## JAMES POPHAM AND BEHAVIOURISM

James Popham from the University of California is a strong advocate of behaviourism. Popham developed a series of filmstrips and related cassette tapes proposing behaviourism as a needed central theme of teaching and learning. Behaviourists believe strongly in the use of measurably stated objectives in teaching pupils. These precise objectives are written prior to teaching learners. Ideally, there is no leeway in determining what will be taught when viewing the written statement of objectives. The teacher then is certain as to what will be taught. He/she may announce to pupils that which will be taught before teaching and learning. Pupils then know what is required of them in terms of subject matter to be acquired. Learners need not out guess the teacher to realize what is expected as to precise objectives to be achieved.

According to Popham, the learning opportunities chosen by the teacher must contain only that which is in the stated objective(s), no more and no less. Evaluation of pupil attainment in mathematics needs to be done in terms of the measurably stated objectives. Thus, a very close alignment indeed is in the offing among the objectives, the learning opportunities, and the evaluation procedures. Validity, a measurement term, is in evidence if the evaluation techniques harmonize with the stated objectives in mathematics.

James Popham with his stress placed upon behaviourism as a psychology of instruction in teaching mathematics advocates the following:

1. vague hazy objectives need to be eliminated or rewritten so that a sharp focus exists in terms of what will be taught.
2. learning opportunities must be very carefully chosen since each needs to guide pupils to attain that which is in the stated objective.
3. evaluation procedures should ascertain if each pupil has attained the precise objectives.
5. sequence of objectives is arranged by the mathematics teacher.

Popham places extremely strong emphasis upon choosing precise, measurable stated objectives for instruction. He places little stress upon choosing learning opportunities, except that they should match up very precisely with the stated objectives. Evaluation is done strictly in terms of what is mentioned specifically in each objective for pupil attainment.

## ROBERT GAGNE AND TASK ANALYSIS OF OBJECTIVES

Robert Gagne (1984) is a leading psychologist in education who recommends a behaviouristic approach in teaching; however, his thinking is more open-ended as compared to Skinner and Popham. Gagne's eight sequential steps of hierarchical learning for pupils may be of considerable help to teachers in planning the mathematics curriculum. The eight steps of sequential learning for pupils are the following: signal learning, stimulus- response, chaining, verbal association learning, multiple discrimination, concept learning, rule learning, and problem solving as being the most complex form of achievement. Gagne was a former mathematics instructor and found task analysis as being a very appropriate way of determining sequence for pupils. We will comment on a few of the levels we believe to be especially relevant in teaching. Stimulus-response psychology is very relevant for mathematics teachers to consider. For example, once pupils attach meaning through the use of manipulative materials that 7+6 and 6+7 = 13, this addition fact may be committed to memory. Thus, on a flash card or computer program the stimulus is 7+6 or 6+7 = ... If correct, pupils should respond with the answer being 13. Drill and practice should not be used prior to meaningful learning by pupils. But, once meaning is there, pupils may need to associate the stimulus and the response in a somewhat rote manner. Gagne's step of chaining might involve pupils using a series of concrete and semiconcrete materials to indicate and show that 7+6 and 6+7 = 13. Which materials might these be? Sticks, corn and bean seeds, paper squares, and buttons, among other items, may be used by the learner in sequence to show a set of seven and set of six and by joining the two sets together obtain a set of thirteen markers. The commutative property may also be shown by a learner. Chaining is involved in that the pupil used diverse materials to show the value of two addends. Multiple discrimination, in the Gagne' hierarchy of objectives stresses pupils noticing differences and likenesses in ongoing lessons and units of study. Analysis is involved here in that pupils separate the relevant from the irrelevant such as in seeking solutions to story or word problems. To do so indicated the need to make separations from what is needed to what is unnecessary. We believe the last three terms used by Gagne are very significant in planning the mathematics curriculum. Thus, concept learning is very relevant. It takes a variety of learning opportunities using different materials of instruction for pupils to understand concepts such as addition, subtraction, multiplication, division, inverse operation, radius, radius squared, radius cubed, and exponents. Understanding concepts are needed on the pupil's part in order that sequential achievement is possible in mathematics.

Gagne's principle or rule learning indicates that learners related concepts so they become usable. A rule or principle such as "to find the area of a circle, square the radius and multiple by the vale of *pi*" is necessary in a specific situation; otherwise pupils could not ascertain the area of a circle. The last idea in Gagne's hierarchy is problem solving. Thus, principles or rules are needed to understand how to solve the problem of determining the area of a square, triangle, or parallelogram.

A strong point in Gagne's hierarchy of objectives is that the teacher needs to go back a step or level if a pupil does not understand what is to be done. For example, if a pupils cannot solve a problem, perhaps he/she does not attach meaning to the involved rule or principle. If the rule or principle is a stumbling block to the pupils progress, he/she may need to go back to learning the meaning of the inherent concepts within the rule or principle.

## JEROME BRUNER AND THE STRUCTURE OF KNOWLEDGE IN MATHEMATICS

Jerome Bruner, professor from Harvard University, advocated a structure of knowledge approach in teaching mathematics. The structural ideas in mathematics would be identified by professional mathematicians in their academic area of specialty. These professional mathematicians then choose key or main ideas for pupil attainment. The structural ideas may be used again and again by learners as they proceed to more complex learnings on sequential grade levels. In mathematics then pupils may attain the following in increased levels of complexity:

1. commutative and associative properties of addition and multiplication.
2. distributive property of multiplication over addition.
3. property of closure.
4. subtraction as the inverse operation of addition.
5. division as the inverse operation of multiplication.

The above examples of structural ideas can be emphasized on sequential grade levels at increasing levels of complexity. For example, first grade pupils may learn that 4+3 = 7 and 3+4 = 7; this stresses the commutative property of addition. At a higher grade level, fifth grade pupils may learn meaningfully that 18,996 + 38, 649 = 38,469+18,996.

Jerome Bruner stressed the use of three kinds of materials in teaching mathematics to pupils. In sequence, these would be enactive, iconic, and symbolic. Enactive materials emphasize the use of concrete materials and other objects for learner manipulation in a hands on approach in learning. Second, pupils learn through the use of iconic materials which include pictures, illustrations, video tapes, video discus, slides, filmstrips, and other audio visual aids. Third, Bruner stresses the use of symbolic materials, such as printed content in textbooks, library books, and other abstract content. This sequence in pupil learning then emphasizes the teacher using concrete, semiconcrete, and abstract materials in teaching.

Jerome Bruner advocates the use of inductive methods of instruction in which pupils discover structural or major academic ideas of a discipline. To emphasize Bruner's approach in teaching, the teacher should attend to the following:

1. The teacher needs to have an excellent knowledge of the structure of knowledge since these key ideas become objectives for learner attainment.

2. To achieve objectives on the pupils' part, the teacher needs to sequence learning opportunities in that individuals experience the enactive, the iconic, and the symbolic in that order.
3. The teacher must appraise pupils to ascertain how many of structural knowledge objectives are being attained by pupils in a spiral curriculum. With a spiral curriculum, pupils meet up again and again in increasing levels of complexity the structural ideas which serve as objectives of instruction.
4. The teacher needs to become a quality asker of questions involving the ongoing mathematics lesson so that pupils can truly learn in an inductive manner. Inductive teaching then assists pupils to achieve the structural ideas.
5. Inductive teaching in mathematics must be used together with the enactive, iconic, and symbolic materials of instruction.

## JEAN PIAGET AND DEVELOPMENTAL PSYCHOLOGY IN MATHEMATICS

Jean Piaget studied pupils in clinical settings for over forty years in Switzerland. He identified different stages that pupils go through in the maturation process. The first stage called the Sensorimotor Stage occurs from birth to two years in the infant's life. Here, parents need to have objects for the young child to manipulate and edxperience in a friendly environment. The child then experiences and perceives objects such as toys in the real environment. He/she may touch, smell, and see the objects. Listening to sounds made by these objects is also salient in sensorimotor learning.

The preoperational stage of development of the child roughly occurs from ages two to seven years. Here, the young child perceives one variable largely. Thus, the preoperational child when viewing two tumblers of the same brand name and size as having an equal amount of water in each, if this is the case. Now, in front of the child, one of the two tumblers of water is poured into a taller thinner tumbler. The child is asked which has more water inside the tumbler. The preoperational pupil will answer the taller thinner tumbler does. The child perceives one variable in that one tumbler is taller than the other and therefore contains more water. If two spheres of clay are held in front of the preoperational child and both are identical in amount, the child say neither has more clay in it than the other. But, if the experiementer flattens one sphere in front of the child, he/she will say that the flattened clay has more in it than does the sphere of clay. Again, the preoperational child perceives one variable only and that being the flattened piece of clay is longer than the spherical lump of clay. Teachers of kindergarten and first grade pupils need to be aware that preoperational pupils lack maturation to notice that there is more than one variable to objects being observed. Preoperational pupils are perceptionally oriented. How something looks to the child is the correct perception or view. They tend to center on one variable such as the larger the area that one of two sets of marbles is placed in, even though both sets have an equal number of marbles, the larger the number of members of that set in the enlarged area. Thus, if a set of six marbles is placed in a larger area, it will have more marbles than a set of six placed in a smaller region.

From ages seven through eleven, Piaget, in his research, found that these learners still needed concrete objects to learn from. Piaget called this the stage of concrete operations. Here, the learner has matured to emphasize reversibility. Thus, the pupil may notice that the order of addends can be changed and yet the sum stays the same. Or, the concrete operations pupil learns that there are number families such as 7+5 = 12 and 5+7 = 12, which can be undone through subtraction within that number family such as 12–5=7 and 12–7=5. Reversibility also indicates that one can go back to an earlier stage of working on a project or activity and come back to the original starting point. One may go back (reversibility) to an earlier stage in unit teaching to further analyse what was done. One can also reverse to the original stage prior to emphasizing reversibility. Thus, the concrete operations development pupils may perceive several variables when reversibility is in evidence.

Additive composition is also a part of the learner's stage of concrete operations. With additive composition, the pupil in perceiving numerous variables, may define, for example, what the identity elements are for addition and multiplication. There are numerous descriptions which can be given in the definition indicating again the pupil's ability to focus on several items at one time. All the definitions possible add up to a sum pertaining to the identity elements for addition and multiplication.

The principle of associativity is also a part of the concept the stage of concrete operations. With associativity, the pupil can add three or more numbers in any order. Or three or more factors may be multiplied in any order and the product is the same. Many tasks may also be taken up in any order and the results are the same or similar. In all facets of the pupil being in the stage of concrete operations, the teacher still needs to refer to and use concrete materials along with the abstract being emphasized.

At about twelve years of age, pupils enter the stage of formal operations. At the stage of formal operations, learners might be able to think abstractly in mathematics without reference to concrete materials of instruction. Learners in all stages of development need to operate or focus on what is being learned for learning to really take place.

There are numerous implications for teaching mathematics when using Piaget's research in teaching-learning situations. These include the following:

1. The teacher must study the maturational levels of pupils in order to know what and how to teach these learners.
2. There can be much wasting of time in teaching what the maturational level of the involved pupil is not ready for. Then too, the teacher must teach what the maturational level of the pupil is ready for in mathematics. Otherwise time slips by without the learner attaining as much as possible.
3. Hastening the readiness of a pupil for learning mathematics does not work. The maturational level will indicate what can/cannot be taught.
4. There needs to be an adequate amount of concrete materials available for teaching since through the age of eleven, the stage of concrete operations is still in the offing.
5. Securing attention for learning is salient since learners do not achieve unless they mentally operate upon the content being presented.

According to Piaget and Imhelder (1969), there are definite factors that impinge upon pupils as they progress in intellectual development. These are biological maturation; interaction with experiences in the natural environment; social activities; and homeostasis, a balance between the self and experiences in the physical environment.

Biological maturation stresses pupils going through the stages of sensorimotor, preoperational, concrete operations, and formal thought. However, there are factors that influence these stages of biological maturation. One factor is pupils interacting with the natural environment. The richness of experiences here has much to do with learners developing biologically. Thus, a stimulating environment in mathematics definitely affects progression in biological development. Working with others or being in groups that stress collegiality and its influence on both biological and the affects of the natural environment. Certainly, pupils learn much from each other pertaining to the world of mathematics. In supervising student teachers and co-operating teachers, we notice how pupils might affect each other very positively in ongoing lessons and units in mathematics. For example, in one class it was difficult for a pupil to understand and attach meaning to why the divisor is inverted and multiplication is stressed in the division of fractions. When this pupil and three others worked together in co-operative learning, one pupil made it very clear as to why the divisor is inverted and then multiplication occurs in the division of fractions.

Homeostasis emphasizes feelings of satisfaction that a solution has been found to a problem. Thus, there is balance between the individual and his/her environment. Equilibration has then occurred. In the previous example, when a learner understood what is involved when fractions are divided with the "Invert the divisor and multiply" rule, the pupil also has reached a state of homeostasis at that point. Homeostasis may be followed again by a desire to know a new fact, concept, and/ or generalization. A good teacher will guide pupils to reach a state of disequilibrium so that an inward desire to learn is involved to seek new information and subject matter.

Piaget emphasizes that what is learned is grouped together in schemes. These schemes provide key ideas upon which future learning of the pupil is based. Schemes are also called structural ideas. Structural ideas or schemes are patterns of behaviour of the individual. The pupil who has been actively involved in learning that 6+4 = 10, may now use these learnings to achieve the new to be stressed such as 6+5=.. and 5+6=... New content might then fit into the older pre existing structures. In other words, previous content acquired in mathematics now sets the stage to learn more of higher decade addition. The involved process is called assimilation. There had to be accommodation so that the old and the new content might be blended.

Piaget (1971) continually emphasizes active involvement of the learner in the mathematics curriculum when writing the following:

> *If we desire... to form individuals capable of inventive thought and of helping the society of tomorrow to achieve progress, then it is clear that an education which is an active discovery of reality is superior to one that consists merely in providing the young with ready made wills to will with and ready made truths to know with.*

## JOHN DEWEY AND PROBLEM SOLVING IN UTILITARIAN SITUATIONS

John Dewey (1859-1952) advocated a utilitarian mathematics curriculum in which school and society would be related. Thus, what is useful in society should provide the basis for the school curriculum. Thus, in mathematics, pupils with teacher assistance identify a problem area. The problem is significant to the learner. He/she feels a definite need to find needed solutions. The problem then must be adequately delimited so that an answer can be found. Data or information is acquired in answer to the identified problem. The answer is tentative and subject to change due to further testing of the results. John Dewey did not consider textbook problems as being lifelike and reality based. Predetermined questions raised by the teacher and objectives written prior to instruction for pupils to attain do not stress problem solving. Rather within context in an ongoing unit of study preferably, the learner or a committee of pupils choose a problem in mathematics which is vital to solve. This is a practical problem to solve which emphasizes being useful and stresses application of content/skills acquired (Ediger, 1997).

Problem solving the emphasizes the useful and the utilitarian in the pupil's life in the school setting. Mathematics is a curriculum area that can truly emphasize that which is functional. Thus, situations such as the following may stress a practical mathematics curriculum with problem solving involved:

1. measuring ingredients for a representative food dish of a foreign nation being studied in social studies.
2. planning and preparing a holiday meal in school whereby each pupil brings a certain amount of a food item.
3. averaging scores of the number of words spelled correctly by a pupil from six sequential weeks of spelling test scores.
4. developing a line graph from pupils individual birth dates in a calendar year.
5. operating a simulated supermarket in the classroom using real or toy money.

The above are merely suggestions for a reality based mathematics curriculum. One needs to remember that John Dewey advocated that problems come from pupils and not from an extrinsic source. The teacher guides learners in selecting and solving problems. John Dewey believed that pupils liked to work on committees rather than individually in solving problems. Learners, too, desired to find out on their own instead of being told how to locate an answer. Pupils were to be active, not passive recipients of knowledge. Creative behaviour is preferred much more so as compared to conformity endeavours.

In summarizing John Dewey's problem solving approach in teaching pupils, the following are salient points:

1. Activity centered approaches are emphasized in teaching in that pupils are the focal point of the curriculum.
2. Mathematics stresses that pupils with teacher guidance select relevant lifelike problems which need solving.
3. A learning by doing, not passivity on the part of pupils, is a must for learning to accrue in mathematics.
4. Purpose and interest on the learner's part make for learner effort and perseverance in solving problems.
5. The role of the teacher is to encourage, help, and assist pupils in attaining solutions to problems.

## CONCLUSION

There are numerous psychologists who may provide teachers with guidance in teaching mathematics. B.F. Skinner advocated a highly structured curriculum in which pupils would make few errors when achieving objectives arranged in an ascending order of difficulty. The programmer arranges the frames of learning in mathematics by using a sequence of read, view an illustration, respond, and check order. A psychology of behaviourism is emphasized here. Responses are either correct or incorrect as given by pupils individually.

James Popham believes in using measurement driven instruction (MDI) with the objectives stated behaviourally. The stated objectives leave no leeway for interpretation. The mathematics teacher then provides learning opportunities which contain only that which is in the stated objective. Appraisal is done in terms of the stated objective to determine if learners individually have been successful achievers.

Robert Gaggne emphasizes a hierarchical arrangement of teacher written objectives whereby the learner attains each in ascending order of complexity. Should an objective in mathematics be too difficult to achieve, the teacher needs to assist pupils individually to go back to a previous goal so that background information may have been attained. Then, the pupil should be ready sequentially to achieve the original objective. We will review the last three objectives Gagne stressed in curriculum development. These are in sequence: concept development, attaining generalizations, and solving a problem, by the learner. The mathematics teacher writes the objectives for pupil achievement. Gagne, a former mathematics teacher, found that the teacher needed to go back tr an earlier level of achievement if a pupil could not attain the preset objective being stressed in the curriculum. Thus, if a learner did not understand how to solve a mathematics problem, he/she might need to go back to studying the related generalization that is inherent in the problem. Should the learner not understand the generalization, he/she may need to study the related concept(s). Once the concept(s) are understood, the pupil is ready to be taught the related generalization. If the generalization is meaningful, the involved pupil might then be ready to solve the problem. Robert Gagne emphasized going back to an earlier level of achievement if the pupil did not attach meaning to what is presently being taught. Sequence in learning mathematics is very important to Robert Gagne. All good teachers of mathematics prizes highly if content, skills, and attitudes are learned sequentially by learners. This may mean reversing to an earlier level of attainment if a pupil does not understand or comprehend that which is being taught presently. The sequence may also pertain to a learner being taught more complex subject matter in mathematics if presently the objectives have been achieved.

Robert Gagne advocated a hierarchy of objectives for pupils to attain in mathematics which meet the following standards:

1. The objectives are arranged so that each pupil may attain an appropriately ordered set of goals which move from the easier to those increasingly more complex.
2. The teacher may place another objective between two others if a pupil makes an error at that point.
3. The problems to be solved tend to be more abstract than those advocated by John Dewey.
4. The objectives are determined prior to instruction.
5. Quality sequence in mathematics makes for fewer learner errors when being engaged in a lesson or unit of study. The teacher sequences or orders the objectives for learner attainment.

Jerome Bruner emphasized that pupils on any grade level attain structural ideas in mathematics. mathematicians at the university level select and agree upon these ideas. The structural ideas are available to teachers who teach pupils. Inductively, pupils are to achieve these structural ideas on an increasingly difficult level as they progress through sequential levels of attainment.

Jean Piaget stressed the importance of pupils going through specific maturational levels such as the sensorimotor, preoperational, concrete, and abstract levels. Biological maturation is salient when teachers ascertain what should be taught to pupils. The stage of concrete operations, for example, has associativity as one of its subcategories. The associative properties of addition and multiplication, using concrete materials, should be taught at this stage (ages seven to eleven ) of learner development.

John Dewey advocated a problem solving approach in which pupils identify and solve problems. The problems are lifelike and practical. The useful and the utilitarian are emphasized. Dewey placed strong emphasis upon democracy as a way of life. Democracy then is more than a political system or a way of governing individuals. Democracy is a way of associating with others and a means of communication. It is a means of involving all who will be affected by a given decision (Dewey, 1916). Democratic means are needed to identify and solve problems. These problems need to be reality based and practical in the societal arenas. Pupils then need guidance to select and solve life-like problems in mathematics. To stress democracy in the school and classroom settings, learners should work co-operatively in problem solving endeavours in mathematics.

The teacher of mathematics needs to use a psychology of teaching which will guide the learner to achieve as optimally as possible. There are diverse psychologies available to provide guidance in helping pupils achieve, grow, and learn in mathematics. Pupils need to be able to use what has been acquired. Meaning is then attached to facts, concepts, and generalizations achieved in mathematics. The National Council Teachers of Mathematics in 1989 developed excellent criteria, goals, and objectives for pupils to achieve. These are listed in their book *Curriculum and Evaluation Standards for School Mathematics*. The psychologies discussed above may well be used to guide pupils in goal attainment from those listed in *Curriculum and Evaluation Standards for School Mathematics*.

## REFERENCES

Bhaskara Rao, Digumarti (1998), *Educational Psychology*, Guntur; Nagarjuna Publishers (in Telugu Language).

Bhaskara Rao, Digumarti, ed. (2000), *International Encyclopaedia of Science and Technology Education* , 11 Vols. New Delhi, Discovery Publishing House.

Dewey, John (1916), *Democracy and Education*, New York; The Macmillan Company.

Ediger, Marlow (1997), *Teaching Mathematics in the Elementary School,* Kirksville, Missouri; Simpson Publishing Company, 78-85.

Gagne', Robert (19y, 96–102.84), *The Conditions of Learning,* New York: Holt, Rinehart and Winston.

Morris, Van Cleve (1976), *Philosophy and the American School,* Boston; Houghton Mifflin Company, 340.

Piaget, Jean (1971), *Science of Education and the Psychology of the Child,* New York; Viking Press, 26.

Popham, James (1970), *Alternative Avenues to Educational Accountability: Appropriate Practice: Educational Objectives: Éstablishing Performance Levels: Modern Measurement Methods : Opening classroom structures: Selecting appropriate Objectives: and Teaching Units and Lessons Plans.* (These are filmstrips and related tapes on behaviourism as it applies to teaching and learning).

# Chapter 19

## SEQUENCE IN MATHEMATICS IN THE PRIMARY GRADES

Primary grade teachers need to assist pupils to achieve meaning in ongoing lessons and units of study. With meaning, pupils understand what is being taught. It does little good to teach pupils that which does not make sense and cannot be understood. Time is wasted in teaching mathematics in situations such as these. Time needs to be used wisely by the teacher in guiding pupils to attach meaning and understanding in content learned.

A definite sequence should then be in order for pupils to be successful learners. The primary grade teacher may use a logical mathematics curriculum. Here, he/she designs learning opportunities in which pupils achieve increasingly more complex objectives. Each step along the way in learning provides a scaffold for the next sequential objective to achieve. Achieved objectives by pupils provide criteria for the teacher to gauge his/her teaching effectiveness. Learning opportunities are arranged so that pupils individually and collaboratively might achieve stated objectives. The teacher arranges the order of objectives for pupil attainment as well as the order of learning opportunities for learners to experience. Meaning and understanding need to be in evidence for each objective that is attained as well as each sequential learning opportunity pursued. The teacher then devises a mathematics curriculum in which pupils experience sequence, success, and meaning in mathematics.

A second approach stresses a psychological sequence. Here, there are broad objectives planned for pupil achievement. However, pupil/teacher planning is involved in determining the order or sequence of specific objectives to be achieved as well as the learning opportunities to be pursued.

There are state mandated objectives which provide constraints in planning the mathematics curriculum. These are measurably stated objectives for pupils to achieve in mathematics. Criterion referenced tests are developed by the state to measure pupil achievement at selected intervals.

The National Council for Teachers of Mathematics in 1989 completed *Curriculum and Evaluation Standards for School Mathematics*. This excellent volume provided a framework for the voluntary selection of objectives for pupil attainment. Quality sequence may then be in the offing for pupils in ongoing lessons and units of study in mathematics.

## ACHIEVING LOGICAL SEQUENCE IN MATHEMATICS

The following situation emphasizes sequential learning opportunities that the student teacher and the regular teacher attempted to provide. First grade pupils are to achieve the objective pertaining to "adding 5+4=..." A variety of learning opportunities were provided for pupils. The student teacher and the regular teacher showed five sticks to pupils and asked how many there were in the set. If a pupil responded incorrectly, the teaching team asked for another response without any ridiculing the person or answer that was not correct. Correct answers were rewarded with verbal praise. After receiving the right answer, the teaching team held up four sticks. The first pupil gave the correct response with four members being in the set. Next, the teaching team held all nine sticks up and asked for the correct number of sticks in the new set. The number sentence "5+4=9" was printed on the chalkboard as well as typed into the computer as each value was given by pupils when responding to the number of sticks in each set as well as the total number with sets combined. A printout of the number sentence was provided to pupils. Meaning theory was emphasized by the student and regular teacher in starting with concrete materials of instruction which were sticks in this case. If pupils responded incorrectly, selected learners were asked to provide reasons for their thinking. In this way teachers analysed reasons for logic used by pupils in thinking mathematically. Reflective thinking is important in reviewing algorithms and methods of reasoning. Reflection by learners is also important in thinking about correct answers that were given. Processes and products are then analyzed in the mathematics curriculum. Improved retention of content should be an end result when pupils reflect upon what has been learned.

Next in sequence, the student teacher and the regular teacher wished for pupils to see the relationship of 5+4=.-- and 4+5=----. Thus, the teaching team held up four sticks and then five sticks with pupils giving a correct answer for the number of members in each set. The commutative property of addition was emphasized by the teacher. Here, pupils built on previously acquired information by realizing that a+b = b+a. "This is one of the most worthwhile ideas that pupils can achieve," according to the regular teacher. "Modern school mathematics of the latter 1950's," she continued, "truly pinpointed the commutative property of addition and multiplication which has value on any grade level be it primary grades or higher education mathematics. This property continues to be as important as ever in teaching mathematics."

Both the student and the regular teacher emphasized that primary grade pupils should experience pictorial materials, following the concrete, in a logical curriculum. The two teachers determined the order of presentation of materials. Here, the teachers had pictures on a chart. The first chart had five cats and pupils were asked to tell how many there were. The teaching team then held up the chart with four illustrated cats. Pupils told how many there were. To develop concepts of addition in depth, the teaching team had pairs of illustrated charts containing dogs, elephants, tigers, lions, and people. The concept of 5+4= – and 4+5= – has the same answer and was being emphasized in intensive or depth teaching. The teaching team determined the order of presenting the learning opportunities in a logical curriculum. As each set of illustrations or pictures was presented, the teaching team wrote the corresponding numerals on the chalkborad as well in the computer.

The transition needs to be made here by pupils in moving from the concrete and pictorial to abstract numerals. In a logical mathematics curriculum, the teacher determines sequence. For a brief review, the teaching team consisting of the student teacher and the regular teacher asked five pupils to come to the front of the classroom. Then four more pupils were asked to come to the front. The student teacher wrote the numeral '5' to indicate the number of pupils in the first set; the numeral '4' was written to show the number of pupils in the second set. Pupils in the two sets were then joined together with a pupil coming forward to write the numeral '9'. The abstract concept of 5+4=9 was clearly written so that all learners could see this number sentence. The two sets of pupils were changed in order of presentation so that learners attached meaning to the commutative property of '4+5=9' or inverse operation. The teaching team stressed consistently that primary grade pupils perceive the concrete and the pictorial stages of learning being related to the resulting abstract number sentence. Also, changing the order of the two addends did not change the sum in addition. To stress the abstract only, the teaching team passed a worksheet to pupils stressing basic number pairs. The number pairs included all previously learned addition and subtraction facts, including the newly acquired learnings in addition. The number pairs were written at random on the worksheet to ascertain what pupils had learned and what needed more emphasis. Each pupil was asked to explain how incorrect answers were obtained. With diagnosis, the student and the regular teacher could better determine logically which the next sequential step of teaching should be. The teachers continued to do the sequencing of learning opportunities for pupils in the ongoing lesson plan. A logical approach was used by the teaching team in that human reason and feedback from pupils determined the order of experiences for learners.

Kennedy and Tips (1993) list sequential steps developed by Madeline Hunter and Douglas Russell that stress a logical mathematics curriculum:

1. Setting the stage
2. Statement of objective
3. Instructional input

4. Modeling
5. Checking for understanding
6. Guided practice
7. Independent practice

According to the above lesson plan, the teacher provides readiness or review of what pupils had learned previously in mathematics (setting the stage). He/she then states the objective(s) for pupils to achieve, as well as choosing learning opportunities so that pupils may achieve the stated objective. In these learning opportunities the teacher models by showing pupils how to proceed or giving examples of how to work a problem or secure an answer to a question in mathematics. The teacher makes certain that pupils are working problems correctly before providing guided or supervised activities to pupils. Within these steps of learning, the teacher in a logical order sequences experiences for learners.

## A PSYCHOLOGICAL MATHEMATICS CURRICULUM

Some students and regular teachers believe strongly in a psychological mathematics curriculum. Here, the teaching team made up of the two teachers assisted pupils to develop their very own sequence in learning. These teachers felt that sequence resides within the learner, not textbooks nor teachers. It is the pupil that needs to determine what comes first, second, third, and so on in learning. Thus, the psychological curriculum is more openended as compared to the logical mathematics curriculum. The mathematics teacher then needs to motivate pupils to pursue what is sequential in their very own minds. The objectives, the learning opportunities, and evaluation procedures in their determination need considerable input from pupils. How might a psychological sequence work in guiding pupils to use what has been learned? Here, pupils with student teacher and regular teacher guidance developed a miniature supermarket with empty fruit and vegetable containers, as well as cereal boxes, among other objects. The 'food products' were placed on different shelves in the classroom. Prices on each item harmonized with numerical values being studied in class. Pupils were told that the marked prices of each commodity might not be the real prices found in supermarkets. Toy money was used by pupils to buy different items from the 'supermarkets shelves.' Thus, pupils might buy a box of cereal for five cents, as marked, and a can of peaches for four cents. Pupils would then determine what 5+4=… . they could use hand held calculators, if desired. Each pupil had adequate opportunities to buy from the miniature supermarket and use what had been learned previously in mathematics. Learners individually and collaboratively sequenced their very own experiences in a psychological mathematics curriculum. The teaching team believed very strongly on pupils using what had been learned so that forgetting might less likely occur; the sequential review was determined by pupils, not the teaching team. Pupils together with the teaching team planned and implemented the use of the miniature supermarket; a psychological sequence was involved in experiencing the integrated concrete, pictorial, and abstract facets of learning.

A second approach in guiding pupils to sequence their very own learning activities is to use learning stations. Here, the pupils and their teachers planned the title for each station as well as the materials for instruction that should be at each station. Learning experiences in using the materials were also planned by pupils with the assistance of the student teacher and the regular teacher. There were an ample number of tasks so that pupils might choose which to pursue and which to omit. Pupils selected sequential tasks to pursue and complete; they were motivated and interested in choices made since learners themselves made the selection.

There are excellent ways for teachers to use in guiding pupils to sequence personal learning opportunities. In a philosophy of constructivism pupils need to find meaning in a contextual situation. Learners then construct their very own knowledge as activities and experiences accrue. Knowledge as a result of learning opportunities pursued is made by the self or selves in a constructivist mathematics curriculum.

## NEEDED IS QUALITY SEQUENCE IN LEARNING

With quality sequence, be it logical or psychological, new content acquired is based upon that which had been achieved. The new is related directly to the old. There is a definite relationship here between what is being learned and what has been learned. Feelings of success, very often, come about due experiencing quality sequence. Jackson and Canada (1995) wrote the following pertaining to their research:

> *This study explored the relationship between self concept as measured by the Tennessee Self Concept Scale and mathematics achievement as measured by the California Test of Achievement in a population of 133 students ranging in ages from 13 to 16 and designated at-risk of not graduating from high school. Results were based on pre/post test data with the intervening treatment consisting of an eight week residential summer program with strong social service, counseling and work components. Significant correlations indicated the student's total mathematics scores increased so did their self acceptance, feelings of worth and adequacy as well as their sense of capacity in distinctions between right and wrong in their conduct.*

From the above study, it is important to notice that as mathematics scores from tests go higher, the self concept of the learner also increases. A carefully planned program of sequential progress for pupils, be it a logical or psychological sequence, might well improve how pupils feel and think about themselves.

An adequate number of workshops for inservice education and staff development need to stress the importance of emphasizing quality sequence for pupils in mathematics. Columbia and Dologos (1993) wrote the following in teacher education programs:

> *In the preparation of classroom teachers we must model our commitment to good teaching to enable future teachers of mathematics to present lessons that reflect the vision of the* Curriculum and Evaluation Standards for School Mathematics *and its companion document* Professional Standards for Teaching Mathematics. *In addition to adopting the modeled strategies, continual reflection on tasks, discourse, environment, and analysis will enable future teachers to integrate the goals of both documents into their evolving instructional philosophy in order to become effective teachers of mathematics.*

*Finally, we must remember that our goal in connecting teacher preparation to the vision set by the National Council Teachers of Mathematics is to ensure that an environment is created in the classroom where students can be successful and confident in mathematics.*

The National Council Teachers of Mathematics (NCTM) is the leading organization in the world for mathematics teachers interested in improving the curriculum in mathematics. Much time and attention has been given by the NCTM in developing objectives for teachers to use in teaching. The objectives are voluntary to use and do provide an excellent framework for determining what should be taught in mathematics, kindergarten through secondary school. Objectives chosen for implementation by teachers (Ediger, 1994) should be emphasized so that learners experience:

1. Meaningful lessons and units of study. With meaning, pupils understand and comprehend that which was contained in ongoing learning opportunities.
2. Interesting content and skills in the curriculum. With interest, the pupil and the curriculum become one, not separate entities. Pupils attend and achieve from ongoing lessons and units of study.
3. Purpose in learning. With purpose for learning, pupils accept reasons for attaining relevant facts, concepts, and generalizations presented....
4. Sequence in learning. With quality sequence, pupils relate newly acquired content with that achieved previously. Previous knowledge obtained provides readiness for the objectives to be attained. Pupils need guidance to perceive relationship of knowledge in teaching-learning situations.
5. Balance among objectives stressed. Thus, knowledge, skills, and attitudes-- three kinds of objectives need to be achieved by students. These objectives interact and are not in isolation from each other. For example, if pupils possess positive attitudes, they should achieve needed knowledge and skills more readily.

David Ausubel, a cognitive based educational psychologist, believes that quality sequence is the most important ingredient to emphasize in teaching and learning situations. Thus, the mathematics teacher needs to start pupils with where they are presently in achievement and stress continuous progress. Previous learning then provide an advance organizer or readiness for the new objectives to be achieved by pupils (Shepherd and Ragan, 1982).

In addition to stressing a cognitive psychology in teaching and learning, there are personal characteristics of the teacher that assist pupils to achieve more adequately in mathematics. Lampert and Eshelman (1995) advocate teachers exhibit patience, curiosity, generosity in listening to and caring about people, confidence, trust, and imagination. These characteristics strongly stress the affective dimension of teachers in the instructional arena. Such traits of the ideal teacher, we believe, must be emphasized in mathematics programs which improve quality sequence in pupil learning. Patient, curious, generous, confident, trustful, and imaginative mathematics teachers will be concerned about each pupil making continual optimal progress.

## CONCLUSION

Schifter (1996) stresses that constructivism philosophy of teaching mathematics does not emphasize a finished point but rather there is further growth and change in pupil development. In a constructivist philosophy of instruction, pupils are doers, not hearers only. When actively involved in ongoing lessons and units of study, pupils reflect or think about what has transpired previously. Teachers and pupils both have attitudes of inquiry when trying out new ideas. Pupils ideas are analyzed; there is room then for growth and change. I believe this change brings on improved sequence for growth in the mathematics curriculum.

## REFERENCES

Columbia, Lynn, and Kathleen Dologos (1993), "Professional Development for Teachers of Mathematics," *Education*, 114, 32-36.

Ediger, Marlow (1994), "Early Field Experiences in Teacher Education," *College Student Journal*. 28: 302-06.

Jackson, Mary H., and Richard Canada (1995), "Self Concept and Math Among Potential School Dropouts," *Journal of Instructional Psychology,* 22; 234-37.

Kennedy, Leonard M., and Steve Tipps (1993), *Guiding Children's Learning of Mathematics.* Belmont, California: Wadsworth Publishing Company, Pages 47-55.

Lampert, Magdalene, and Angie S. Eshelman (1995), "Using Technology to Support Effective and Responsible Teacher Education: The Case of Interactive Multimedia in Mathematics Methods Courses," paper presented at the annual meeting of the American Educational Research Association, San Francisco, April, 1995.

Shepherd, Gene and William Ragan (1982), *Modern Elementary Curriculum,* New York: The Macmillan Company, Pages 22, 23, 39, 309, 342, and 346.244244

Shifter, Deborah (1996), " A Constructivist Perspective on Teaching and Learning Mathematics, *Phi Delta Kappan,* 77: 492-99.

# Chapter 20

# OUTPUTS, INPUTS, AND THE MATHEMATICS TEACHER

Numerous speakers and writers in education talk about the desirability of outputs from pupils largely or only. Thus, test results from pupils which show good achievement are wanted. Inputs, according to these speakers and writers, are of secondary or minimal importance. Let us analyze the advocacy of outputs with minimal attention paid to inputs.

## TEST RESULTS AND OUTPUTS

Test results appear to be objective to many. They provide numerical data to show learner achievement. A pupil, for example, is on the fiftieth percentile on results from a standardized or norm referenced test. Or, a pupil is one standard deviation above the mean according to test results. Further way of expressing pupil results from testing would be to say a pupil is working on the 6.2 grade equivalent or is on stanine five.

A realist in educational philosophy desires to have preciseness in stating where a pupil is in academic achievement. Much emphasis is placed upon validity in that tests should measure what they purport to measure, such as academic achievement or personal-social adjustment. Consistency of results be it split-half, alternative forms, or test-retest approaches are needed to indicate reliability. Correlational results in numerical terms are needed to show degrees of correlation in validity and reliability. Correlations then show the strength of relationships between two or more variables, such as the strength of relationship between two achievement tests or two IQ tests.

Measuring pupil progress, according to realists, becomes the major or only way of ascertaining pupil progress. Measurably stated objectives are advocated in that pupils reveal if they have/ have not attained any one objective. A yes or no situation is involved here. Precision is needed to show how well a pupil is doing in school. Behaviourism as a psychology of learning is being emphasized. Teaching toward ends becomes a major goal of the teacher. The ends are the measurably stated objectives for pupils to attain. Testing is necessary to reveal if a pupil is successful in goal attainment. Numerical results are in the offing which communicate clearly to parents how well an offspring is doing in school. Stress then is placed on outcomes from the learner; inputs become relatively unimportant.

Standardized norm referenced achievement tests do not have related predetermined measurably stated objectives for pupils to achieve whereas criterion referenced tests do. Thus, for criterion referenced tests, a teacher may announce to pupils, prior to instruction, what they are to learn from the teaching and learning act. This provides security to learners in that they now know what is expected of them in terms of achievement or outputs.

Communication with parents becomes easier when a precise numeral can be given pertaining to the offspring's achievement. It is also easier in the accountability movement to hold teachers accountable for learners attaining that which is stated in the predetermined objectives. These objectives are usually developed on the state or district level. By having access to the measurably stated objectives, prior to instruction, the teacher selects learning opportunities so that learners may achieve the measurably stated objectives. With the related criterion referenced tests, the teacher measurably stated in the measurable objectives. Reliability is present if pupils tend to receive consistent results in and on the same test be it test-retest, split-half, and/or alternative forms of reliability.

To every action, there appears to be an opposite and equal reaction, a law of physics, which appears to be true in methods of determining pupil achievement. Among others, the following are weaknesses of using measuring procedures only, to determine learner achievement:

1. The test results are not objective in that human beings wrote the test items for both norm and criterion referenced tests. Human beings choosing what goes into a test in terms of content in test items emphasizes a bias and subjective thinking.
2. 'Objectivity' is brought in after the test items have been tried out on learners in pilot studies to develop numerical results, such as percentile ranks, standard deviation scores, stanines, and correlations among others.
3. 'Objective' test items are limited as to what can be measured. Too frequently critical and creative thinking, as well as problem solving are omitted from norm and criterion referenced tests. These processes are difficult to measure numerically.
4. Tests are external to the teaching and learning situation. They do not measure what is contextual or that which is sequential in learning opportunities. Norm and criterion referenced tests are developed by those who are outside of the local classroom in which pupils are tested as well as outside the framework where teaching and learning occurred.
5. Tests cannot measure such items as quality oral communication, skill in construction experiences or experimentation, among others. They are very weak in measuring personality and social traits of pupils.

A further major weakness pertains to educators and lay people believing that the ends only count in terms of pupils achievement. Accountability of teachers then is related to how well pupils do on tests, regardless of ability levels or socio-economic statuses of the learner. Little stress then needs to be given to inputs or means to an end. The ends are the precisely stated objective (s). How can quality instruction occur unless there are adequate materials of instruction to use so that the objectives may be achieved by learners?

We recommend that adequate attention be given to inputs so that any teacher has adequate materials of instruction to use in teaching. Pupils might attain as optimally as possible when interacting with quality materials of instruction.

## EXPERIMENTALISM IN TEACHING

Experimentalism as a philosophy of education advocates that one can only know experience, not the real world as it truly is. To experience means to interact with the natural and social environment. Thus, the teacher needs to have adequate learning opportunities so that pupils might have rich experiences in the curriculum. These experiences need to be lifelike and real, not rote learning and memorization. The teacher here needs to provide a variety of realistic activities which assist pupils to attain vital goals of instruction. What is this vital goal or goals?

Experimentalists realize that change is all around us. We experience change, not sameness nor consistent stability. With continuous change, problems arise which need solutions. The world is no longer the same but has modifications. These modifications or changes make for the necessity of identification of relevant problems. Thus, the pupil with teacher guidance needs to select relevant problems. The ultimate goal of instruction then is to have pupils engage in problem solving experiences. The problems are selected in context, not in isolation from the ongoing unit of study. There are subsidiary flexible objectives inherent in problem solving. Thus, in addition to the selection of relevant problems (a subsidiary objective), the pupil needs to learn to develop a hypothesis which is a tentative answer to the problem (subsidiary objective two). The hypothesis needs to be tested in a lifelike situation (subsidiary objective number three). A fourth flexible subsidiary objective for the pupil to attain is to revise the hypothesize if necessary. Problem solving here stresses the complete act of thought. Time is necessary for pupils to be engaged in problem solving activities. The teacher stimulates, challenges, and encourages pupils to achieve, grow, and develop.

With problem solving, pupils need to interact with materials that relate to reality, the social and natural environment. Predetermined objectives do not harmonize with experimentalism and problem solving. The teacher then cannot state predetermined problems for pupils to solve unless learners accept these as their very own. Otherwise, pupils should identify problems in context in ongoing lessons and units of study. The complete act of thought or problem solving procedures need to be stressed.

Which activities should be available to assist pupils in problem solving? a multimedia approach should be used. Concrete (excursions, objectives, realia, construction endeavours, creative and formal dramatics, and models, among others), semiconcrete (video disks, cassette tapes with accompanying filmstrips, slides, video tapes, among others), and abstract learning opportunities (computers and accompanying software, radio, cassette tapes, oral and silent reading of content, internet and resource personnel, among others) should be in the offing to solve problems.

An experience centered curriculum requires many materials of instruction. Ends or objectives to achieve emphasize problem solving by pupils with teacher guidance. The cost of inputs will be relatively high since there needs to be subject matter available from multimedia to solve problems. The outputs are also important in that pupils need to identify and solve relevant problems relating school and society which become one, not separate entities. Numerical results of pupils achievement is not feasible nor possible.

Experimentalists advocate that pupils work in committees to solve problems since in the societal arenas, collaboration is emphasized to choose and solve problems.

## EXISTENTIALISM AND THE CURRICULUM

A third philosophy of education to implement is existentialism. Existentialists are strong in pupils making decisions to the maximum extent possible. Decision making by learners is of utmost importance. A learning stations approach may be implemented. An adequate number of stations need to be in evidence so that pupil may choose which tasks to complete at different stations. Each station has concrete, semiconcrete, and abstract materials of instruction for pupils. The tasks are printed on small cards at each station. The learner may then select sequential tasks to complete. With an ample number of tasks at each station, the pupil may omit those not possessing perceived purpose. Co-operative learning or individual endeavours may be chosen; the tasks selected may or may not stress problem solving. Existentialists tend to emphasize tasks for learner choice which reflect the human dimension. Thus, learning activitites reflect content pertaining to the tensions and anxieties that individuals experience in the life every day.

The individual pupil should do the choosing of tasks to pursue, not the committee or group, unless the pupil chooses to engage in group work. Tasks at the different stations should have those that stress individual as well as committee endeavours. It will not be possible here to secure numerical results in terms of learner achievement. Tests are minimized by existentialists when obtaining data pertaining to achievement. Rather the pupil reveals progress, among other ways, through research in reading, writing prose and poetry, dramatic endeavours, pantomiming, art work, story telling, and making of objects and items, among others. Again, the feeling, dimension is very salient when pupils reveal in processes and products that which has been learned. People posses feelings, thought, and action when participating in daily activities. Subject matter to be learned should reflect the human dilemma with its anxiety, stresses, and dread. Many materials of instruction will be necessary when existentialism as a philosophy of education is implemented. Audio visual aids, reading materials, art items, and other materials of instruction need to be there. Many inputs are needed so that pupils may reveal progress in a variety of ways such as in the quality of written work, dramatizations, reading endeavours with related discussions, and art products, among others that stress creativity, not conformity behaviour.

## PHILOSOPHY OF IDEALISM

A teacher adhering to idealism stresses a subject centered curriculum. The academic areas receive much emphasis here. The abstract learning opportunities of listening will, speaking clearly, reading effectively with comprehension, and writing feuently should receive priority in a subject centered curriculum stressing vital academic content. Subject matter learned needs to be challenging, accurate, and relevant. Materials of instruction should include reading for a variety of intellectual purposes, technology to stress pupils interacting with and listening to vital subject matter, computers and word processors for writing activities, and models to improve speaking effectiveness. Inputs are important here in that costs are involved in having pupils attain vital objectives of instruction. Outputs could being in testing and measuring; however, there are many other useful procedures to ascertain what pupils have learned. These include using portfolios, discussing academic subject matter, listening to and analyzing the contents pertaining to a significant debate involving the academics, writing for a variety of purposes, and reading significant content involving vital concepts, facts, and generalizations.

Idealists tend to emphasize intellectual development of pupils as being of utmost importance. Thus, higher cognitive objectives are of primary significance, not affective nor psychomotor objectives. Affective (attitudinal) goals become salient if cognitive objective are being achieved better than would otherwise be the case. The same can be said of psychomotor ends. Attaining relevant psychomotor ends are important to the degree that they assist learners in attaining cognitive or intellectual goals. Mental development is extremely significant in its development according to idealism as a philosophy of education.

Many inputs are needed when pupils are taught in a manner emphasizing intellectual growth . There should then be an adequate number of trade/library books as well as audio-visual aids being comprehensive in number so that pupils may be guided in developing appropriate thinking skills. Basal textbooks need to be challenging and on diverse reading levels. Concrete materials used in teaching must reflect higher levels of intellectual achievement. Inputs then are very important so that pupils do well taught by a teacher or teaching team stresses idealism as philosophy of education.

## CONCLUSION

Each philosophical school of thought in education has implications for helping to determine the amount of money involved in ascertaining how much of costs there will be in terms of inputs. Realism, focusing upon ends in teaching, requires the least in input when stressing financial input needed to buy school supplies. However, that could be debatable. For a teacher to assist pupils to attain behaviourally stated objectives, he/she must select appropriate learning opportunities so that learners attain optimally. Realists do view ends of instruction much more so than the means or learning opportunities to achieve objectives.

Experimentalists, existentialists, and idealists as philosophies of teaching and learning do require considerable emphasis being placed upon inputs. Thus, to supply teachers here with materials of instruction requires considerable money. The experimentalist teacher bases instruction upon experiences provided in the curriculum. Experiences need to be rich and abundant so that the pupil with teacher guidance may identify and solve problems. Learning stations for an existentialist teacher also require a variety of concrete, semiconcrete, and abstract learning opportunities. Pupils may then select, from among alternatives, that which has interest, purpose, and value in learning. The idealist teacher focuses upon abstract materials of instruction to emphasize a subject centered curriculum. However, the concrete and the semiconcrete materials may be needed so that pupils achieve well in the symbolic domains.

The authors recommend the following:

1. Using materials of instruction which harmonize with the individual styles of learners in achieving more optimally.
2. Applying the best of each of the four philosophical approaches in learning. Thus, quality precise objectives will be stressed in teaching. Problems solving will receive much stress since life itself consists of identification and solutions to problems. Decision making strategies also will receive much attentions since individuals need to select from among alternatives in life and living. Abstract thinking is salient since ultimately learning stresses thinking symbolically. Since the concrete and semiconcrete world of learning may not be available at a given time and place, thinking in the abstract truly is vital.

## REFERENCES

Bhaskara Rao, Digumarti (1997), *Teacher and Education,* Guntur; Nagarjuna Publishers (in Telegu Language).

Bhaskara Rao, Digumarti, ed. (1998), *Reforming School Education,* New Delhi; Discovery Publishing House.

Ediger, Marlow, and Digumarti Bhaskara Rao (1996), *Science Curriculum,* New Delhi; Discovery Publishing House.

•••